Between Melting Pot and Mosaic

BETWEEN MELTING POT AND MOSAIC

African Americans and Puerto Ricans in the New York Political Economy

ANDRES TORRES

TEMPLE UNIVERSITY PRESS

Philadelphia

Temple University Press, Philadelphia 19122

Published 1995
Printed in the United States of America

♾ The paper used in this book meets the requirements of the American National Standard for Information Sciences—Permanence of Paper for Printed Library Materials, ANSI Z39.48-1984

Text design by Nighthawk Design

Library of Congress Cataloging-in-Publication Data

Torres, Andrés, 1947–
Between melting pot and mosaic : African Americans and Puerto Ricans in the New York political economy / Andrés Torres.
p. cm.
Includes bibliographical references (p.) and index.
ISBN 1-56639-279-9 (cloth : alk. paper).—ISBN 1-56639-280-2 (pb : alk. paper)
1. Afro-Americans—New York (N.Y.)—Economic conditions. 2. Puerto Ricans—New York (N.Y.)—Economic conditions. 3. New York (N.Y.)—Economic conditions. I. Title.
F128.9.N3T67 1995
305.8′96′07307471—dc20 94-18151

In memory of my father,

Andrés Ismael Torres

CONTENTS

LIST OF TABLES

ACKNOWLEDGMENTS

This study has its genesis in the early 1970s, with reports from the U.S. Census indicating that Puerto Ricans had the highest poverty levels of any group in New York City and other urban centers. Puerto Ricans were faring worse than African Americans, the group that most Americans identified with socioeconomic disadvantage. At the time, it struck me that the joint examination of New York City's two largest minority communities would be an interesting project that could help illuminate important issues in urban political economy. Both communities shared the conditions of poverty and unequal status in the larger community, and it seemed clear that a comparative analysis of the two would provide some useful insights. This volume, which was many years in the making, is the result of that analysis.

Without the support of family, friends, and colleagues, I would not have had the confidence to transform my early interest into a book. The very idea of rendering intelligible something as complex and dynamic as the New York experience seemed an overwhelming task. That I have ventured to author a chapter in the continuing story of the Great Metropolis is greatly due to the many people who assisted me along the way.

I wish to acknowledge the support of David M. Gordon, who prompted me to conduct my dissertation research on the subject and imbued me with his enthusiasm for the study of political economy. Many students have been the recipients of his careful guidance and encouraging advice; I am thankful to be numbered among them. I am deeply grateful to Frank Bonilla, for his wisdom, feedback, and sustenance during my years at the Centro de Estudios Puertorriqueños, Hunter College. Also crucial were the many discussions with Centro staff, a testing ground for ideas formulated in this book.

Several persons helped improve earlier versions of this work with their comments: Gilberto Arroyo, Janis Barry-Figueroa, Edwin Meléndez, Michelle Naples, Palmira Ríos, Carmen Vivian Rivera, Clara E. Rodríguez, Thomas Vietoricz, Rhonda Williams, and anonymous reviewers with the *Review of Black Political Economy* and Temple University Press. Participation in research and policy networks enabled me to interact with scholars and analysts concerned with issues of race and class in urban America. I am grateful for the opportunity to be involved in this dialogue: the Inter-University Program for Latino Research (IUP), the Strategy Development Group of the Boston Foundation's Persistent Poverty Project, and the Poverty and Race Research Action Council (PRRAC).

In addition to those already mentioned, many others provided technical assistance and contributed materials, ideas, and commentary. I would like to thank a few in particular: Paul Bartlett, Paul Cooney, Armengol Domenech, Angelo Falcón, Jill Hamberg, Deborah Hersey, Jim O'Brien, Nélida Pérez and Amilcar Tirado (of the Centro Library), Philip Rivera, Camille Rodríguez, Digna Sánchez, Walter Stafford, and Frank Vardy. I value the support and advice extended me by colleagues at the College of Public and Community Service, University of Massachusetts-Boston, especially James Green, Patricia Reeve, Michael Stone, and Miren Uriarte.

I benefited from the assistance of all these individuals, whether or not they agreed with the arguments made in these pages.

Thanks, too, to Doris Braendel of Temple University Press for persevering with this project and for prodding me on with her contagious energy and professional advice. Patricia Sterling made my writing much more accessible with her excellent copy editing, and Joan Vidal ushered the manuscript through the final stages with efficiency and humor.

From all of the aforementioned and from many other quarters, I received support of an intangible nature. Help came in numerous guises: an embrace, a pat on the back, a motivational lecture. Longtime companions of the soul spurred me on when my stamina waned: Ballerina, Jawbones, Percy, and Rosalita. I was encouraged by successive cohorts of coworkers and colleagues and by several branches of my family tree: Torres, Ayala, Rivera, Carrillo.

I am most indebted to my immediate family, who allowed me the most precious resource, the time and freedom to pursue this project. Over the years, they sacrificed numerous hours to this endeavor, sometimes unknowingly. I thank my mother, Bienvenida; my wonderful children, Rachel and Orlando; and my wife and steadfast friend, Carmen Vivian, without whom this work would have remained an unfulfilled effort.

Between Melting Pot and Mosaic

INTRODUCTION

New York has spawned more than its share of metaphors. The most compelling of these allude to the city's status as a locus of racial and ethnic relations. Numerous writings and works of art, extensive theorizing, social research, and policy analysis are all bent on endorsing, amending, or debunking the idea that U.S. and, particularly, New York society has evolved from "melting pot" to "mosaic."

The power of the melting pot image resides less in its historical accuracy than in the fact that so many people have taken it to be true. Myths and legends have a life of their own. Despite ample evidence to the contrary, the view persisted well into the twentieth century that New York was a giant cauldron homogenizing all newcomers into a single entity. The orthodox view believed in a natural progression from immigration to settlement to assimilation, resulting in a common identity as Americans. The idea had a tenacious grip on the American imagination.

For this reason, the revisionism that began with Nathan Glazer and Daniel Moynihan's *Beyond the Melting Pot* (1963) had a profound influence. Questioning the conventional myth was bound to raise eyebrows, but it was an appropriate response to the obvious fact of ethnicity's continuing resiliency in postwar New York.

Glazer and Moynihan attempted to show that immigrant groups (and their descendants) do not necessarily jettison their cultural baggage in the settlement process. Instead of dissolving into a single entity, they compete intensely, and ethnic identity and language continue to figure in their political, social, and economic activities. The authors also pointed out that the vitality of ethnic identity is nothing to be alarmed about. In fact, part of America's uniqueness is its capacity to accommodate a multiplicity of heritages. What binds disparate people together is the democratic ideal and freedom of opportunity. In the long run, differences in heritage—although important and enduring—become subsumed under a common macro-identity. Cultural pluralism should be celebrated.

More recently, a new image has struggled for acceptance: the idea of the "grand mosaic." This image is unlike the ethnic revisionism of a generation ago in that it springs from a different source and implies a different basis for social relations in the United States. Popularized by New York City's first African American mayor and sharing roots with "rainbow" terminology, the metaphor exalts the idea of racial diversity as central to the American experiment. In portraying social relations in terms of color, it overcomes a weak spot in previous traditions.

Both the orthodox (melting pot) and revisionist (beyond the melting pot) views presumed that the indispensable foundation of American identity was European tradition. The first was concerned with the incorporation of successive waves of foreigners from the Old World: Germans, Scandinavians, Irish, Jews, Italians, Poles and various other East Europeans. Ignored were the nonwhite "others": Native Americans, African Americans, Mexican Americans, Puerto Ricans, and Asian Americans. These had such a peculiar relation to U.S. society that they were not even contemplated as ingredients in the pot. Similarly, the revisionist tradition, although quite aware of the condition of minority groups, presupposed a set of criteria for successful participation in American plural society: middle class values, English-language dominance, and acceptance of Western political and cultural ideals. For minorities, gaining entry into the American dream still meant surrendering their identity of origin.

The new revisionists who endorse the mosaic as a hopeful and forward-looking concept do not themselves agree on the desired basis for a common identity. This ambiguity leads to some confusion and not a little anxiety. If not Europe, what? Multiculturalism? Cultural relativism? Afro- (and other) centrism? Nevertheless, the new metaphor has entered the vocabulary of those who argue for a broader, more tolerant vision of the city and nation. Whether or not it fully describes the real world, it is a powerful idea.

In New York, the defeat of Mayor David N. Dinkins in 1993 portended the death of the mosaic idea. According to the victors, Rudolph Giuliani's election represented a return to a bygone era when New Yorkers celebrated a common identity as participants in an American Dream. This claim that we could now begin to focus on the things that unite us harked back to earlier assimilationist conceptions.

But the claim is far from true, and here the Latino vote offers some interesting lessons. Despite a campaign heavily targeting Latinos, Giuliani failed to win new votes from that community. Even with the well-known Puerto Rican politician Herman Badillo as Giuliani's running mate, Hispanics gave close to two-thirds of their support to Dinkins. Also, many were angered that even though so many white Democrats crossed party lines to support the Republican candidate, they refused comparable support to his Puerto Rican running mate.

These results call attention to an important subplot in the racial-ethnic drama of post–World War II New York: the relation between African Americans and Latinos. Few analysts acknowledge the role of the latter in helping to forge the mosaic coalition, yet since the 1950s, blacks and Hispanics—particularly Puerto Ricans—have been drawn together in an alliance of survival. From the early years of postwar migration through the War on Poverty of the 1960s and succeeding years of backlash and insurgency, the two groups saw their fortunes as mutually linked. Their search for a share of power culminated in 1989 with Dinkins's election. Even Dinkins's defeat demonstrates the stability of the coalition, since Giuliani was unable to split the partners. Having Badillo on the slate may have made it easier for whites to vote for Giuliani, but it failed to persuade Hispanics to break with Dinkins. Latinos had valid complaints about their treatment during the Dinkins tenure, but they were convinced that a Republican administration would represent a setback for them.

The potential for mosaic politics is not limited to the black-Latino axis. It appeals as well to Asian Americans and white progressives who have faith in the ability of our society to welcome newcomers. In its demographics and cultural life, New York looks more and more like a microcosm of the world, befitting its claim to be a global city. This may be disconcerting to conservative and moderate whites, but there will be no turning back of the clock. Having finally gained access to some levers of power, minorities are unwilling to accept a return to the days of exclusion and neglect.

All signs indicate that we have entered a period of deadlock, in the city and in the nation. It may last for years, perhaps even decades. No one knows how it will be broken. The assimilationists are not likely to succeed in persuading minorities to return to their previous condition of marginality, but those who argue for a politics and culture of diversity must convince the traditionalists that minorities seek not a victory but a share of the dream. Still, as metaphors go, the future seems to be more accurately prefigured in the mosaic than in the melting pot. In any event, the fundamental obstacle to the mosaic notion is the continuing problem of poverty, not the transitory return to a conservative political regime. In 1989, one of every five city residents lived in poverty. Among African American and Hispanic New Yorkers, the proportion was 25 percent and 33 percent, respectively. Among New Yorkers of other nonwhite races (mostly Asian), the rate was 29.4 percent.[1]

Ironically, it is in minority communities that the idea of the "gorgeous mosaic" has been embraced most enthusiastically: the least powerful are advancing the most encompassing and egalitarian notion of social relations. But this optimism clashes with the unhappy reality of gaping differences in socioeconomic conditions. Social harmony requires a material, economic basis as well as a foundation in mutual respect and tolerance. At present, the absence of even minimum socioeconomic parity among racial and ethnic groups threatens to ruin *all* forms and images of the ideal society. It would be futile to define the African American–Puerto Rican experience within the terminology of race relations, for in reality, both groups occupy an ambiguous space, somewhere between melting pot and mosaic.

This book explores the nature and causes of continuing poverty and inequality among these two largest of New York's minority groups. It also devotes considerable space to a comparative analysis of African Americans and Puerto Ricans in their economic and political efforts, relative to each other and to New Yorkers at large.

Why focus on these two groups? Broadly, because examination of their history may illuminate deeper sources of inequity in all of the urban United States. More narrowly, because they are the "poverty constant" linking the New York of the early postwar period to the Global City it is today. Although each group has its own distinctiveness, they have shared a common experience over the last half-century, mostly as citizen-outsiders trying to get a foothold in the big city. History has drawn them together—as wary rivals, beleaguered allies, and sometimes even victorious partners—in ways that few social scientists have appreciated. It is not clear whether the lessons of this episode in the history of inter-minority relations can be generalized far beyond the borders of the great metropolis. For reinforcing the commonality of purpose and history, a significant overlapping of cultural legacies and geographic proximity may account for the intermingling of African American and Puerto Rican fortunes. Generally, Latinos and African

Americans outside New York have not been exposed to this collective history.

Nevertheless, addressing their New York experiences jointly has the advantage of raising a set of interrelated issues that are important to contemporary discussions about urban America. First, this dual treatment surmounts the common tendency to classify poverty as an exclusively African American dilemma. Because of smaller population size and regional concentration, the Puerto Rican "problem" is given scant, usually patronizing, attention in the general scheme of policy discussions. Many Americans, perhaps fatigued by talk of racial inequality, do not welcome reminders that yet another body of U.S. citizens live a harsh and tenuous reality. Moreover, some African Americans may see their own survival as contingent on obtaining undivided sympathy for their plight; sharing the stage with others seems only to dilute their case. No wonder that awareness of the Puerto Rican dilemma has been barely perceptible. Perhaps this book will help correct that disregard.

Second, an important paradox comes to light in contrasting the experience of these two groups. How do we explain the greater inequality and powerlessness of Puerto Ricans, a people who bear a lesser burden of racism? I contend that the answers lie somewhere in the interplay between political and economic dynamics affecting the two communities. Their respective evolution within U.S. history; their mode of incorporation in the city's economy; the impact of subsequent changes in that economy, such as evolving labor segmentation; and forms of political action, community infrastructure, and strategies for socioeconomic mobility: all these have something to do with each group's development and with their relative status.

A third theme is the reconfiguration of New York's race relations that began in the Puerto Rican migration of the early postwar years. What had been essentially a dual society of black and white discovered in its midst a culturally distinct and itself *multiracial* community. Drawing upon Spanish, African, and Indian origins, Puerto Ricans maintained a set of attitudes and customs that challenged the racial order, however faintly, by questioning its perverseness. Their presence forced American society to listen to a new voice that asked, "How does the dominant culture intend to deal with non–African American minorities?" and "Does one really have to choose between black and white?"

Today, with residents arriving from all over the globe, the city hears the sentiment expressed ever more vociferously that we must begin to reconceptualize race relations beyond black and white. A sad, indeed dangerous, irony inherent in the condition of African Americans and Puerto Ricans has to do with their relative standing vis-à-vis the new immigrants who have flocked to New York since the 1970s. Dramatic changes in the city's demographic and racial composition have contributed to a shifting of attention away from *native minorities* such as African Americans and Puerto Ricans. By 1990 Puerto Ricans were no longer a majority among Hispanics; Dominicans, Colombians, Ecuadorians, and other Latin Americans had increasingly made their presence felt. Within the black community an influx of Jamaicans, Trinidadians, Haitians, and other Caribbean people significantly raised the proportion of African-origin foreigners. There was an equally impressive growth in the population of Chinese, Koreans, and other Asians.

These new cohorts, largely from the Third World and in effect constituting a population of *immigrant minorities*, are imprinting a new diversity and complexity on the New York landscape. Undoubtedly, their place in the scheme of things will keep growing, and no serious discussion of the city's political economy can afford to ignore them. Will these groups avoid the poverty and deprivation plaguing native minorities?

There are dismaying signals that some political and intellectual circles are encouraging the new immigrants to accept the mantle of "model minorities." If these non-European groups succeed in their quest for a piece of the pie, so the argument goes, the claims of Puerto Ricans and African Americans can be rightfully ignored. For if native minorities—who are citizens, after all—cannot achieve progress, while immigrants advance up the social ladder, then something must be wrong with them. The possibility of foreign-born contingents leapfrogging U.S. citizens in the social structure has not gone unnoticed. The implications for social harmony are problematic, especially if native minorities perceive that newcomers are being accorded a more favorable reception.

Beyond these issues is a theme of even broader scope. It is not the thesis of this book that African Americans and Puerto Ricans are passive victims of some conspiracy, or that racism condemns them to eternal deprivation. On the contrary, their historical record demonstrates an extraordinary capacity for self-organization and active intervention in the world about them. But I do argue that these efforts are ultimately constrained and shaped by the dynamics of class and race within the larger society.

The interplay between these forces, in the context of changing economic and political trends, conditions the potential for progress. To theorize these relationships within a specific historical conjuncture is the task of Chapter One.

CHAPTER ONE

Class, Race, and the Reproduction of Inequality

Like the national economy, the economy of New York City in the second half of the twentieth century has experienced two periods of economic activity: one of growth, one of decline. Writers have debated why the postwar boom ended, but few deny that sometime during the late 1960s or early 1970s the world's most prosperous economy entered a phase of stagnation and decline, from which it still struggles to emerge.

The Meanings of Class and Race

The regional manifestations of the nation's journey through boom and bust set important boundaries on the potential fortunes of all New Yorkers. Class membership shapes the degree to which one may take advantage of an expanding economy and, conversely, find shelter in periods of decline. The great divide is between those (workers) who have nothing but their labor to sell and those (capitalists) who are in a position to employ labor for their own profit. This primary *interclass* conflict between workers and capitalists, a driving force in economic change, takes several forms.[1]

Capital and labor struggle over the labor process, as capital seeks to maximize profits from the production of goods and services. Employers may use a number of strategies to increase labor productivity within a firm: intensifying the pace of work, reducing labor costs, substituting machines and new technologies for human labor. Within the larger society, capitalists may seek to strengthen their hand by promoting legislation that holds down labor costs: preventing occupational health reforms, enacting anti-union measures, freezing the minimum wage. Workers counter by organizing in unions and associations. The bargaining power afforded by these entities provides labor with its main safeguard at the workplace. And trade unions too exert influence in the political process, supporting legislation and candidates that reflect their interests.

Intraclass conflicts occur as well. Capitalists compete among themselves: they struggle over markets, technology, and resources, and they attempt to sway government in favor of their specific industry or region. Workers in rival strata or subclasses divided along occupational lines also take adversarial positions, as when craft or professional workers organize to limit entry into their field. *Labor market segmentation* (defined below) leading to increasing stratification within the labor force, is a principal cause of rifts in the working class.

Like class divisions, race-based processes are also fundamental features of capitalist development. Since the beginning of European settlement in North America, economic and political developments have been bound up with a system of racial hegemony. Here the great divide is between Europe and the "Other": from the outset, the ideal of equality has had to contend with the ideology of white supremacy. Despite a dissident egalitarianism espoused in some political and cultural arenas, racial unity has rarely been a pervading theme or even a conscious goal of American life. Whatever the young republic's self-image as a rebellious offspring of Europe, the United States has returned to the fold with a vengeance, perceiving itself as the caretaker of Western civilization. Americans of non-European origin have been accepted into the family only to the degree that they adopt the Eurocentric world view.[2] Racial and ethnic minorities, those groups whose histories and cultures hail from non-European sources, encounter a system of racial domination that pervades every aspect of life.

Hegemony based on an ideological premise of racial superiority has served concrete and material functions. It legitimated the conquest and genocide of indigenous populations and the enslavement of Africans in both North and South America. Later, it licensed the annexation of territories inhabited by multiracial peoples, first in Mexico, then Puerto Rico. Toward the end of the nineteenth century, after the abolition of slavery, the mechanisms of domination underwent a revision; an array of coercive institutions and laws kept Native Americans, blacks, Hispanics, and Asians subordinated, segregated, and marginalized.

The economic logic underlying racial hegemony takes several forms. On a macro level, the capitalist class employs racism in a "divide and rule" fashion to undermine the bargaining power and political unity of a multiracial working class. Under certain circumstances, segregated labor allows capitalists to achieve higher-than-average profits. It is not only capitalists, however, who benefit from discrimination. Exclusionary hiring practices that limit the supply of labor can work to the advantage of white workers as well, by pushing up their wage level. In other words, racial hegemony may require the support, or at least the tolerance, of substantial segments of the white working class.

Historically, racially based attitudes made it easier for employers to allocate cheaper labor to special purposes. When labor shortages in crucial industries were overcome by importing racial and ethnic minorities (Chinese to build the railroads, Mexicans and Puerto Ricans to work agricultural fields), opposition to bringing in non-Europeans was met by devising legislation that clearly circumscribed the rights of these workers, thereby affirming their second-class status in the United States. Their visible "otherness" made them easy targets for such compromises.

Although these overt forms of hegemony have been largely eradicated, minorities continue to be subjected to discriminatory practices by dominant groups and institutions.[3] For decades minority workers were excluded from better-paying jobs in many industrial sectors, and in government as well. Hiring bias is still evident in such industries as construction and financial services. Racial wage differences and occupational segregation prevail across the labor market. Subtle and covert forms of discrimination still pervade rental housing, mortgage lending, access to entrepreneurial capital, and educational services.

But history teaches that social oppression breeds active response on the part of the oppressed. Just as labor organizes to resist class domination, racial/ethnic minorities undertake *ethnicity-based strategies*, hoping to establish an autonomous foothold in a racially divided society. Disadvantaged groups seek to transform racial and cultural difference from a barrier into a resource, recasting racial identity as a bonding mechanism and a basis for self-esteem and group pride. Such people rarely remain passive bystanders; the pursuit of ethnicity-based strategies makes them active social agents for change. Social protest, political insurgency, civil disobedience, and economic and cultural movements are examples of how minorities act to change their condition. Racial hegemony, like class oppression, is a two-way affair: it generates a countering response, which can be threatening to capitalist development.

Undoubtedly, an enormous weight of disadvantage, an immense power differential, afflicts those groups who are thwarted simultaneously by class *and* race hegemony. Their situation illustrates the complexities inherent in these categories, for identities of class and race cannot be easily demarcated. Class cannot be equated simply with economic status, race with physical appearance or culture. Each individual is a product of countless experiences and influences and displays a range of identities, attachments, and loyalties. At times, depending on circumstances, white working class persons will find more in common with their black counterparts than with wealthy whites; minority capitalists often find little common ground with majority business people. In short, no class or race designation determines a predictable set of beliefs and behaviors for all situations.

This complexity can be clarified by considering the meaning of racial identity for the various nationality groups among white Americans. The idea of a "white" race did not emerge until the sixteenth century; its origins were clearly associated with the need to justify black slavery in the Americas.[4] Eventually, all European settlers in the New World—including those in the various waves of immigration from the eighteenth into the twentieth century—were taught that they belonged to a homogeneous racial group, distinct from the Native American, African, and Asian populations.

Nevertheless, this superimposed racial identity could not do away with the hierarchy of prejudice that ran through European history and was transposed to the United States. Between Anglo-Saxons and Latin Europeans or Christians and Jews, among scores of ethnicities and languages, bitter hostilities had accumulated in the Old World. Many were reproduced in the new setting. The story of the urban United States is largely the story of European immigrant groups fighting their way into the mainstream, often battling the very adversaries they thought they had left behind: the Irish confronted the descendants of their colonizer; Jews once again had to deal with the torment of anti-Semitism. Keeping in mind these long-standing and multilayered conflicts is crucial to understanding how racial identity becomes modified by nationality, language, and culture.

The same applies to African Americans and Puerto Ricans. Until they hear a few words spoken, most Americans cannot distinguish between a U.S.-born black and a Haitian or Jamaican. Each is classified in the official surveys as "black," but they display variations in customs and historical background. For Puerto Ricans the meaning of race is perhaps even more complex, since racial identity in Puerto Rico is unlike that of the mainland United States. The Puerto Rican migration brought New York face to face for the first time with a multiracial people, and the migrants found that their assumptions about race, class, and culture were greatly at variance with practices and expectations in the new society. Inevitably, these facts had a jarring effect on the group's adaptation, including their perceptions of one another in the context of race. Would their multiracial identity unravel in the face of America's white-black dichotomy?

All of this accentuates the point that the great schisms of class and race veil more intricate rifts and tensions internal to each category. Systems of class- and race-based hegemony are the principal institutional structures facilitating capitalist reproduction, but their efficacy is subject to myriad contradictions and countervailing influences.

Labor Segmentation

The Effects of Stratification

By the middle of this century, transformations in the production process and technological change had generated an essentially dual system of employers: large corporations on the one hand and peripheral firms on the other. This differentiation, in turn, created a stratified labor force in which workers encounter differing sets of opportunities, working conditions, and rewards, depending upon which stratum, or "segment," an individual is attached to. For example, persons with similar educational backgrounds often display wide differences in earnings because they happen to work in dissimilar segments.

Industrial dualism and labor segmentation form the structural basis for the inequalities and divisions among U.S. workers in the postwar period. The socioeconomic position of a particular class, class stratum, or racial/ethnic group will be dependent largely on its siting within this nexus of industry and occupation, the segmentation structure.[5]

According to one important group of analysts, the labor force is divided into three parts: the *independent primary, subordinate primary,* and *secondary* segments.[6] Workers in both primary segments are employed by large institutions and corporations. Those in the independent primary segment are usually defined as "professionals" (such as lawyers, editors, college professors); their work offers a degree of autonomy and independence. Workers in the subordinate primary segment (typically, office clerks or factory workers) are often unionized; these jobs provide certain protections and security in a regimented work environment. Workers in the secondary segment (usually employed by the smaller marginal firms that constitute the other half of the industrial dualism described above) ordinarily make less money and enjoy fewer benefits and safeguards than their counterparts in the primary segment; they frequently hold their jobs at the discretion of their employers.

Across segments, variations in labor market outcomes—wages, working conditions, potential mobility—are determined largely by the characteristics and job structures of given companies, rather than by the attributes of the workers themselves. Segment differences are fairly rigid because, according to David Gordon, "the structures defining jobs within each segment are not easily adjusted to changes in labor market conditions or labor supply proportions . . . [and] firms cannot easily change the ways in which they organize production or hire and promote workers."[7]

The distinction between independent primary and subordinate primary jobs arises primarily from the difference in the skills required to get hired. Employment in independent primary jobs—for example, as a teacher or an accountant—calls for a combination of general and professional skills, acquired primarily through formal education. Subordinate primary jobs require job-specific skills, attained primarily through a relatively short training process, either within the firm or externally.

There is no major difference between the skills of workers in the subordinate primary segment and those in the secondary segment. A subordinate primary worker usually has the same basic skills as a secondary worker performing similar tasks. Yet because the two are employed in different segments of the labor market, they typically receive different rewards and occupy different statuses. What really distinguishes the economic position of these two workers is the nature of their employers: that is, the characteristics of the firms they work for.

Historical and institutional factors may well account for a differential allocation of labor across these two segments. Two groups of workers distinguished by race, ethnicity, or gender may have similar levels of schooling and skill, yet different proportions of their members will work in subordinate primary and secondary jobs. At various points in U.S. history, discriminatory practices excluded entire groups from jobs in the subprimary segment. For many years, for example, African Americans could not obtain entry-level jobs in banking firms, utilities, and insurance companies; the same was true for Latinos and Asians. Likewise, women were systematically blocked from male-dominated occupations. Some members of these groups were relegated to lower-paying, secondary jobs as laborers, maintenance workers, and domestics. Others were totally excluded from employment in the industrializing economy, confined to subsistence farming or public relief.

Although training and experience are important in getting and keeping a job in any segment, a worker's pay also depends on which of the three segments he or she is employed in. Education and labor force experience (how long one has been employed, and in what capacity) are essential ingredients for securing wage increases in the independent primary segment, whereas collective bargaining via the union-management relation most often governs wage-setting in the subordinate primary segment. In the smaller enterprises typical of the secondary segment, there often exists an informal bargaining process between individual workers and the boss. An employer may favor particular workers and reward them with higher pay or special privileges. Employees are retained as long as they exhibit loyalty and responsiveness to employer dictates. For secondary workers the influence on wages of experience and education is less consequential. Increased education and training are likely to improve earnings only if they become the means to move the worker out of the segment.[8]

Aside from its effect on income, segment location may determine attitudes and behavior. One's class consciousness, or political viewpoint, or attachment to an occupation or a firm will be influenced by one's segment location. Occupational or company attachment is usually lowest in secondary jobs. The lack of class solidarity within U.S. labor partially mirrors the cleavages wrought by labor segmentation.[9] In addition to the obstacles brought on by racial, ethnic, and gender conflicts, an equally great or greater barrier to working-class unity has its basis in labor force segmentation.

Segmentation and Racial Hegemony

The effects of racial discrimination on labor force segmentation—and vice versa—are exemplified in the experiences of African Americans, Mexican Americans, and Puerto Ricans.

Throughout most of U.S. history, African American labor was effectively kept separate from the rest of the labor force.[10] Even after slavery was abolished, an extended era of racial segregation limited employment, residential, and educational opportunities. Until well into the twentieth century, most blacks were excluded from the expansion brought on by industrial capitalism and confined largely to sharecropper status or unemployment. This extended experience of racial hegemony conditioned the subsequent insertion of black labor into the segmented labor force. To say simply, as many analysts do, that the problem with African Americans is a lack of education is to give short shrift to the root causes of unequal opportunity among races in U.S. history.

Denied access to educational skills and union power, and often victimized by discrimination in hiring, blacks were effectively excluded from primary jobs during the period of transition leading to segmentation in the early twentieth century.[11] Their confinement to secondary jobs had as much to do with racial oppression as with the class processes that determine how white workers are allocated across segments.

Racial dynamics may have other consequences, however, having to do with the response to social oppression discussed earlier in this chapter. The political struggle of racially oppressed groups can provide the impetus for the creation of new jobs and may even help to transform industries, affecting the segmentation process from the demand side of the economy. For example, during the 1960s the civil rights and Black Power movements actually led to an enlargement of the public sector, and vigorous activity by blacks in the labor movement contributed to a new wave of trade union organizing.[12]

The history of Mexican Americans, the second largest racial/ethnic minority, reveals another kind of interface between segmentation and racial processes. In effect, the communities of Mexican origin that populated the U.S. Southwest from the mid-1800s through the first few decades of the 1900s constituted an "internal colony."

The United States, victorious in the Mexican American War of 1848, picked up vast tracts of land inhabited primarily by Mexicans and Native Americans. Over time, with the penetration of U.S. capital into the region, Mexican labor was funneled into a specific range of low-paying jobs. Whether as agricultural day laborers, mine workers, or ranch hirelings, their plight was unvarying: distanced from the rapid industrialization occurring in the North and lacking many of the civil liberties accorded to most U.S. citizens, these workers were subject to dual wage systems, debt peonage, and extreme labor repression.[13] After World War II, Chicanos were integrated into the broader U.S. class structure through the labor segmentation process, but they still retain important elements of the colonial relationship. Overwhelmingly relegated to secondary labor, they have remained residentially segregated and politically powerless in many areas.

For the residents of Puerto Rico, U.S. control began in 1898 and underwent minor modifications during the first half of the twentieth century. But the close of World War II provoked a change in the political environment. The difficulties of maintaining direct authority over the territory, at a time of mounting world sentiment for decolonizing the Third World and when island support for political independence was at a peak, forced the United States to redefine its relationship to the possession. In the compromise that was struck, the U.S. government turned over some autonomy to Puerto Rico, while still retaining dominion over economic, legal, and military matters. An important outcome was the promotion, by U.S. and cooperating Puerto Rican authorities, of a massive migration, with New York as the primary destination. Ostensibly, the idea was to insulate the island's economic development ("Operation Bootstrap") from the pressures of population growth.

On the demand side of the New York labor market, the migration made partial economic sense: some light manufacturing and marginal service sectors had expressed a need for unskilled labor, and Puerto Ricans were natural candidates to alleviate the shortage. Thus it was only logical that close to 90 percent of the migrants would end up in the secondary segment, as small-factory operatives, manual laborers, and service workers.

This was fundamentally a politically driven migration, an offshoot of the nation's perceived international interests. Embedded in this perception was a long-held, racially clouded view that Puerto Ricans were not yet ready to handle their own destiny as an independent nation and certainly not prepared for the first-class U.S. citizenship implied by statehood. Political exigency clashed with economic rationality, however, and Puerto Ricans found themselves eventually outnumbering the available opportunities for mainland employment. The grim reality of being a surplus, residual population, somehow dropped en masse into the metropolitan cauldron, was to become a permanent aspect of the New York Puerto Ricans' culture, politics, and life. The reception accorded these new multiracial and multi-lingual arrivals reinforced their anxiety about their future.

Ethnicity-Based Responses to Racial Hegemony

Adapting segmentation theory so that it fully appreciates racial/ethnic diversity requires looking at several key questions. What is the response of racially subordinated groups to their conditions of domination? What forms does this response take, and to what extent do they conflict with or complement one another? What are the possible connections between this response and labor market segmentation? How may these relationships affect employment and wage levels for different minority groups? The following statement of how these issues interface constitutes the framework for much of the qualitative and empirical discussion in succeeding chapters.

Forms of Ethnicity-Based Struggles

Racial domination systems are buttressed by a comprehensive array of laws, policies, and ideologies that have the effect of keeping racial/ethnic minorities marginalized and disenfranchised. Voting rights are systematically circumscribed in a way that limits minority political participation, either through gerrymandering practices or by means of administrative restrictions that render inoperative the principle of "one person, one vote." Public allocation of resources—in education, health, and housing services—routinely favors upper-income and non-urban communities, where African Americans and Hispanics are few and far between. The mass media and the dominant culture continually warn of the dangers presented by those Americans who remain unassimilated and on the fringes of the economic and social mainstream. All these practices and attitudes augment the economic system's capacity to reproduce itself.

Although all workers are dependent on the sale of their labor skills for survival, racial/ethnic labor confronts the additional obstacle of subjugation. A primary response is the pursuit of *ethnic political power,* in which subordinated minorities consciously organize in their own self-interest.

The "pursuit of political power" refers to efforts at group advancement which take place in the public realm and seek to reform or radically transform state-related institutions, functions, and policies. Such efforts can be (1) "civic," as manifested in voter registration and electoral campaigns, civil rights drives, and struggles of oppositional militancy such as the Black Power and Chicano Power movements; (2) educational, as in the promotion of government-supported educational institutions (historically, black colleges); (3) entrepreneurial, as in minority capitalism initiatives that are subsidized by the state (small business loans, first-source contracts, set-asides).

Responses to discrimination may also follow an *indigenous*, or internal, course. Often, groups seek to enhance collective resources and power independent of interventions in the public (state) sphere. Examples of this approach can similarly be found in the civic, educational/cultural, and entrepreneurial realms. Minorities may create a range of self-help organizations to promote social progress: mutual aid, cultural, religious, labor, women's, and youth associations. The tradition of Puerto Rican "hometown clubs"—whereby migrants in the diaspora coalesce with compatriots from their birthplace towns—illustrates this option. Other examples include the establishment of autonomous alternative schools. The expression of indigenous *economic* activity took on increasing significance during the 1970s and 1980s with the development of immigrant enterprises, which exploit kinship and ethnic ties to promote group economic advancement.

While essentially "nonpolitical," indigenous approaches are not to be construed as contradictory to or exclusive of political power strategies. Indeed, the success of political power often depends on the establishment of indigenous strategies and institutions. Table 1 summarizes examples of ethnic struggles for political power and of indigenous self-help activities, both subsumed under the general category of ethnicity-based strategies.

Catalysts for Ethnicity-Based Strategies

Ethnically oriented interventions would be less necessary in the presence of a broad class-based challenge to the capitalist accumulation process. Since racially subordinate populations are overwhelmingly working-class people, they would perceive it in their interests to pur-

Table 1
Ethnicity-Based Strategies

Political Struggles (public domain)	Indigenous Activities (internal)
Civic	
civil rights	mutual aid groups
oppositional militancy	hometown clubs
electoral	youth associations
	women's associations
Educational/cultural	
desegregation	alternative schools
open admissions	religious organizations
bilingual education	cultural organizations
community control	
preschool enrichment (Head Start)	
Entrepreneurial	
minority capitalism	immigrant enterprise
small business development	credit unions
community economic development	
set-aside programs	
economic boycotts	

sue a transformation of capitalist society into one that subordinates the profit motive to social criteria and needs. A class unity bringing together working and poor people of all races and ethnicities would offer the best chance to bring about such a change. But multi-racial, anti-capitalist coalitions have been rare in U.S. history, and most were short-lived experiments in which racial divisions ultimately brought about their downfall. During the period of Reconstruction in the post–Civil War South and in the Great Depression years, significant mergings of white and black constituencies occurred, but they did not endure.

In the absence of such a comprehensive unity, especially since World War II, the rivalries among ethnic components of the population continue to be an important element in the competition for jobs and economic resources. The debility of working-class power—and the correlative fact of continued capitalist dominance—is in no small part due to the lack of intraclass racial harmony.

Among racial/ethnic minorities, the need to seek political power is accentuated by the lack of access to wealth-producing assets. Most people who read reports of socioeconomic status do not realize that these accounts normally compile only annual income totals: earnings from wages and salaries, self-employment, and such sources as social security, pension benefits, and welfare payments. On the basis of these census data, the average level of household income is determined for various groups or classes of people, and from these figures other estimates are devised: the level of poverty, the shape of income distribution, and so on. But excluded from this picture are people's *assets* such as real property, stocks, and business holdings. Factoring these in exposes the immensity of the racial gap in economic status.

The great majority of racial/ethnic workers have zero net worth; the difference between their assets and their debts is negligible. One needs a sizable annual income in order to accumulate, through savings and investment activity, significant assets. Asset ownership, or at least access to capital, is what enables entrepreneurship. As the saying goes, "You need money to make money."

But what about all the entrepreneurial energy displayed by immigrants during the past two decades? Have they not overcome the handicap of being "outsiders" in a very competitive environment?

It is true that among recent immigrants, especially Asians, commercial ventures have flourished significantly. Several new developments, however, supported the rise in immigrant enterprise during the 1970s and 1980s. Notably, the increasing availability of venture capital transferred from distant shores such as Hong Kong, Taiwan, and South Korea enabled the bankrolling of U.S.-based economic activity; the success of these Far Eastern economies encouraged capital export in search of new markets. In addition, the first wave of immigrants from these countries in the 1970s was largely a self-selected cohort of educated and skilled persons, a contingent that formed a critical mass of small business operators and merchants. Then the later immigrant flow, primarily made up of low-wage workers, supplied a pool of labor that could be employed in many of the immigrant businesses.

These circumstances allowed some groups to initiate niche-creating activities and establish an economic foothold in a number of local areas. What is significant is their ability to trigger a process of economic mobility without reliance on ethnic political power in the public domain. As of 1990, for example, there were no elected officials of Asian American origin in state or city government in the New York area. Yet this apparent success has to be qualified. Despite a significant stratum of professionals and entrepreneurs, vast numbers of Asians continue to live under harsh conditions; others avoid official impoverishment only by working excessive hours in either family businesses or sweatshops.

Moreover, the seeming achievement of these Asian "model minorities" has not exempted them from racial discrimination.

But for most racial/ethnic minorities, who lack funding from abroad, the entrepreneurial path toward social and economic mobility is essentially closed. As historically subject peoples, their capacity to accumulate capital has been delimited through a variety of institutions and mechanisms, leading to a class structure composed overwhelmingly of persons whose sole source of earnings is the sale of their labor. Among African Americans, Native Americans, Mexican Americans, and Puerto Ricans there is no "national bourgeoisie" of consequence. The absence of a dynamic capitalist class restricts the scope of economic enterprises that can be generated from within these groups.

Nor is educational attainment seen by many as anything but a limited route to social progress. The quality of public education in urban schools fails to keep pace with that found in suburban or private schools, and the payback for a high school diploma or even for a college degree is perceived to be declining, especially for minorities. Groups with the same educational qualifications as their white counterparts repeatedly find themselves with higher unemployment or lower earnings rates.

Under these circumstances, ethnicity-based political power emerges as a prominent response to the conditions of persistent inequality and discrimination. The apparent futility of relying on human capital or entrepreneurial strategies accentuates the appeal of the political option. The civil rights movement of the 1960s and its constituent claims for affirmative action and equal opportunity testify to the effort to exercise political power. Other forms of political action, electoral or directly militant, become attractive options. Minority labor seeks to exert political power as a way of compensating for barriers in the labor market and the society generally.

The State as a Site of Struggle

The governmental sector emerges as a prime target of ethnicity-based political power strategies. To the extent that racial minorities hold some sway within government, their political power is enhanced. Because the state can create landmark legislation or reinterpret past laws in ways that broaden or interdict the potential for group progress, and because it redistributes incomes and resources through tax and expenditure policies, government is a site of conflict and an instrument for control or regulation.

Not until the early 1960s was there sufficient pressure to expand civil rights for blacks in the South, and it took the full force of the national government to bring this about. In the mid-1960s the Great Society of Lyndon B. Johnson initiated a far-reaching array of social programs—the most direct state intervention to deal with poverty since the Great Depression. The subsequent backlash stifling this progressive moment of social activism was itself a product of political struggle, with the balance of power tipping in favor of conservative forces. From Richard Nixon to George Bush the national state (with the Jimmy Carter exception) steered away from liberal social policy. The political movements that generated the victories of the 1960s and early 1970s were unable to sustain all of their initial accomplishments.

These shifting fortunes attest to the state's capacity for accommodating class and social conflict, even as it supports the stable reproduction of capitalism. It is neither a neutral institution, adjudicating disputes between class interests, nor a perfectly honed instrument of control for the dominant class. The state bends and adapts; it deflects strategic challenges to capitalist control but must make concessions to the democratic process.

Government is also an economic power in its own right. Access to government employment depends partially on such nonmarket factors as group political power and patronage. Beginning in the 1960s the changing racial composition of the labor force and the existence of antipoverty programs and affirmative action policies increased minority employment in the public sector. In addition to its role as employer, government wields economic power through its purchase of goods and services and its investment in physical infrastructure. It can also influence the direction of private-sector activity through tax legislation and incentive programs. Metropolitan and regional jurisdictions compete to attract capital. Government policies, sensitive as they are at all levels to political pressures, may very well favor certain economic sectors or industries and thus, directly and indirectly, affect the social conditions and status of labor.

Finally, political power enters into the process of interethnic competition for employment and wage growth. In the absence of class solidarity, labor groups may be forced to organize along lines of specific self-interests. Racial/ethnic minorities may perceive themselves as confronting one another in a zero-sum game over employment opportunities.

For racial/ethnic communities seeking some measure of control over their destiny, then, the state is a site of struggle where each group's share of available resources, jobs, and incomes may be determined by its success in wielding political power.

Class and Race, Growth and Stagnation

Growth and stagnation define the two phases of economic change in the post–World War II period. In order to trace the relationships between economic change, class, and race, one must look at the impact of these two primary interactions on (1) the *labor market,* (2) the *state,* and (3) *politics.* How do class and race mediate the effect of economic change on these three levels, each of which is of crucial importance to the social conditions of racial/ethnic minorities.

The labor market allocates labor inputs into the production process. The timing and manner of incorporation of racial/ethnic labor is influenced by such factors as the stage of economic development and the degree of class and racial stratification within the labor force. Historically, the restricted nature of minority labor's incorporation has led to its continued economic and political vulnerability.

The state, because of its political and economic functions, is a site of class contention and racial conflict. In their various roles and identities, capital and labor, whites and minorities, compete or ally with one another for influence over the state's power.

Politics is broadly conceptualized here as a realm encompassing ideology, culture, social movements, and race relations. The political consequences of class conflict and race-related discord, especially in their urban context, interact with broader economic conditions to affect the status of these groups.

Growth: 1945–1970s

During the postwar growth phase, the dynamics of race and class were manifested in several important ways, accounting for the dramatic but contentious infusion of African Americans and Puerto Ricans into the New York economy. These developments include (1) the consolidation of labor segmentation through a national capital-labor accord; (2) the allocation of racial/ethnic labor into secondary jobs; (3) the remaking of the city's politics with the first mass migration of non-Europeans, from the South and Puerto Rico; (4) the political insurgency of the 1960s.

1. The segmentation process that had evolved in the labor market during the pre-World War II era became consolidated in the early post-war years through a de facto agreement between large corporations and industrial unions. The accord basically guaranteed stable employment and wage increases to unionized workers in exchange for labor peace. During the 1940s and 1950s, workers not covered by collective bargaining and those in declining industries—including most minority labor—were relegated to the "secondary" labor segment with substandard wages and working conditions. In the 1950s and 1960s, labor organization intensified within the public sector, elevating the quality of many jobs held by white ethnics, including Irish, Italian, and Jewish workers.

2. The migration of new labor, racial/ethnic U.S. citizens from the South and Puerto Rico, was crucial in solving the labor shortages arising in New York during the boom years of the early postwar period. Many and varied were the forces joining to bring about the largest inflow of fresh migrants since the early twentieth century. Changing economic and political conditions in their home regions fomented a substantial movement of African Americans and Puerto Ricans. Blacks were, on the one hand, propelled outward by dire poverty and the rigid segregation of living and working arrangements in the rural South and, on the other hand, attracted by hopeful employment prospects and liberal racial policies in the North. A major transformation in Puerto Rico's political relation to the United States precipitated a parallel flow. Island residents had had free access to northern U.S. cities for almost fifty years, but not until the 1940s were large numbers induced to migrate.

There were several labor market consequences of these population flows. The ready availability of these new workers aided the consolidation of the labor stratification process that was under way at the time. Retirement and intergenerational mobility among white ethnic groups had created a vacuum that low-wage labor could fill in several manufacturing and service industries. The new migrants became prime candidates for secondary jobs in garment production, building maintenance, the hospital sector, and the tourist industry. They gave new life to the process of ethnic succession in the labor force, described by some as an "ethnic queuing system." Their entry seemed to be following an age-old pattern of beginning at the bottom rung of the economic ladder.

Little did they realize that upward mobility was not to be in the cards; that fact would not become clear for another two decades. Lacking significant capital resources, advanced skills, or political clout, African Americans and Puerto Ricans had virtually no leverage in the city's economy. Bearers of a racial and cultural heritage distinct from that of European-origin New Yorkers, they often found their racial/ethnic character used as a screening device to sort them out from the better jobs. Given the workings of racial hegemony, they found few advantages in their identity as *native* minorities.

3. In transforming the population profile, however, native minorities also forced accommodations in the functioning of the state sector and transformed irrevocably the political life of the metropolis. An important characteristic distinguished them from European immigrants. Both groups had been systematically denied the full rights associated with democracy: African Americans through their experience of slavery and segregation, Puerto Ricans through a colonial status imposed in 1898. Here were two groups who, like Native Americans, had reason to question the veracity of U.S. claims to moral superiority; they were not immigrants but citizens who could doubt that the American Dream was meant for them.[14]

Their historical experiences conditioned native minorities to be doubtful of the classic immigrant adaptation model. First-generation European immigrants, many having fled persecution or poverty in the Old World, were generally grateful to reach American soil. In the new terrain they could share in the fruits of democracy by means of hard work and patience. But African Americans and Puerto Ricans were wary of the mythology of the Promised Land and sustained mixed feelings about a country that had already deprived them of their full rights and repressed their cultural autonomy.

Their knowledge of this deprivation tempered the enthusiasm of these groups once they had migrated to the metropolis. It gave rise to an unwillingness to wait generations for social mobility, a skepticism regarding the use of standard political methods, and an inclination toward political militancy. Although this attitude reinforced their outsider status in the eyes of established groups, it had an important consequence: it engendered a focus on making the state accountable to minorities through social programs, the protection of civil liberties, and the stimulation of economic development. Compared with the private economy, government was seen as much more accessible to the influence of political might.

4. For most minorities, prosperity's rewards seemed unattainable even into the 1960s. Internationally, U.S. leaders boasted that for the first time in history a nation had extended democracy and affluence to all its populace. But on the domestic front, continuing poverty and racial discrimination showed this to be a misleading claim. One of the great inconsistencies of the boom years was that racial/ethnic minorities were being excluded from an equal share in the benefits of economic growth. The response to a perceived obstructionism on the part of the status quo was a resurgence of ethnicity-based struggles. On the New York stage the drama was played out intensely throughout the 1960s and into the early 1970s. On numerous fronts African Americans and Puerto Ricans engaged in movements for social and political equality, often in tandem, occasionally at odds.

Where alliances between the two groups failed to materialize, certain advantages generally gave the edge to blacks in any interethnic competition. One was numerical superiority. Another was that African American patterns of migration and settlement, social and religious institutions, and political organizations made for a more fully developed *community infrastructure.* And not to be overlooked is the simple fact that African American history, initiated at the birth of European settlement in the New World, is an indispensable part of the American story. Puerto Rico, on the other hand, passing from Spanish to U.S. colonialism at the end of the nineteenth century, was not only a later arrival, but its inhabitants' insertion into the mainland scene has been essentially regional, affecting chiefly the Northeast and Midwest. The implications of this difference for the perceived validity of the two groups' respective claims for equality seem obvious: in the minds of most enlightened white Americans, their country owes a greater moral debt to African Americans than to Puerto Ricans.[15]

Two other factors have also worked against acknowledgment of Puerto Rican rights. For one thing, few citizens understand the history of the island and its essentially colonial relationship to the United States; during most of the twentieth century, mainland residents considered it another foreign country. Therefore, Puerto Rican migrants were seen as *immigrants,* not as fellow Americans relocating from one U.S. jurisdiction to another. Gaining legitimacy for their demands was confounded by confusion in the public mind over the exact place of Puerto Ricans within social and legal domains. International considerations also came into play. In key government circles it was thought that to concede a special U.S. obligation to Puerto Ricans was to open a can of worms; it meant agreeing that somehow the Puerto Rican "problem" derived from the colonial conditions of U.S. domination throughout the island's history. At a time of rising world concern over colonialism in the Third World, the United States could hardly afford this embarrassment.[16]

Stagnation: 1970s to the Present

If native minorities could not fully share the benefits of growth, the subsequent long-term decline—which spelled serious difficulties for many New Yorkers—occasioned a steady fall in living standards for most African Americans and Puerto Ricans. From the late 1970s on, their prospects were shaped by key features of the local political economy: (1) a business-led restructuring drive, consisting of major revisions in corporate organization and methods of production; (2) a political backlash that facilitated capitalist efforts to reduce the scope of the state; (3) for native minority communities, the failure of political gain to generate substantive economic progress; (4) the economic impact of new immigration from Third World countries; (5) an alteration in race relations brought about by the new immigrant presence.

1. In New York's service industries, restructuring consisted of employer strategies that streamlined labor costs by making greater use of part-time workers and downscaling management bureaucracies. Manufacturing, depleted by the flight of capital to low-wage regions, was revived by small producers who were able to reap a reward from newly arriving immigrants: substandard working conditions mushroomed, as employers used undocumented labor for production. Restructuring was not limited to high finance and advanced technologies; it bred an expansion of the informal (underground) economy as well. In the 1980s, restructuring also encompassed a set of public policies espoused by the Reagan administration: freezing the minimum wage, relaxing health and occupational standards, and relentlessly challenging union power.

2. The problems of a stultified economy, compounded by a declining tax base as middle-income families accelerated their out-migration, severely circumscribed the maneuverability of the government sector. While minorities continued to insist that the state act on their needs, the voices of opposition to these demands grew louder, nationally and

locally. Based on fears that were fiscal and racial, a backlash movement emerged in the early 1970s that dramatically slowed the pace of social reform and curbed the insurgency of racial/ethnic minorities.

A series of important effects originated in this backlash. The principles of equal opportunity and activist government were severely questioned, as were specific remedies such as affirmative action and bilingual education. A taxpayer revolt further undermined the strength of the public sector. Having watched native minorities appeal to ethnic identity as a galvanizing force for political empowerment, white ethnics too began to assert their heritage. On the political front a fundamental realignment occurred as the Republican Party successfully courted white working-class voters in the South and urban North, splitting the New Deal Coalition that had been the bedrock of Democratic Party success. All this provided a severe test of race relations and a challenge to the idea of cultural pluralism.

In the next decade, as Washington relegated more and more functions to local government and revoked earlier commitments to fighting poverty, America's urban centers seemed without a solution to the problems of declining resources and worsening poverty. Less than twenty-five years after the War on Poverty was announced, it was declared a moot issue. Less than a decade after escaping bankruptcy, New York City once again, in the late 1980s, stood on the brink of fiscal collapse.

These developments had some bearing on the relative economic status of blacks and Puerto Ricans. Arguably, the cumulative weight of two waves of economic dislocation—manufacturing flight in the growth years, capitalist restructuring in the decline period—seemed to have wrought singular havoc on Puerto Rican conditions. Historically, with their greater attachment to the manufacturing sector, and smaller presence within the shelter of public employment, and with their political power still diffused, Puerto Ricans were even less effectively positioned than African Americans to withstand the ravages of economic change, political and racial backlash.

3. As the late 1970s ushered in economic restructuring and political backlash, African Americans and Puerto Ricans increasingly saw the electoral arena as the principal option for political action, and their community movements turned less and less to militant activism. But despite measurable gains throughout the 1980s, there was little evidence that these were translating into economic progress for the two groups. Were the new realities such that political advancement would

not necessarily elicit economic progress? This possibility raised doubts about the efficacy of ethnicity-based strategies and the prospects for African American–Puerto Rican unity. What factors would condition those prospects? How would race and class aspects, between and within the two groups, shape the possibilities of alliance?

4. The expanding presence of immigrant minorities from Latin America, the Caribbean, and Asia revamped the local labor economy in two important ways. First, the newly available supplies of low-wage labor facilitated the restructuring process in several sectors. Many analysts unfortunately have associated the idea of restructuring with the substitution of capital for labor and the displacement of low-wage labor by professional/technical workers. The long-term shift toward a services economy has given credence to these assumptions. But in major urban centers where immigration has been strong, manufacturing sectors have been remade by means of a new reliance on simple production techniques, piecework, substandard pay, and in some instances even a return to homework.

Immigrant labor satisfies a necessary condition for these new modes of operation: foreigners accustomed to a poverty-level standard of living, fleeing a homeland racked by political turmoil and deprivation, are content to accept inferior working conditions and pay. Initially, these are even seen in a positive light, given the workers' memory of instability and social strife in their country of origin. Only time will tell how long they may tolerate these exploitive circumstances.

As individual entrepreneurs and, more important, as family teams, immigrant minorities have made their mark in the world of small business. Their enterprises include restaurants and eateries, grocery and vegetable stores, garment production, travel agencies, and others. In the 1970s and 1980s small entrepreneurship became a prime path of social mobility for minority noncitizens, whose political power was even more lacking than that of native minorities. With kinship networks facilitating labor recruitment and a sense of ethnic identity helping to suppress internal class differences, the new arrivals found that small business offered an important solution to the problem of outsiders attempting to compete in postindustrial New York.

For the most part, their new enterprises were confined to their own ethnic neighborhoods. Vibrant *enclaves* began to flourish throughout the city, each tied to a network of commercial strips: Colombians and Ecuadorians in Astoria, Queens; Chinese, once confined to lower Manhattan's Chinatown, expanding into sections of Queens; Jamaicans and

Haitians in Crown Heights and Flatbush; Dominicans in Washington Heights. Following the route of European ethnics and native minorities, these communities have acted as an initial staging ground, with residential concentration, social networks, and commercial activity all feeding each other and strengthening group identity and mobility.

But small entrepreneurship is not likely to propel group economic mobility unless it transcends the enclave. For the most part, collective economic progress comes when a group creates *niches* in the larger economy as some have done. Perhaps the outstanding examples are the Chinese restaurants and Korean vegetable stores that service New Yorkers throughout the city. In this, they are following the well-worn route traversed by others, such as Italians and Greeks with their eateries. Whether other immigrant minorities will successfully expand their use of small entrepreneurship remains to be seen.[17] Can the new groups escape the fate that awaited African Americans and Puerto Ricans, who approach the twenty-first century still deeply entrenched in poverty? The answer depends on the future trajectory of the economy and the workings of class and race in the coming decades.

5. In the political and cultural realm, the infusion of new immigrants has had an influence no less extraordinary than their impact on the local economy. Theirs has been a transforming presence, modifying existing assumptions and relations regarding race, ethnicity, and ideology. Their energetic drive to insert themselves into the political and social life of the city adds further complexities to racial and ethnic relations.

New intersections take place on several levels: between native minorities and whites, native minorities and immigrant minorities, English-speakers and non-English-speakers, citizens and non-citizens. The arrival of new groups of non-European origin may affect African American–Puerto Rican relations as well. For example, is there a basis for increasing alliances between Puerto Ricans and Dominicans, or African Americans and Jamaicans? Will culturally based identities of Pan-Africanism and *latinismo* usurp the historically based bonds uniting native minorities? The intricacies of these influences are multiple, and their eventual outcomes unpredictable.

By tilting the population balance and converting America's premier urban center into a "minority" city for the first time in its history, immigrant minorities have also brought about a renewed polemic on cultural issues. For decades the reigning ideology of cultural pluralism pictured the United States as a country where different groups could bond politically and socially while still retaining their cultural heritage. The assumption remained, however, that the nation would continue to be essentially an extension of Western civilization and its traditions. Now, a more diversified and potent "Other" is challenging prominent precepts of western traditions, especially ethnocentrism, consumerism, and belief in the primacy of individual over collective rights.

Through growth and stagnation, the dynamics of class and race can be seen as shaping the conditions under which people advance or languish. The trajectory of African Americans and Puerto Ricans within this context illustrates principal characteristics of their history in post-war New York.

CHAPTER TWO

The Regional and Urban Context: 1945–1990

Except for some hardy optimists, historians judge America's days of glory to be things of the past. Explanations vary as to the sources of stagnation, but few doubt this basic tenet. Some place the causes beyond our borders in international competition or excessive military intervention. On the domestic front, the possible culprits include everything from welfare statism to runaway laissez-faire capitalism. Diagnoses abound, theories are plentiful, yet we seem not very close to a consensus. Even as the early 1990s brought the Cold War to an end, the United States seemed no nearer to recovering the economic hegemony it enjoyed in the early postwar years.

A similar sense of gloom pervades discussions about America's premier metropolis. New York's "Golden Age" of growth—the vibrant years from the late 1940s to the late 1960s—was replaced by crisis in the 1970s and recurring stasis in the 1980s. Certainly there have been astounding changes and advances in some areas, but the distressing fact is that many city dwellers were left behind during the vaunted "go-go eighties." Downtown Manhattan basked in hyper-development at the expense of the rest of the city. Hundreds of thousands of new jobs were created, but by and large they were designed for either the highly trained or the easily exploitable, relegating many to the margins of the labor economy. Fortunes were made, but poverty and homelessness grew also.

Residents of the New York area have faced the double jeopardy of national decline linked to the weakening of their great city. And within the metropolitan center, down the hierarchy of geographic and social space where subpopulations of classes and racial/ethnic groups contend, the least powerful were the most vulnerable of all.

This chapter depicts the major trends in the flow and ebb of New York's economic vitality, with particular focus on transformations in the *economic base, population, and labor force*. As in the national picture (and as noted in Chapter One), two principal phases can be discerned: a growth period from the end of World War II, reaching a plateau in the late 1960s; then, following a transition period of crisis in the 1970s, the stagnation era beginning in the 1980s and continuing to the present.

From Golden Age to Crisis

Economic Base and Sectoral Diversity

The early postwar period found New York an already mature city, the premier urban center of a country just beginning to assert international hegemony. Several features characterizing the city's economy endowed it with an aura of singularity and dominance. It was a place highly connected to the economic fortunes of the nation, well diversified in its industrial base and offering important advantages to business enterprise.[1]

The truly dynamic urban economies are those that produce goods and services used by other regions of the country. A locality seeking a strong economic base must aspire to more than self-sufficiency, must be able to do more than just satisfy local needs. It must be linked to a larger economic entity—be it a region or a nation or the world—by meeting that entity's demand for the locality's output. Indeed, the economic foundation of a city is made up of its "basic" (or "export") industries, those that produce primarily for consumption in other areas.[2]

New York's bond to the rest of the country was established in key areas such as apparel goods, printing and publishing, financial and insurance services. These were the city's traditional "basic industries" in the sense that they were the motor of its growth; the remaining sectors made up its nonbasic industries, which survived primarily by servicing these basic activities. Basic industries drive change because increases or decreases in their level of production or employment are reflected in nonbasic sectors. Thus an increase in the nation's demand for the products of New York's basic industries could spur an expansion of activity in the city's non-basic sectors. In the mid-1950s some 40 percent of economic activity in the New York Region was oriented toward the national market, an indication of the robustness of the area's economy.[3] Significantly, the bulk (two-thirds) of these export-tailored activities involved manufacturing. An essential component of the city's distinctiveness lay in its character as a production hub of export goods.

Employment patterns by industry indicate the diversity of the city's economy. In 1950 manufacturing supplied 30.1 percent (1,040,000) of total jobs, leading all sectors (Table 2). All services, including financial, insurance, and real estate sectors, accounted for 24 percent (835,000), and the trade sectors represented 21.8 percent of all jobs. This balanced mix of basic and nonbasic industries, manufacturing and service sectors, buffered the area against alterations in the national economy during the recessions of the 1950s and 1960s. Not overly dependent on a particular industrial sector, the regional economy was relatively sheltered against the nation's business cycles.[4] In the ensuing decades, however, the striking expansion of the services sector and the rise of the global economy would cause fundamental changes in New York's economic base.

Table 2
New York City Employment by Industry, 1950–1990
(in thousands)

Year	Total	Mfg.	Constr.	T., C., P.U.	W/R Trade	F.I.R.E.	Misc. & Services	Gov't.
1950	3,448	1040	122	330	750	330	505	370
1955	3,431	1010	115	325	735	350	520	375
1960	3,538	947	127	318	745	384	609	408
1965	3,577	865	111	318	748	390	684	462
1970	3,743	766	110	323	735	458	788	563
1975	3,286	537	80	270	634	420	772	574
1980	3,302	496	77	257	613	448	894	517
1985	3,488	408	106	232	638	508	1040	557
1990	3,566	338	115	229	608	520	1149	607

Sources: Port Authority of New York and New Jersey, *Report*, 1980, 1984, 1992; Herbert Bienstock, "New York City's Labor Market," *City Almanac* 12, no. 4 (1977) 5 (for 1950 and 1955).
Notes: Figures represent all persons (residents and nonresidents) who were employed in the city. Abbreviations stand for the following industry categories: Mfg.—Manufacturing; Constr.—Construction; T., C., P.U.—transportation, communication, public utilities; W/R Trade—wholesale and retail trade; F.I.R.E.—finance, insurance, real estate; Gov't.—government, all levels. Because of adjustments in the data collection process, figures are not exactly comparable across all years.

The Advantages of Doing Business in New York

The first-time visitor to New York is struck by—indeed, may find appealing—the city's density of population and whirlwind of activity. Long-time residents often tire of this intensity of life, preferring the calm and expanse beyond the metropolitan core. Yet these attributes offer clear advantages to certain types of enterprises.

Few cities can promise businesses the benefits of "external economies" as New York can. These are benefits that accrue when a clustering of economic activities allows a firm to realize cost savings. On the production side, a company faces lower costs if it belongs to an industry that is geographically concentrated rather than dispersed. That industry's suppliers will naturally congregate in the area, making it less necessary for individual firms to carry large inventories or maintain long supply routes. Workers will be attracted to such a region, providing a ready supply of labor. On the output side, firms have access to large markets nearby for sale of their products and can reduce transportation costs below what they would be if all markets were distantly located.[5]

But the conditions giving rise to external economies are not to be found everywhere. By definition, these advantages are available in the context of intensively utilized spaces, and a preferred spatial location—like all resources—commands a high price. Consequently, the savings engendered by these economies must outweigh the other costs, such as rents and taxes, associated with doing business in highly attractive sites.

By midcentury New York offered extensive rentable space, a wide variety of specialized suppliers of industrial materials and services, and a labor supply quite diverse in skills. Furthermore, the region touted an excellent array of transportation facilities, especially freight services.[6]

Certain kinds of businesses particularly appreciate direct access to these resources and facilities. The producer of ladies' apparel operates under conditions of continual uncertainty, especially given the volatility of consumer tastes. Entrepreneurs in this field need to be extremely agile in deploying machinery and labor to meet changes in fashions. They cannot afford to be bogged down by huge plants and assembly-line processes that take a long time to establish or modify.

Job printers produce goods that vary constantly not only in volume but also in content. Since the printing design for each magazine or greeting card differs from the previous one, the printer must rely on machinery that can be specialized for a limited time. These producers prefer to contract out the design and layout functions to neighboring companies that specialize in this type of work. Advertising and legal services are just two of many other industries that count on this spatial proximity to producers, suppliers, and consumers.

Historically, New York's appeal to businesses has resided in its capacity to extend the advantages of an enormous pool of facilities and resources, enabling rapid access and face-to-face contact among suppliers, producers and consumers. Since the nineteenth century the city has served as a location center for numerous enterprises that can benefit from this singular clustering of economic resources and activity. By one account, nearly one-third of the region's jobs in the mid-1950s were located in such enterprises.[7]

As a result, it is no wonder that small firm size has been a characteristic of New York's business sector. As one moves deeper into the core of Manhattan and the central business district, the potential benefits from agglomeration economies multiply. The gathering of firms intensifies, with carting services and the subway system serving as inexpensive conduits of materials and labor. But the intense competition for space by industries functioning under constant uncertainty makes for a fairly small scale of operations of these establishments. Traditionally, average firm size has been smaller in New York than elsewhere.[8] As a center of concentrated economic activity, the area has also been an ideal site for spawning new enterprises and products. This role as "incubator" has gone hand in hand with the external economies and small firm size that have characterized the industrial structure.

The city noted for small shops and lofts bustling with factory workers has been no less famous for the office buildings piercing the skyline. The numerous small factories had their counterpoint in the skyscrapers that housed America's major corporations on Wall Street and Madison Avenue. For New York was also a "headquarters city," offering attractions to businesses that were a world apart from the garment producers but could nevertheless take similar advantage of the city's features. Manufacturers such as General Motors situated their support operations in the city, away from the auto assembly lines. They desired easy access to the capital markets where funds could be raised and to the lawyers, accountants, advertising professionals, and managers who congregated in the region. Giant banking and insurance companies needed to be close to the financial nerve center of the country. The annual survey of "Fortune 500" companies provides a simple indicator of the importance of this function: by 1957, 144 of the top companies had located their central offices in New York, far and away the highest figure for U.S. cities.[9]

The firms capable of profiting from a New York location nevertheless faced a range of obstacles. The economic law of supply and demand guarantees that intensely utilized space will exact high rentals. In time, workers will insist on higher compensation, pushing their wages beyond that received by workers in other regions. The local government, charged with the responsibility of maintaining the physical infrastructure, transportation facilities, and public safety, will pass on much of this cost to businesses through the tax system. Business owners must deal with the high cost of living, the congestion, and stresses of the urban life-style; these too enter into the benefit-cost calculations of entrepreneurs.

Firms must constantly weigh the benefits and costs of doing business at particular sites. The very conditions that helped to establish New York's prominence in the twentieth century harbored as well the sources of its vulnerability. With its industrial diversity intact and its continuing appeal to dynamic enterprises, however, the balance persisted in favor of the positive aspects until the 1960s, obscuring the signs of impending difficulties.

Constraints on Economic Success

Like natural organisms, consumer goods can be thought of as passing through a life cycle: birth, rapid growth, maturity, and extinction. These cycles will vary in length, depending on the public's preferences, the cost of production, technological change, among other factors.

The radio exemplifies the way changes in product life cycle can affect an industry's location. By the early part of the century radio manufacture was established in New York, feeding off the qualities that made the city unique for industries still in the experimental phase. With the end of World War II, however, previously pent-up consumer demand assured a ready market, allowing manufacturers to switch to standardized production and assembly-line methods. Under these circumstances, it was preferable to locate production facilities in areas of lower labor and freight costs. It became feasible to pass up the attractions of face-to-face contact and access to a large pool of diversely skilled labor, because these attributes were no longer as important as having the physical space to build large production centers. During this period the industry came to be dominated by a small number of large companies, firms that could grow to maturity serving the national market for radios. In this transition, New York lost many of these companies to other regions.

Likewise, as other products that had been "incubated" in New York achieved acceptance in the market, entrepreneurs found it wiser to use large machines to routinize the production process—counting on a large volume to cover the enormous costs of capital equipment[10]—and again, some expanding producers transferred operations to locations where space and labor were less costly.

A variant pattern of plant relocation occurred in the ladies' apparel industry, spurred in this case by the development of the truck. Rail transport, previously the only available method for moving supplies and goods to markets outside the city, was too costly for garment producers to consider locating outside the urban ring. But once trucking emerged as a relatively inexpensive substitute for rail shipping, garment producers could use these new vehicles to spin off various phases of the production process. The more specialized steps of designing and cutting could still be done in city locations, but assembling and sewing could be performed in areas of cheaper labor. Trucks delivered patterns, components, and supplies to the sewing factories and returned the completed products to the city for the final stage: sales.[11]

In these and other instances, changes in consumer demand or in technology, coupled with increasing relative costs, encouraged businesses to leave the city or farm out portions of their activity. Already by the 1950s and early 1960s the scale had started to tip against the traditional advantages of locating in New York. The external economies that had traditionally sufficed as a magnet of attraction were increasingly outweighed by the appeal of relocating.

Another aspect of this gradual change in fortune was manifested in the city's weakened ability to function as an incubator for newer, risk-taking enterprises. In the past, when expanding industries moved out, replacements often found their way to the city because it was still a place where new product concepts and designs could be tried and tested. But as communication networks and skilled labor pools became more decentralized, other regions—especially suburban areas in the Northeast—competed more effectively to provide a favorable environment for experimentation and innovation.[12]

It is important to keep this point in mind: well before the much-publicized dual crisis of manufacturing flight and fiscal collapse that befell the New York area in the mid-1970s, manufacturers had been steadily leaving the city. Between the early 1950s and the early 1960s some 200,000 manufacturing jobs were lost, about a 20 percent decline.[13]

A retrospective evaluation of Raymond Vernon's 1960 projections for the New York region illustrates how unanticipated was the fall-off in the manufacturing sector. Vernon's expectations of total employment growth were actually too conservative, but he misread greatly the eventual *composition* of the industrial structure. The decline in manufacturing turned out to be much deeper than he forecast, while the services sector grew faster. In the late 1960s, with the advantage of hindsight, Dick Netzer observed how Vernon had underestimated the velocity of the change from a "goods-handling to a service-producing economy":

> In the entire metropolitan region, the number of production-worker jobs has actually declined significantly since the early 1950's, and in New York City the decline has been considerably sharper. . . . Regional employment in the industries with a primarily white collar character . . . was projected to rise by roughly 400,000 from 1956 to 1965; the actual increase has been closer to 700,000. For New York City, the projected increase was about 75,000 and the actual increase about 240,000.[14]

In a subsequent review Netzer pointed out two problematic features of this shift. First, the drop was not offset by growth in other parts of the region, as had happened in the past; second, job losses were permeating all manufacturing industries, even though these industries nationally had increased their employment by 25 percent during the 1960s. Together with the decline in the city's favored status as an incubator for new manufacturing activities, these changes were so marked that the average firm size of city establishments rose during the 1960s and early 1970s.[15]

Crisis and the Beginnings of Stagnation

As the gradual but steady exodus of manufacturers during the 1950s and 1960s culminated in a virtual stampede from 1969 through the mid-1970s, the city faced an unprecedented decline in employment. Annual reductions accumulated so persistently that by 1977 nearly one of every six jobs had been lost. From the historic peak of 3.8 million jobs in 1969, the city's total employment fell to below 3.2 million in 1977.[16]

Complicating the picture was the widespread nature of the decline, which affected even the previously expanding services industries. Paralleling the out-migration of manufacturers was the flight of large corporations that for many years had maintained headquarters operations in the city. As other states and localities enticed New York's office complexes with lower rents, lower taxes, and a skilled labor force, large firms reestablished their administrative centers elsewhere. From a total of 139 headquarters offices in 1967, the figure plummeted to 98 in 1974.[17] Moreover, from 1969 to 1976 major losses were registered in other sectors of the private economy: one of three jobs in construction, one of five in the transportation and public utility industries, one of six in wholesale and retail trade.[18] The one key area to evade the contraction was local government—yet even in this sector, employment plunged with the fiscal crisis of 1975.

These slump conditions are brought into greater relief when placed in comparative perspective. From the early 1970s the New York Region sustained a continuous slacking off in its performance relative to the rest of the country. Its share of national output, population growth, job creation, and personal income dropped steadily throughout the decade. Between 1972 and 1982, for example, the gross regional product fell as a proportion of gross national product (GNP) from 12.3 percent to 10.9 percent. There was a similar erosion in the region's share of total employment (from 9.7 to 8.6 percent) and aggregate personal income (from 12.5 to 10.0 percent).[19] Not only was the U.S. share of global economic activity descending from the peaks of the early postwar era, but New York was suffering inroads on its proportion of national wealth and resources. Whatever phenomenon can be considered the cause—the economic rise of the "Sunbelt" or a power shift away from the Northeast—the Big Apple was beginning to sense the demise of its once undisputed dominance on the national scene.

New York as a Center for Business Services

This confluence of deteriorating circumstances concealed signs of the economic strength that remained, however, especially in various service industries. While losing its preeminence as a manufacturing center, the city was successfully managing the transition to centrality in not just national but international finance. The "globalization" of the

U.S. economy during this period was manifested in the rising importance of international trade as a proportion of total economic activity nationwide. Between 1961 and 1982, for example, the ratio of imports and exports to total GNP rose from 9 percent to 18 percent, a truly significant change.[20] This trend offered an opportunity to those U.S. urban centers that could ride the waves of this change.

As U.S. corporations diversified their operations beyond national borders, they required expanded access to international capital markets. As foreign producers and financial institutions increased their presence in the U.S. economy, they sought entry points to American consumer and capital markets. New York City, long the financial hub of the nation, became an ideal site for serving these new types of activities. An analysis of the largest U.S. banking firms in 1967–69 showed clearly the continued preference for a New York location, even as industrial corporations were finding other places more attractive.[21] By the mid-1970s the city had emerged as capable as ever of serving as a central point for international commerce and finance. Of all *foreign* corporations with offices established in the United States, more than 60 percent had their headquarters in New York.[22] And soon to overlap these activities was the 1980s explosion in corporate mergers and takeovers, requiring sizable accommodation and support from financial institutions. This financial focus, along with a booming real estate industry, gave the city a reprieve while many other industrially based localities were floundering.[23]

An additional source of resilience was the expansion in business services triggered by the corporate trend toward lean organizational structures. Traditionally, large companies had maintained internal support divisions in such spheres as accounting, marketing, advertising, law, and human resources, usually at their headquarters locations. One response of corporate America to the increasing competitive pressures of the 1960s and 1970s was to unload these functions and hire outside firms to perform them less expensively.[24] Seeing this as a way of trimming their top-heavy organizations, companies that remained in the city often instituted such economies, creating a demand for "advanced" corporate services, especially in complex areas dealing with international affairs.[25]

With its sheer size and intensity of activity, then, New York persisted as the premier American city in a number of areas. Although its growth patterns were not altogether promising, its stock of assets and capabilities still made it the leading urban center. Even at the worst point in its mid-1970s downturn, the area continued to be the largest consumer market in the world and the leading business center for wholesale and retail trade and for manufacturing activity. Still the magnet for skilled labor, still offering the largest supply of office space, and still maintaining the most extensive transportation and distribution system in the country, New York possessed the wherewithal to retain its position as the leading U.S. city.

The Picture in Manufacturing

Nevertheless, despite renewed vigor in the services sector, the city's situation in manufacturing was increasingly dismal. Wage increases in New York had always outpaced those in other regions, and from the point of view of employers, this was an unfavorable feature of doing business in the city. They could disregard this problem as long as they could draw on the numerous advantages of being located in the area, but by the late 1960s these advantages were insufficient to anchor producers. For years the highly unionized labor force had realized wage gains that kept local pay beyond the national average. Given the region's high cost of living, these increases simply preserved the standard of living for the typical worker; however, in the context of wage comparisons among regions the New York worker, skilled and unskilled, was becoming too "expensive"—an additional reason for companies to uproot their operations in pursuit of a better "business climate."

As many manufacturing firms left, the available supply of labor competed for fewer job opportunities, dampening the potential for income growth. The balance between labor supply and demand now shifted against the worker. By the early 1970s the wage differential between factory workers in the city and the rest of the country was beginning to narrow. From 1970 to 1976 average pay for workers nationally rose 54.5 percent, while increasing only 44.4 percent in New York City.[26] Throughout the decade manufacturing workers in the city consistently received smaller wage increases than workers in the nation as a whole.

Quite possibly, the large influx of immigrant labor during this period contributed to the slower pace of wage increases, by expanding the pool of unskilled labor.[27] Manufacturing in general continued its decline throughout the 1970s, but there was some growth in sectors such as apparel, furniture, and footwear as foreign capital and immigrant labor combined in new enterprises, very often in small family businesses. Conditions were being set in place for the flourishing of the "new immigrant" enterprise that would distinguish the 1980s.[28]

As the decade closed, key elements in the economic base and structure appeared conditioned for a new era of growth, and many hoped the city was poised for a rebound. Important developments in population and labor force trends rounded out the phase of expansion and crisis. They also remind us that prosperity is not evenly distributed, for a question remains to be answered: who was hurt most by the decline, and who was best positioned to benefit from the envisaged recovery?

Jobs and People: Changing Population, Changing Labor Force

The curtailing of population growth by midcentury was perhaps the clearest indication that New York City had reached economic maturity. Thereafter, sheer numbers would cease to be an engine of economic growth and prosperity. No longer could a rising tide of population and economic activity be expected to lift all boats; no longer could pursuers of the American Dream be confident of a growing pie. It would be another two decades before this reality set in on Americans as a whole, but New Yorkers had begun to encounter it by the 1950s. The stability of the city's population level was a harbinger of relative decline for the United States. From then on, the principal change in population had to do with demographic composition, not size. And as population characteristics changed, so did labor force patterns, contributing to important trends on the supply side of the labor market.

Throughout the postwar years and until 1970, New York City's population remained at just under 8 million persons; the steady emigration of whites—reducing their share by 25 percent—was offset by the inflow of African Americans and Puerto Ricans, who jointly constituted 33 percent of the city by 1970. This twin pattern of white out-migration and minority in-migration fundamentally transformed the racial/ethnic makeup of the city.[29]

As whites left the city (in a suburbanization trend affecting urban areas across the nation), this largely middle-class emigration had damaging effects on New York's tax base. When middle-income groups leave, they deprive a city of vital resources, for the taxes they pay, as homeowners, workers, and consumers are the bedrock of municipal finances. An additional loss is represented by direct job transfers, especially among professional and managerial labor.[30] Many emigrants from New York in effect took their jobs with them: as suburban commuters they retained employment slots that otherwise might have been passed on to a city resident.

The inflow of African Americans from the South and Puerto Ricans from the Caribbean followed a pattern true for the Northeast and Midwest: many cities found that increasing shares of their population were going to African Americans and Latinos (primarily Mexicans, Puerto Ricans, and Cubans). Along the northeast corridor from Boston to Philadelphia, the Puerto Rican population expanded significantly during 1960–70, doubling in most places except for New York.[31] By the 1960s the northward black migration was tailing off, but black urban populations continued to grow as a result of high birth rates. In many places, rising minority shares were more than offset by departing whites, so that total population and labor force size actually declined. Nationwide, many of the cities with the largest numbers of African Americans experienced losses in total population during the 1960s.[32] In New York and other cities the increase in share of minorities took place in the context of stagnant growth and white flight—hardly optimal circumstances.

Throughout New York's history the immigration process had functioned as an equilibrating mechanism that mitigated but did not eliminate labor supply shortages.[33] In contrast to the relatively high unemployment and low participation rates that characterize today's labor market, New York was often plagued with a shortfall of workers. This happened because of the city's dynamic growth and because it served as a point of entry for many European immigrants who were only "passing through" to other regions of the country. Their "temporary" stay may have lasted as long as a generation, with the children of immigrants often moving outward. Nevertheless, it signified a steady outflow that created difficulties for employers seeking low-wage labor. Not until the 1960s did labor supply begin to exceed demand consistently.

As the region entered the postwar boom of the late 1940s, new sources of labor were needed. In the 1920s and 1930s, legislative changes and Depression conditions had reduced European immigration. The northern movement of African Americans and Puerto Ricans reflected a turn to domestic sources of low-wage labor, and these groups constituted the first wave of immigration—actually an internal *migration*—in the postwar period.[34]

By 1970 the combined effect of white out-emigration and minority in-migration had significantly transformed the New York labor market. In the metropolitan area about half of the net growth in employment went to African Americans and Puerto Ricans. Although the manufacturing sector had ceased to be dominant in the profile of jobs, its employment base was still large enough to accommodate sizable numbers of workers, and Puerto Ricans were still concentrated in this sector. Growth in public sector areas such as hospitals, health services, and school-related services—and, in the private sector, the hotel industry—offered opportunities to other less-skilled minority workers. Finally, as the educational levels of African Americans and Puerto Ricans rose, some found entry into the higher-paying clerical and professional positions that increased during this period.[35]

Crisis in the 1970s stimulated new changes in the demographic profile. In the first half of the decade, as the city endured its crunching falloff in jobs and economic activity, total population fell by some 300,000 persons—the first time in its history that such a large decline had been registered.[36] Added to the steady exit of white New Yorkers was a slowdown in migration from Puerto Rico and the South.[37] There were signs also of an exodus of African Americans and Puerto Ricans who had established themselves in the city during the previous decades. As conditions worsened and the quality of life deteriorated, some sectors within the two groups appeared to be repeating the behavior of earlier, European-origin immigrant groups that had left the city after an initial period of settlement. But as the postwar migration of African Americans and Puerto Ricans tailed off, it was followed by the arrival of large numbers of foreigners from the Caribbean, Latin America, and Asia. By the late 1970s, close to 80 percent of all immigrants to New York City came from these areas.[38] The city was witnessing the beginning of the third great influx of *new* New Yorkers in the twentieth century.

Labor Market Contours

Various attempts have been made to describe the characteristics and workings of the New York City labor market prior to the restructuring surge of the late 1970s and 1980s. These approximations recognized the stratified nature of the local labor market and other characteristics that further conditioned its functioning, including trade union influences and racial/ethnic patterns. The picture emerging from these studies is very unlike the textbook image of a smoothly operating environment in which demand and supply forces generate a full-employment equilibrium.

Forms of Stratification

A standard view in the early days portrayed two parallel "employment systems" in New York: one consisting of a highly competitive labor market in which small firms predominated; the other made up of larger, capital-intensive enterprises with "internal" labor markets the norm.[39] During the 1940s and 1950s, in the heyday of U.S. corporate power, internal labor markets were an important means by which firms could induce valued employees to stay with the company. Career ladders were set up with the understanding that over time, loyal and productive workers would move up the corporate organization. Other rewards included fringe benefits, pension plans, and regular wage increases. Even during recessions these employees would be kept on board rather than laid off for fear that they would not return once business picked up.

During the 1970s, further study added more weight to the view of the economy as basically split into two systems or labor markets. Beyond this simple dichotomy, however, important variations were identified. In some instances, union power led to highly structured employment systems *within* the smaller light manufacturing and service industries. That is, job security was not correlated exclusively to large firm size; unions afforded some measure of strength to workers in the garment production firms, for example. Conversely, some very large establishments showed evidence of a two-tier employment system, one part very competitive and the other very structured. Financial institutions and insurance companies illustrate this pattern, and compared with other cities, New York has always had a large proportion of such enterprises.[40] These exceptions to simple dualism implied that the New York labor market was dominated by competitive employment relationships.

Labor segmentation theory offered further variations on the theme of stratification. One model visualized the labor market as comprising four segments, in contrast to the tripartite breakdown discussed in Chapter One. The fourth segment represented craftworkers, such as plumbers and electricians, who had previously been considered part of the independent primary segment. This modification reflects the different way these workers obtain their jobs: unlike professionals, they rely primarily on union-sponsored apprenticeship programs. The unique role of unions and the lesser significance of formal educational credentials distinguish these high-wage workers from independent primary workers.[41]

Table 3 estimates the variation in the segmentation structure over time, based on a subsample of census data for the New York Standard Statistical Metropolitan Area.[42] During the 1960s the independent primary segment was the fastest-growing component, rising from 15 to 22.7 percent of the regional labor force. Simultaneously, the share of secondary jobs shrank by ten percentage points to 29.9 percent. The other two segments remained stable. In other words, a significant upgrading in the job structure appeared to have occurred during the decade. This picture was revised considerably during the 1970s, as the secondary segment expanded once again, returning to its 1960 level.

From 1960 and 1980 the most important change was a shuffling of weights among the three primary segments. The proportion of independent primary jobs increased from 15 to 21.8 percent, at the expense of independent primary craft and subordinate primary jobs. Whatever the significance of these shifting boundaries and weights (see Chapter Four), it remains clear that jobs and workers continued to be demarcated in the labor market.

Unionization

New York is a union town if ever there was one, but in ways that differentiate it from the great industrial cities of the Midwest. The prevalence of highly competitive industries and small firm size present

Table 3
Segmentation Structure of NYSMSA, 1960–1980

Segment	1960	1970	1980
Independent primary	15.0%	22.7%	21.8%
Independent primary craft	7.4%	8.0%	3.7%
Subordinate primary	38.8%	39.4%	36.0%
Secondary	38.8%	29.9%	38.5%
N =	4,338	4,364	4,577

Source: Andrés Torres, "Human Capital, Labor Segmentation and Inter-Minority Relative Status" (Ph.D. diss., New School for Social Research, 1988).

difficulties for the trade union movement. Among the European immigrants, traditionally sympathetic to labor organizations, who constituted much of the labor force in the early days, recruitment was fairly easy. But local unions could not match the clout of the big steel, auto, and electrical unions based elsewhere. Throughout the 1940s and 1950s, the constantly threatened profit margins of New York industries forced unions to constrain their demands for wage increases.[43] Large organizations such as the International Ladies Garment Workers Union (ILGWU) faced persistent criticism from membership for their lack of militancy.[44]

By the end of the 1960s the rate of unionization in the goods-production sector was still very high. Upward of 85 percent of workers in manufacturing plants belonged to labor organizations—a considerably higher proportion than in other major cities, where 70 percent was the norm.[45] With a sympathetic public attitude toward the trade union movement and a generally liberal political environment, union membership bestowed certain advantages and protections, even for those working in the declining sectors of industries.

Nowhere is New York's labor uniqueness more evident than in the case of the public sector, where unionization is higher than in almost any other city. Employees in the uniformed services (police, fire, and sanitation) and transit workers organized labor unions in New York well before their counterparts in other cities did so. Collective bargaining rights were achieved in the rest of the government sector beginning in 1958, again earlier than in most other municipalities. Because of the size of the public employee labor force (200,000 in the mid-1970s) and the complexity of managing government in so large a city, the local government has always bargained with more unions than has any other city.[46]

Unionization has been significant in other areas as well: the hotel and restaurant industries and the not-for-profit sector, including hospitals, colleges, and social service agencies. Only in the financial and business services sector have employers been able to deter labor organization. But even though this has been among the fastest-growing fields, the anti-union trend has not been generalized to the rest of the labor force.

Historically, the impact of unionization on the New York labor market has been to provide a measure of protection for workers who lack advanced educational preparation. In most industries, union members' wages compared favorably to those of their counterparts in other regions. Even light manufacturing workers in the city who received only a subsistence wage were at least better off than southern employees, who were generally non-union. Among the mass of workers within the city, unionization has constituted a dividing line, segmenting better-paid from less-well-paid workers.

Racial/Ethnic Queues

Adding further to the complexity of the labor market are its racial/ethnic characteristics. The interaction of industry and ethnicity manifests itself in different ways. Historically, marginal industries in New York have depended upon an "ethnic queue" of newly arriving workers to meet their demand for low-wage labor. As one group exhausts this function over the course of a generation, new groups are needed if the industry is to continue. The classic example is the garment industry, where women have historically made up the majority of the work force. Succeeding generations of operatives in this sector were supplied by Jewish and Italian immigrants until the mid-1920s. In the 1940s, African Americans, followed quickly by larger numbers of Puerto Ricans, filled the ranks as the preceding groups aged and retired.[47] The decline of the industry in the 1960s averted the need to bring in another round of migrants. But with the reorganizing of manufacturing beginning in the 1970s, new sources of labor had to be found, and these were to be recruited from among Third World immigrants.

Ethnicity comes into play in a number of occupational categories. Observers of the New York scene remark that ethnic groups tend to be concentrated in particular industrial sectors. As Dale Hiestand and Dean Morse note, there has been "a widespread image of the 'Jewish' school teacher, the 'Irish' policeman and fireman, the 'Italian' sanitation worker, and the black and Puerto Rican health worker."[48] One reason for this clustering is that since discrimination often bars entry to preferred areas, groups subject to bias will gravitate to the remaining jobs in the labor market. Another is that particularly among craftworkers and the uniformed services in the public sector, jobs may be "passed on" from one generation to another. Ethnic groups use family and cultural ties to increase their chances of getting into an apprenticeship program or lining up a job interview. Although perceived as having less status and prestige than professional jobs, these positions are attractive because they offer higher salaries and better job security than are available for similarly educated workers in less structured occupations. Conversely, compared with such occupations as teacher and health care worker, the educational credentials called for are less demanding.

Dualism, segmentation, unionization, and racial/ethnic queuing: each adds an element of complexity to a large metropolitan labor market.

Stagnation and Restructuring

The crisis-ridden 1970s brought to a definitive end the postwar expansion era, a turningpoint in the city's economic evolution. The 1980s initiated a new phase that promised a return to prosperity. This hope was premised on the evidence of a prodigious growth in jobs.

The decade began with a recession, but there followed a major expansion largely driven by a national boom. Not until the Wall Street crash of 1987 did the pace of job creation decelerate. From 1977 to 1989, employment in New York City rose almost 15 percent, reaching 4.16 million jobs. This represented an addition of half a million jobs.[49]

But on deeper inspection, it could hardly be said that a new golden era was on the horizon. Despite a swelling number of jobs, the employment base in 1989 had not been restored to its 1969 peak of 4.275 million. True, the suburban areas surpassed their levels of two decades earlier, but this was minimal consolation to New York City residents whose access to the regional labor market is often restricted. The city's share of employment in the tristate area had fallen from 51 percent (1969) to 40 percent (1989).[50]

Further dampening the prospects for optimism were trends in earnings, income distribution, and poverty that suggested not a new prosperity but the beginning of a prolonged stagnation. Even after accounting for the ups and downs of the business cycle during the 1980s, most signs pointed to New York's inability to recover its glory days. Even more apparent was its incapacity to secure a rising standard of living for its inhabitants. Most significant was the *de-linking* of job growth and earnings growth: for the first time in the modern era, a booming economy failed to lead to rising wages for the vast majority of workers. On the average, city residents outside of Manhattan, home to the professional elite, had *zero* earnings increase between 1979 and 1989—despite a 10 percent rise in employment during the period for those who lived in the outer boroughs.[51] Obviously, the new jobs were low-paying work that brought down the average wage level for all workers.

Why the great discrepancy between activity generated and results obtained? There is no shortage of analyses attempting to explain New York's economic fortunes in the 1980s. For those who define this period essentially as one of stagnation, not prosperity, there is broad agreement on the key factors. The implicit consensus is made up of two connected arguments: (1) the end of U.S. economic hegemony, beginning in the late 1960s, occasioned the opening of U.S. markets to foreign competitors and reinforced the flight of domestic corporations abroad; (2) globalization led to a dual *restructuring* response in the United States—(a) corporate strategies to cut labor costs and streamline internal structures, and (b) state policies designed to complement employer strategies.

Restructuring was a calculated move to place U.S. industry in a "competitive" mode with foreign industry. Examples abound of the capitalist-led effort to reassert U.S. hegemony. On the industrial front, these include "flexibilization" techniques such as increased hiring of part-time and temporary labor, thus reducing the size of the labor force eligible for health and other benefits. Another practice (described above) became popular: diminishing professional staff by eliminating corporate services units in legal, financial, and advertising areas and contracting these functions out to independent firms specializing in such tasks.[52]

Complementing this overhaul in industrial practices was a set of public policies instituted nationally that had devastating effects for labor and urban centers. Beginning with the Air Traffic Controllers strike, President Ronald Reagan sent a clear message to organized labor: the capital-labor accord of the postwar era is over. This was seconded by a range of anti-labor measures that entailed a freezing of the minimum wage, relaxation of occupational and health standards in the workplace, and a weakening of labor's rights to organize. The results were crystal clear: by the end of the decade, real wages for full-time workers in the United States had stagnated, and unionization in the private sector had fallen from 18 to 12 percent, the lowest since the 1920s.

In urban centers, workers and residents were doubly thrashed by government policy. New York and other cities were jolted by unprecedented reductions in federal aid, even as the poverty population grew. Besides adapting to a declining tax base, fed by the continuing out-migration of middle-income families, the city now had to contend with greater fiscal responsibilities as the national government turned over many functions to local jurisdictions. Throughout the decade and into the 1990s, New York was forced into a financial straitjacket.

Of course, there were those who refused to be swayed by these dreary trends. They saw the twenty-first century prefigured in office towers and luxury condominiums, in the hustle and bustle of Wall Street, in the amazing technological advances of postindustrial New York. But outside the central business district, a different future was in the making.

Majority Minority City

As successive reports on the 1990 census were released by the government, they were greeted in the media with thinly disguised alarm. "What will the U.S. be like when whites are no longer the majority?" read a cover page of *Time*. Headlines in the *New York Times* declared: "Now, Whites Are Minority in New York," and "Middle-Class Flight Feared by New York City Experts."[53]

Population counters from the Census Bureau had confirmed with hard numbers what everyone knew from daily observation: the nation was continuing on its course toward a radically different America. Nationally, three components of this trend could be identified. On the average, Americans were aging, and there were fewer births. Native minorities were sustaining fairly vigorous birth rates but not as high as those of a decade earlier. And finally, the pace of immigration from the Third World was continuing to skyrocket.

In large metropolitan centers these factors were accompanied by an outflow of whites. On balance, though, the principal cause of New York's demographic shift in the 1980s was the huge numbers of new immigrants. Indeed, the influx was large enough to raise the city's total population—reversing the decline that had occurred during the 1970s—and to justify dubbing New York a "majority minority city."

Table 4 shows the extent of this transformation. Of an official population of some 7.3 million people in 1990, whites accounted for 43 percent of the total. Given their 52 percent share in 1980, the magnitude of this trend is truly remarkable. Hispanics increased the most in absolute numbers, with a net addition of 377,122 individuals. The Asian population grew at the fastest rate, doubling its numbers during

Table 4
New York City Population by Racial/Ethnic Origin: 1980, 1990

	1980	1990
Total	7,071,639	7,322,564
White	3,703,203	3,163,125
Black	1,694,505	1,847,125
Hispanic	1,406,389	1,783,511
Asian/Pacific Islander	239,338	489,851
Native American	9,907	17,871
Other	18,297	21,157

Source: New York City Department of City Planning, "Components of Population Change by Race and Hispanic Origin or Descent, 1980–1990," (unpublished report, Population Division, May 1991), Table 1.
Note: Persons identified as Hispanic are excluded from other categories. The Native American figures include Innuits and Aleuts.

the decade. Blacks, including those not born in the United States, maintained their proportion at about 25 percent.

The rise in minorities (or "people of color," which has increasingly become the term of choice) was evidenced across large sections of the city. There were two exceptions. Manhattan actually attracted a net immigration of whites (36,401)—perhaps a measure of the gravitational pull of the financial services sector on young professionals—and this, along with a below-average rise in the number of Asians and Hispanics and a decline in blacks, made Manhattan a borough in which whites remained half of the population. And in the smallest borough, Staten Island, Euro-Americans still claimed a significant majority. The bulk of the increase in minority population took place in the Bronx, Brooklyn, and Queens, precisely where most immigrants have settled.[54]

It is a commonplace that America's minority groups are a diverse lot, but repetition does not make it any less true. To imagine New York's minorities—native and immigrant—as a monolithic cohort is to exaggerate the centripetal influence of "otherness" in America. Discrimination and exclusion distance minorities collectively from a share in the dream, but they do not erase the differences in history, language, and culture among them. Place of birth differentiates African Americans from Caribbean-born blacks such as Jamaicans and Trinidadians and Haitians, for the last of whom language imparts further variation. Among Latinos, race, language, and culture intermingle with various national origins to produce a wide variety of historical experiences. Asians—including Chinese, Koreans, Japanese, Cambodians, and Vietnamese—contribute an equally impressive array of differentiated heritages and cultures.

Restructuring and Labor Markets: The Skills Mismatch

By the mid-1970s the rising population of diverse minorities accompanied a new predicament confronting the New York labor market: the alarmingly reduced proportion of the resident population that was gainfully employed. The employment-to-population ratio is thought to measure the underutilization of human labor better than the unemployment rate, for at least two reasons. For one thing, when persons who have been laid off become discouraged by fruitless job hunting and decide to give up the search, they "disappear" from the official unemployment statistics. For another, young people—especially school dropouts—who have never worked for wages will not be counted among the ranks of the unemployed until they have lost their first job. The employment-population ratio, on the other hand, reflects the effects of structural economic change on these as well as other groups, and its continuing decline had city officials worried. From 1970 to 1976, for example, this ratio fell from 30 to 22 percent among New York youth—only half the figure for youth across the country. Among young blacks, it fell to 13.5 percent; black youth nationally were twice as likely to be in the labor force.[55]

Such signs of a serious incongruity between the two sides of the employment relation engendered new debates regarding the functioning of the city's labor market. Many became concerned that New York was facing a serious "skills mismatch" which, if left unaddressed, would damage the long-term prospects of both employers and workers. The mismatch notion pointed to a perilous discrepancy between the skills held by the city's residents and the skills required by the city's employers in the transformed economy. That is, too few labor force participants were prepared to step into the jobs being generated by the postindustrial economy.

Mainly, this problem was a byproduct of the rise of service industries—especially finance and the retail trade—which spawned a dramatic expansion of professional, managerial, and technical jobs. During the 1960s these amounted to almost *two-thirds* of the 200,000 new jobs created in the city. Add the fact that on the average, salaries in these occupations were about twice as high as in other categories, and we see how crucial these occupational sectors were.[56] In fact, such higher-echelon jobs were least affected by the downturn in the city's economic fortunes during the 1970s. Between 1972 and 1982, for example, the proportion of employed New York City residents who held professional, technical, managerial, and administrative positions rose from 24 to 30 percent, and this figure excludes the positions filled by commuters.[57]

The mismatch hypothesis claimed that the rising service economy was skewing the occupational distribution from blue-collar to white-collar jobs; as professional labor became more attractive, the demand for unskilled workers plummeted. But this basic argument represented a one-sided perspective on the matter. It was also true that the educational system was failing to produce sufficiently well-trained personnel for the real world of work. This was a principal issue, since historically, the educational requirements for labor force entry had been higher in New York City than elsewhere.[58] Some traced the educational "gap" to the school system's inability to adapt its methods and content to changing labor market needs. Antiquated courses and teaching methods were far removed from the exigencies of the rising service economy.

Another aspect of the education problem was the rapidly shifting demographic composition of the student population. These shifts came into conflict with an administrative and teaching corps that was ill prepared and, in some cases, resistant to servicing minority children who brought with them a new set of traditions and cultural practices. Some even maintained that the new populations entering the system en masse during the 1950s and 1960s—primarily African Americans and Puerto Ricans—lacked the wherewithal to succeed academically; the burdens of poverty and disrupted family life made it impossible for many children to persevere in the educational process. In any case, educational institutions—for whatever reasons—seemed incapable of meeting industry's need for skilled labor. For Robert Wagner, Jr., former chancellor of the New York City school system, the educational side of the mismatch had become the key problem by the early 1980s: "When 85% of all the new jobs being created in the city require a high school education and 42 percent of those entering the city's high schools don't graduate, it strikes me that we have a very significant problem."[59]

Further contributing to the skills mismatch was the siphoning-off of huge numbers of high-paying jobs by commuter labor, a pattern that had first come to light in the 1960s. Even as the number of professional and managerial jobs rose by some 125,000 between 1960 and 1970, 75,000 of these jobs—60 percent—went to suburbanites. It appears that most of this job loss was due to the heavy out-migration of professional New Yorkers who now commuted to work.[60] The trend continued unabated in the next decade, which saw an increase (by 46,000) in the number of persons commuting to jobs in the city.[61] The city had to contend not only with macro-economic forces generating a demand for high-skilled labor and with deficiencies in the educational system but also with the constant outflow of white-collar migrants who retained their city jobs.

Finally, there was the persistent problem of discrimination in the arena of higher-paying jobs, a practice that ascribed a distinctly racial character to the mismatch. In the private sector most of whatever minority employment gains occurred during the 1970s were in the lower echelons of the occupational structure. Walter Stafford's study of race and gender patterns of employment in New York industries described the persistent influence of race and ethnicity in job stratification: "Blacks and Hispanics are tightly segmented in a narrow range of industries in the city's private sector. . . . [They] are virtually excluded from 130 out of 193 industries. . . . Despite their increasing number of college graduates, [they] are poorly represented in professional jobs."[62]

Evidence continued to accumulate that, independent of concerns about the allegedly insufficient qualifications of minority applicants, employers were resisting the full and fair incorporation of minority professionals throughout their institutions. It appeared that American corporate culture, like the school system, was having difficulty adapting to the new minority entrants. A long history of antidiscrimination battles predated the concessions made by large corporations during the 1960s and 1970s, but by and large there were only modest inroads made. Even for minority applicants brandishing college degrees, entrée into the professional strata seemed limited.

In short, the worrisome divergence between the demand for and supply of skilled labor contained an apparently irreducible racial component. Whatever the effect of other factors, one simple reality seemed to be an ingrained resistance in corporate America to opening up its boardrooms and executive offices to all. Barriers were more penetrable in the public sector, where political pressure could be brought to bear on discriminatory hiring.

Not all observers agree with the foregoing analysis of the mismatch problem. While recognizing the danger of a sizable disparity between the demand for and supply of skilled labor, some have identified a different set of causes and effects. Perhaps the growing services sector was succeeding in absorbing large numbers of entry-level workers as clericals and laborers. Or perhaps it was inaccurate to associate the mismatch with the expanding services sector; might the root of the problem really be that social ills prevented many young people from completing their schooling in the first place? Also to be considered were signs of a substantial "informal" economy, operating beyond the reach of state regulation, where many immigrants might be found. Debates about the skills mismatch—its sources and solutions—would continue unabated through the 1980s and into the 1990s.[63]

This chapter's look at the general context shaping opportunities for labor in New York since the mid-1940s shows that changes in technology and the competitive position of regional industries influenced the hiring and firing decisions of employers, while changes in the quantity and "quality" (that is, educational background) of workers determined the size and suitability of the available pool of labor. The institutional and structural features of the labor market—dualisms, stratification of all kinds—helped to decide who would gain access to employment and what level of wages they would receive.

The trends of the 1970s transposed the problem that had historically plagued New York industry. Previously, the concern had been to find new cohorts of unskilled workers, as manufacturers searched for low-wage labor to replace an aging labor force. As of 1960, with the region still a manufacturing center, the share of elite jobs in managerial, professional, and technical areas (comparable to the independent primary category in Table 2) was still relatively small, only about 15 percent. Before the explosion in the services sector, New York—always a magnet for the skilled and educated from elsewhere, and equipped with an educational system that produced sufficient numbers of trained personnel from within the local population—did not have to deal with shortages of these workers. Now the dilemma was inverted: where were the service-oriented employers to find highly-skilled labor? And where were less-skilled persons to find employment?

The picture appeared quite dismal to New York's two largest minority groups. The summary presented here is too schematic and sparse to do justice to the rich experience lived by African Americans and Puerto Ricans through the years of growth, crisis, and stagnation. The collective actions carried out by communities struggling to establish their place in the political economy merit separate treatment.

CHAPTER THREE

African Americans and Puerto Ricans in New York

Despite important differences in historical experiences, African Americans and Puerto Ricans share a similar socioeconomic status. Nathan Glazer and Daniel P. Moynihan were among the first to recognize the parallel: "To a degree that cannot fail to startle anyone who encounters the reality for the first time, the overwhelming portion of both groups constitutes a submerged, exploited, and very possibly permanent proletariat."[1] The marked debility of their position relative to the citywide standard is clearly reflected in several indicators, as shown in Tables 5 to 7.[2] Patterns of labor force participation, unemployment rates, and median family incomes indicate that the gaps between native minorities and whites have persisted for decades. Nevertheless, there are discernible differences *between* the two minority groups.

The figures show that historically, labor force participation rates among males have been comparable for the two groups (Table 5). Only in 1970 was there a differential of more than 1 percent. The similarity ends with the female rates. In 1950, 48 percent of black females and 40 percent of Puerto Rican females were officially in the labor force. By 1980, the difference increased markedly: 51 percent to 34 percent.

As for unemployment (Table 6), there has been a gradual narrowing of the difference. By 1980, joblessness was slightly less for Puerto Rican males (11.7 percent) than for black males (12.6 percent). Although unemployment was higher for Puerto Rican females than black females in 1980, the gap was smaller than in 1960. It is also of note that for most New Yorkers, employment indicators were worse in 1980 than in 1960,

Table 5
New York City Labor Force Participation Rates: Total, Black, Puerto Rican, 1950–1980

	1950	1960	1970	1980
Total NYC				
Male	75%	79%	71%	70%
Female	35%	40%	41%	47%
Black				
Male	77%	79%	72%	65%
Female	48%	50%	46%	51%
Puerto Rican				
Male	76%	79%	66%	66%
Female	40%	38%	27%	34%

Source: Andrés Torres, "Human Capital, Labor Segmentation, and Inter-Minority Relative Status" (Ph.D. diss., New School for Social Research, 1988).
Note: Labor force participation is defined as the percentage of the working age population that is employed or actively seeking employment.

Table 6
New York City Unemployment Rates: Total, Black, Puerto Rican, 1960–1980

	1960	1970	1980
Total			
Male	4.4%	3.5%	5.4%
Female	5.1%	4.3%	5.8%
Black			
Male	6.8%	5.2%	12.6%
Female	6.5%	4.8%	9.8%
Puerto Rican			
Male	9.3%	6.1%	11.7%
Female	10.6%	7.7%	12.4%

Source: Andrés Torres, "Human Capital, Labor Segmentation, and Inter-Minority Relative Status" (Ph.D. diss., New School for Social Research, 1988).

reflecting a declining capacity of the local economy to provide jobs across the board.[3]

The foregoing figures suggest a persistently, if slowly, narrowing gap in employment status. Information on median family income, a principal indicator of overall socioeconomic status, suggests a contrary pattern (Table 7). By 1980, family income for blacks (from all sources) was 275 percent of what it had been in 1960; for Puerto Ricans it was 228 percent. If well-being is measured by this standard, Puerto Ricans were

Table 7
New York City Median Family Income: Total, White, Black, Puerto Rican, 1960–1980

	1960	1970	1980
Total	$6,091	$9,682	na
White	$6,365	$10,378	$21,515
Black	$4,432	$7,150	$12,210
Puerto Rican	$3,811	$5,575	$8,705

Source: Andrés Torres, "Human Capital, Labor Segmentation, and Inter-Minority Relative Status" (Ph.D. diss., New School for Social Research, 1988).

falling behind African Americans. Differences in wages and salaries—a better indicator of labor market activity—were similarly persistent.[4] Even more problematic was the widening gap between both minority groups and white families, whose income in 1980 was 338 percent of the 1960 figure.

In sum, attending the expanding gap in family income between native minority and white socioeconomic status were additional, if smaller, differentials between African Americans and Puerto Ricans. Surely it is no consolation to poverty-stricken blacks to know that they have a relative "advantage" vis-à-vis Puerto Ricans. But it may be important for all concerned to appreciate the different faces of poverty and the varied routes to subordinate economic status.

How are we to understand the sources of the difference? Simply put, the argument here is that African Americans were better positioned to withstand the ravages of economic and political change that characterized the New York postwar experience. Through phases of economic growth, crisis, and stagnation, through periods of political insurgency and backlash, they attained a measure of self-generated protection. Although equally determined to establish their claims, the Puerto Rican community faced a somewhat different set of historical legacies, contemporary opportunities, and constraints. It is these variations in experience that this chapter addresses.

In assessing the development of the two groups in comparative perspective, we ask history to reveal the ways in which they have contended with change. The ability to take advantage of change is crucial. Similarly important is the ability of a group to shelter itself from the worst effects of economic and political transformations. The interaction between economic dislocation and racial subordination places a premium on the capacity of groups to use political power.

As subordinated minorities, African Americans and Puerto Ricans have continually had to confront barriers of racial/ethnic discrimination. Under such circumstances the capacity of a group to assert control over its political and economic future is fundamentally influenced by the level of its *community infrastructure:* the underlying foundation of organizations, networks, and traditional group practices that bind it together. This notion encompasses a range of historical and institutional features of a community's development: patterns of migration and settlement; residential characteristics; social and religious institutions; and political organization. The interplay of these in the development of the community, along with ideological factors, determines the group's readiness to overcome the barriers to social mobility.

Comparative Community Infrastructures

Migration and Settlement

Three features affecting a migrant group's eventual prospects for social mobility in its new location are (1) time of arrival, (2) the economic conditions surrounding its initial entry, and (3) the pace of its incorporation. As noted earlier, U.S. society is often viewed as embodying a "queuing system" in which each of successive groups of migrants establishes a foothold and struggles for social and economic mobility until it attains its particular form of accommodation. Scholars have debated the role played by such factors as the cultural characteristics of the group, discrimination, political activity, and a host of other influences. But it has been generally presumed that in time the descendants of first-generation migrants will find their niche within the larger society.[5]

The significance of time of arrival, which establishes a group's place in the queue, can be illustrated by comparing the African American and Puerto Rican migration experiences. Although there had been a community of free blacks in New York since well before the Civil War, the abolition of slavery and the breakdown of the plantation economy in the American South signaled the beginning of the first major migration of blacks to the North.[6] Since northern capital relied on European immigrant labor until World War I, this initial flow was relatively modest. In 1890 African Americans constituted only 2 percent of New York City's population. By the onset of World War II, however—when

Puerto Ricans numbered only 61,500—the black population had increased almost sevenfold, to a level representing over 6 percent of the entire population (see Table 8).

Thus, before the massive Puerto Rican migration that took place following the termination of World War II, a significant black community existed, nourished by several decades of migrant labor. Their prior migration in substantial numbers conferred on blacks an important advantage relative to Puerto Ricans. From a purely chronological standpoint, African Americans attained earlier entry into the labor market and had a longer period of time to build the indigenous social, political, and cultural organizations that would strengthen their community structure.

The economic conditions existing at the time of initial mass migration are similarly important for eventual patterns of migration and settlement. During the first three decades of the twentieth century, as New York City's economy steadily grew, African Americans were hired as domestic service workers and manual laborers; in the government sector they were brought on primarily as heavy laborers in maintenance jobs.[7] The Depression years seriously interrupted this

Table 8
New York City Population: Total, Black, Puerto Rican, 1900–1990 (in thousands)

Year	Total	Black	%	Puerto Rican	%
1900	3,437	68	2.0	0.3	—
1910	4,767	98	2.1	0.6	—
1920	5,620	160	2.8	7.4	—
1930	6,930	341	4.9	44.9	—
1940	7,455	458	6.1	61.5	—
1950	7,892	748	9.5	246.0	3.1
1960	7,782	1,088	14.0	613.0	7.9
1970	7,895	1,668	21.1	846.7	10.7
1980	7,072	1,695	24.0	860.5	12.1
1990	7,323	1,847	25.2	896.8	12.2

Sources: Figures for 1900–1970 from Charles Brecher and Emmanuel Tobier, *Economic and Demographic Trends in New York City: The Outlook for the Future* (New York: Temporary Commission on City Finances, 1977), pp. 66, 85, 88; 1980–1990 from New York City Department of City Planning, "Components of Population Change by Race and Hispanic Origin or Descent, 1980–1990" (unpublished report, Population Division, May, 1991).

Note: For 1900–1930, the black population includes other non-whites. For 1940–90, it includes all foreign-born, non-Hispanic blacks.

gradual absorption, but World War II instigated a new demand for black labor. With the exception of the 1930s, African Americans were finding their way into the local labor force, albeit in the marginal and unskilled occupational strata.

For Puerto Ricans the relevant conditions were different. During the 1920s an incipient community was coalescing (though not on the African American scale), and like blacks, the earliest arrivals found work only in the less-skilled, marginal sectors of the economy as laborers and factory workers. The women concentrated in informal activities such as piecework sewing and child care, in addition to taking in lodgers. As children in Puerto Rico many had been trained in garment needlework, so these women formed the nucleus of an ideal labor supply for the garment industry in New York. Those who couldn't find employment in the factories or as pieceworkers at home often made garments independently and sold them door to door. Others were employed in cigarmaking and as domestics.[8]

But not until the postwar years did Puerto Ricans arrive in large numbers, and by the early 1950s New York was entering a period of long-term decline in the types of jobs to which unskilled migrant labor typically flocks. Puerto Ricans had little difficulty in obtaining employment in light manufacturing, usually as machine operatives in the garment industry. But this early success was deceptive because it occurred near the beginning of a long-term secular decline. Puerto Ricans, though essentially replacing earlier generations of Jewish and Italian factory workers, were being employed in stagnating industries.[9]

The difference in migration patterns is further highlighted by the contrast in the pace of arrival of the two groups. In its two decades of greatest expansion (1910–30), the African American community increased by a factor of about 3.5; the Puerto Rican community, in its equivalent period (1940–60), by a factor of 10. Average net annual Puerto Rican migration to the mainland between 1898 and 1945 was less than 2,000. In the three years 1946–48, more Puerto Ricans arrived than in all previous years combined.[10] The post–World War I migration of African Americans was moderate by comparison, exhibiting no explosive changes. In contrast, the Puerto Rican migration reached extremely large levels in a fairly compressed time span, with more Puerto Ricans coming to New York than blacks in the 1950s.

One of the consequences of a fairly gradual incorporation was that it permitted the original African American settlement to play an important role in the leadership and development of the burgeoning community. Between 1897 and 1913 the United Colored Democracy was pressuring to negotiate municipal positions, and other black organizations lobbied for federal jobs located in the city. Though these were low-wage, segregated positions, they provided evidence of the incipient political influence of New York blacks.[11] During the 1920s the number of municipal jobs held by African Americans rose steadily, also thanks to political connections. Black voter support was encouraged during the 1929 New York mayoral election by the Colored Citizens Non-Partisan Committee, which included W.E.B. Du Bois among its members. The committee endorsed the reelection of James J. Walker, citing his record in increasing city jobs for African Americans during the 1920s.[12]

The Depression years, though halting many of these advances, occasioned an upsurge in political activity centered on more militant struggle. Again, an already established community leadership, tempered through decades of involvement in local politics, steered many of these insurgent campaigns and movements. Led by the Reverend Adam Clayton Powell, Jr., the Greater New York Coordinating Committee on Employment fostered several campaigns to expose discriminatory practices in hiring by major utilities. For years, companies such as Con Edison and the New York Telephone Company had resisted hiring African Americans, and only under public pressure and boycott activities did they finally relent in the late 1930s. In 1939 Powell spearheaded a highly visible movement to secure white-collar jobs for blacks at the New York World's Fair. Other organizations, many based in Harlem and supported by more radical elements, emerged to confront the Depression-era crises in housing, employment, and social welfare. Groups such as the Workers Alliance advocated for home relief (welfare) clients and organized protests against evictions.[13] On the labor front, figures such as A. Philip Randolph became national leaders, organizing workers in the railroad industry. The Brotherhood of Sleeping Car Porters, which since 1925 had had its national headquarters in Harlem, was finally recognized in 1937, and other labor leaders helped to unionize retail workers in Harlem stores.[14]

In the Puerto Rican community too, during its early days of settlement in the 1920s, vigorous social and political activities were taking place. If not as perceptible to the larger body politic as those of the black community, these undertakings nevertheless absorbed the energies and concerns of the migrants. Several coalitions were formed, some to advocate for changes in the political status of the island, others to contend with problems of discrimination and social adjustment in the new society. Like migrant communities everywhere, the new residents relied on informal networks of family and hometown relations to find jobs, obtain translation assistance, and secure shelter.[15] With a fairly stable population size from the 1920s through World War II, the community seemed to be developing a steady base of organizational capacity.

The sheer size of the postwar Puerto Rican migration, however, appears to have overwhelmed the infrastructure of the prewar community. The social mobility of migrant populations proceeds best when there is a balance between the established settlement and newly arriving contingents. If ethnic and kinship networks are to succeed as conduits in the migration process, the settled contingent must avoid being engulfed by the newcomers. Massive immigrations can "swamp" the community infrastructure of compatriots already present. The rapid pace of Puerto Rican migration during the late 1940s and early 1950s apparently upset the necessary equilibrium between arriving migrants and settled community. The previously established community was not sufficiently consolidated to provide leadership and influence, given the speed and size of the new migration.[16]

Residential Patterns

Coinciding with the larger population base of blacks was the greater density of black residential communities, especially in the years after World War II. The population distribution of African Americans has enabled a degree of political representation within the city's civic structure, a correlation noted by historians since the early part of the century. By 1920 the northward migration of blacks ensured a large enough base in Harlem to given them near-majorities in two state assembly districts. This increased share of population accounted for a qualitative improvement in African American political influence, according to Gilbert Osofsky.[17] Though still underrepresented when compared with their share of the total city population, the proportion of elected black officials is higher than that of Puerto Ricans. Areas such as Harlem, Bedford-Stuyvesant, South Jamaica, Morrisania, and Crown Heights are so largely populated by African Americans that they are almost always assured of control over the structures of political representation and social service programs based in these communities.

Two factors have led to this configuration: racial segregation in housing, and public housing policy. The modest level of black political power resulting from the population density of the black community was an ironic consequence of the long history of racial segregation to which blacks have been subjected. Historically, they found themselves prohibited from integrating residential areas by the discriminatory practices of landlords and real estate agents. Now, although it has been illegal for decades to deny housing to a minority person, the laws are nearly impossible to enforce because there are many landlords and few regulatory bodies. Moreover, it is extremely difficult to prove discrimination in court, and most victims are reluctant to pursue lengthy court battles. Constrained further by limited economic means and persistent housing shortages, the African American community has been crowded into a relatively small number of areas.

Public housing projects, important for minorities and the poor, have also shaped the residential pattern of blacks. In the early 1960s these developments helped preserve an appearance of residential integration in some neighborhoods because many were located in areas adjacent to white neighborhoods.[18] At that time, however, about 40 percent of all public housing was occupied by African Americans, representing a fairly stable residential environment for a significant sector of the black community.[19]

Neither of these factors have had the agglomerative effect on Puerto Ricans that they seemed to have on blacks. Although apparently less affected by housing discrimination than blacks, their later arrival and generally lower socioeconomic conditions forced Puerto Ricans into an even more vulnerable position during the period of worsening housing shortages for the poor.[20] Forced to accept whatever residential housing could be found, they often lacked the political connections to compete with other groups for public housing, including the working-class whites who also sought entrance into the projects. The Puerto Rican community was thus characterized by greater dispersal and fragmentation in residential patterns. Even in so-called "Puerto Rican areas," Puerto Ricans often have to share resources and political power with other groups: in Williamsburg, with Jewish residents; in East Harlem and the South Bronx, with Italians and Jews in the past and currently with blacks; on the Lower East Side, with Asians and Jews.[21]

After reviewing the conditions inhibiting the residential concentration of Puerto Ricans during the 1960s, Joseph Fitzpatrick concluded that it was "obviously much more difficult to maintain the cohesiveness of a stable Puerto Rican community" than had been the case for earlier immigrant groups.[22] As Glazer and Moynihan noted, the East Harlem area was prevented from becoming an even greater population base of Puerto Ricans because of "the vast program of slum clearance and public housing which broke up the Puerto Rican concentrations as soon as they were formed and prevented new concentrations from forming."[23] Subsequent disruptions occurred on Manhattan's West Side when a large Puerto Rican community was displaced to make way for the Lincoln Center complex, and again in the 1970s when the South Bronx was practically depopulated by housing decline and arson.[24]

These conditions resulted in the chief distinction between housing patterns in the two native minorities: the African American residential base tended to be concentrated and geographically contained; Puerto Ricans had to contend with housing that was comparatively more dispersed and unstable.

Religious Institutions

Further differences can be seen in the religious institutions of the two groups, which appear to have evolved with different functions and roles. In the black community the churches are essentially indigenous, fostered and led by African Americans. Historically, they have contributed to the building of self-reliant mechanisms for community development and participation in the larger society. In the 1920s there were 160 churches in Harlem alone, many of them storefront operations. Organizations such as the Peace Mission led by Father Divine ran small businesses as part of their fund-raising activities, as catalogued by Jervis Anderson: "grocery stores, lodging houses, shoeshine stands, barber shops, dry-cleaning establishments, newsstands, and little food shops that served fifteen-cent dinners."[25] Even the mainstream black churches, which often felt threatened by the local storefront churches, exercised considerable autonomy within the national Protestant denominations with which they were affiliated.

One can hardly evaluate the political activity of the African American community without taking into account the influence of these religious organizations and leaders. From the late 1930s when he assumed leadership of the 14,000-member Abyssinian Baptist Church, Adam Clayton Powell, Jr., steered his congregation's participation in the great social and political events of the African American community, right on up to the era of the civil rights movement. Following his father's liberal tradition, Powell preached a "social gospel" that identified the church with the social and political needs of the black community.[26] As Glazer and Moynihan observed: "In the Negro communities of New York, as elsewhere in the country, it is difficult to underestimate the importance of the Negro Churches. These churches . . . play a role in politics that the churches of no other [ethnic group] can aspire to, or would dare to."[27]

This vital influence of the church is attributable in part to the exclusion of blacks from mainstream political structures, both nationally and in New York. With many routes of access to the political mainstream blocked, African Americans turned to their religious heritage and customs as a means of self-empowerment—another instance of an oppressed population creating its own mechanisms for social mobility.

Charles Green and Basil Wilson believe that the decline of traditional party politics in the 1960s gave even greater scope to the political activity of religious organizations in the black community of New York.[28] Surveying a number of church groups that had been involved in social and political issues during the 1970s and 1980s, they discovered an impressive array of community activities. Using varied strategies and tactics, the churches carried out social agendas that included electoral campaigns, anti-bias programs in the areas of housing and employment, and local economic development initiatives. Sometimes working by themselves but often participating in multiracial coalitions, they helped foster an upsurge of church-based community organizations in the city.[29]

The religious involvement of Puerto Ricans presents quite a different picture. Although the great majority are nominally Catholic, the Church's religious and social influence among them has fallen far short of what one would expect, given the often hostile environment that awaited the migrants.[30] With no Puerto Rican clergy and a severely limited economic foundation in Puerto Rican areas, the Catholic Church in New York City has not been particularly aggressive in the promotion of policies and programs to enhance the community's political strength.

Much like the Spanish-origin Church in Puerto Rico, the city's Catholic institutions have confined their activity to a strictly spiritual function. Even during the 1960s, in the heyday of community involvement, the Church leadership—predominantly Irish-American—resisted the efforts of parishioners and clergy who wanted a greater orientation to social action; it preferred instead to focus primarily on "pastoral" functions. In this the Church hierarchy was largely responding to the wishes of its traditional base of conservative white ethnics, who were little attracted to the notions of "liberation theology" that were pushing the Church toward social action in Latin America. But in failing to do for Puerto Ricans what it had done for Polish, Italian, and Irish immigrants—that is, to serve as a conduit for social mobility—the Church lost many potential members among the new migrants. And the Puerto Rican community was denied a potentially important mechanism for building community infrastructure.[31]

In more recent years the growth of autonomous Protestant groups, independent of established churches and led by Puerto Rican clergy and laypeople, has begun to fill this vacuum. In addition, although their influence on the political life of the community is only beginning to be manifested, Protestant denominations have increased their involvement in community issues in some areas such as the South Bronx, where both Puerto Ricans and African Americans reside.[32]

Political Organization

The greater population base and longer historical presence of blacks has engendered a broader network of political and cultural institutions.[33] The first black official was elected in 1917, and during the 1920s New York's cultural and political life was increasingly influenced by the African American experience. The "Harlem Renaissance" highlighted the early period of black influence in the city, as Roi Ottley and William J. Weatherby note: "A new phase in the development of New York Negroes took place in the early 1920's, when black men began to emerge from 'the ghetto of segregated life,' and to appear actively in the world of music, art, theater, and literature. . . . This development was national in scope but its most conspicuous stage was Harlem."[34]

Many national and local organizations emerged in the New York black community responding to the full gamut of politically related issues: civil rights, labor, social services, and international solidarity. The harsh conditions of the Depression years encouraged an even greater development of these organizations. Social unrest reached a climax in the great Harlem riots of 1935, which became a focal point for black unity in the period.[35] In comparing black political organizations and leaders in New York City to those in Chicago, James Q. Wilson commented: "In New York . . . the Negro press and civic leaders level a steady stream of criticism against the city regarding school segregation, inadequate school facilities, alleged police brutality. . . . Legal suits . . . are more common. . . . The number and strength of voluntary associations dealing with race issues are higher in New York."[36]

Evidence from the period of social activism of the 1960s seems to indicate that African American political institutions, compared with those of the Puerto Rican community, were more solidly developed. As noted earlier, one reason may be that the pre–World War II Puerto Rican community—with its active but still embryonic array of community institutions—had in effect been swamped by the mass migration of the late 1940s and 1950s.

Other features of the Puerto Rican experience may also have contributed to the relatively slow development of political organizations. One important influence was the New York branch of the Commonwealth Office of the Puerto Rican government.[37] Established in 1948 to assist arriving migrants, it was a subsidiary of the island-based government and recognized by U.S. agencies as an official entity aiding Puerto Ricans in the settlement process. The office assumed responsibility for such functions as monitoring a program of contract farm workers; referring arrivals to employment opportunities, housing assistance, and social services; and familiarizing Puerto Ricans with the legal and cultural realities of life on the mainland.

Despite these laudable goals, retrospective assessments of the Commonwealth Office's activities have expressed some disapproval of the way it inserted itself into the life of the expanding community. Some analysts see this organization, which assumed such a dominant role in servicing and supporting the newly arrived migrants, as having had a deterrent effect on the development of a locally based leadership and organizational capacity.[38] New structures of settlement installed from a distance in the postwar period tended to supersede the prewar community organizations and thereby helped to preempt the autonomous development of Puerto Rican organizations and networks in the continental United States. James Jennings notes the dependence of the New York organizations on the Puerto Rican government:

> Perhaps this is one reason why it has taken so long for Puerto Ricans to begin to organize themselves politically. . . . Any association that New York City government had with the Office of the Commonwealth was usually tempered with prior consultation with the Office of the Commonwealth. Earlier ethnic groups . . . would elect their own to bargain with the City's political and government leaders. . . . The Office of the

> Commonwealth has hindered the development of patron-cliency in the Puerto Rican community. Political leaders, patrons, were unnecessary so long as Puerto Ricans were represented by the Commonwealth Office.[39]

Another factor apparently affecting the development of local political institutions has been the pattern of return migration and turnover within the Puerto Rican community. Unlike most European immigrants, Puerto Ricans did not "burn their bridges" by leaving their homeland. U.S. citizenship, modern transportation systems, and economic instability at both points promoted the constant flux of Puerto Ricans between the island and the mainland.

Oscar Lewis attributed this continuous movement to the special difficulties of Puerto Ricans in attaining acculturation into U.S. society.[40] But it can also be interpreted as a result of the accelerated integration of Puerto Rico into the general U.S. economy after World War II. Indeed, this migration pattern parallels the even more fluid movement of capital: with no tariff or legal obstructions to bar the flow of labor, U.S. corporations could establish operations in Puerto Rico as easily as they would move from New York to the South. In this view, the perennial two-way migratory flow has occurred essentially because of the marginal conditions of existence to which Puerto Ricans are subjected both in Puerto Rico and on the U.S. mainland.[41]

The instability emanating from these conditions has the further consequence of undermining the infrastructure so essential to the development of a community. If Puerto Ricans are forced to be constantly on the move in search of residential and economic security, the long-term building of local community structures is subverted. Political power at the community level requires involvement of families and individuals in all spheres of civic activity: schools, social service agencies, churches, volunteer associations, and local government. A distressed community can ill afford sizable turnover in its population, especially within its leadership strata; that this turnover may largely be beyond its control only complicates the problem.

There are indications that with second- and third-generation Puerto Ricans this tendency has been less operative, but there is still no clear pattern of stability. In the early 1970s, when U.S. recessionary conditions drove unemployment higher, there occurred a large net return migration to Puerto Rico. A further complication is the more recent trend of second-generation migrants returning to Puerto Rico.[42]

Finally, the language factor must be taken into account in assessing both economic and political activity. The fact that Puerto Ricans and other Hispanics are Spanish-speaking has tended to confine these groups to low-paying jobs in which English-language proficiency is not required.[43] Language difference was also an important force in maintaining the political weakness of the community during the crucial years immediately following World War II: until 1964 all citizens in New York state were required to pass a literacy test in English before they could register to vote.[44]

Community Infrastructure and Political Power

It appears, then, that the conditions of poverty and marginalization that have historically afflicted both groups have had dissimilar effects on the evolution of their respective community infrastructure. For African Americans these very conditions may have contributed to an inward consolidation of indigenous and autonomous institutions; for Puerto Ricans they have tended to fragment and disperse the community's potential strength. In short, the relative strength of black community infrastructure seems to have resulted in greater potential for exercising political power.

Of course, since measuring "community infrastructure" and its corresponding political power is not as easy as counting the number of cars coming off an assembly line, comparisons between groups are fraught with limitations. But research and reasoned judgment have generally led to the conclusion that a more developed level of political power evolved within the African American community than in the Puerto Rican. Referring to the early postwar period, Adalberto López states, "Compared to modest achievements of blacks and Chicano 'politicos,' those of Puerto Ricans were insignificant. There was not among them even a counterpart of the black NAACP or the Chicano LULAC [League of United Latin American Citizens]." And Oscar Handlin remarked in 1959 that the development of both political awareness and group consciousness among Puerto Ricans was taking place "more slowly than among Negroes."[45]

Authors who express the view that blacks have attained greater integration into the political mainstream have used a range of indicators to approximate the idea of assimilation, or integration. Some have seen a relative underdevelopment in electoral activity for Puerto Ricans.[46] In their survey of involvement in voluntary organizations, Stephen Cohen and Robert E. Kapsis found that Puerto Ricans had lower levels of participation than blacks. Dale Nelson concluded not only that community activism was lower among Puerto Ricans than blacks but that it did not appreciably increase among second-generation Puerto Ricans—contradicting the expectations of most assimilation hypotheses.[47]

The implications of the relative strength of black community infrastructure are brought into relief by research studies showing that political power leads to improved employment opportunities for minorities, especially in the public sector. Interpreting black political power as an expression of ethnic political activity, P. K. Eisenger found that rising political activity led to increased civil service hiring of blacks. Ethnic representation is crucial because group leaders who attain positions of power within the larger political structures generally remain accountable to their constituents. After conducting a study of national affirmative action data for 1973 and 1978, Eisenger concluded that the electoral potential of black population size is the principal determinant of black municipal employment. For the "prestige" occupations he found virtually no independent effects of the educational characteristics of the black population on black employment. Political power, measured by potential voting population, was the central factor affecting public sector employment.[48]

Thomas R. Dye and James Renick confirmed this association between minority political power and local government employment. Focusing on those categories of city jobs in which minorities have historically been underrepresented, they found that

> for blacks and Hispanics, employment in top city jobs appears to be a function of political power, as it is reflected in city council representation. [This] is more important in gaining city employment in administrative, professional and protective [police, firefighters] positions than any other single factor, including income and educational levels.[49]

Struggles for Social Equality and Economic Mobility

Insurgency

The end of World War II brought a resumption of economic and social struggle among African American New Yorkers. On the economic front, groups such as the National Association for the Advancement of Colored People (NAACP), the Congress of Racial Equality (CORE), and the Urban League spearheaded various campaigns targeting employment discrimination.[50] By the end of the 1950s this pressure was beginning to produce results, according to Charles Abrams:

> Major gains have . . . been made in New York City in the communications industry, in clerical work generally, in the services industries and a breakthrough has been made in department stores. . . . There are now Negro brakemen and yard conductors in the Pennsylvania Railroad, reservations clerks and other workers on the airlines, tellers in banks, clerks in insurance companies, drivers on trucks, etc. The breakthroughs, even where not substantial numerically, are important because they open up new fields of opportunity and aspiration.[51]

In the following decade, as their population rose and Great Society programs fed new resources into the public payroll, blacks expanded their presence in government employment. A 1964 study of employment patterns within the municipal labor force reported that "of some 177,500 fulltime employees of the 66 surveyed agencies, about 23% were Negro and 3% were Puerto Rican. In comparison, about 14 percent of the [city's] population in 1960 was Negro and 8 percent was Puerto Rican."[52] Clearly, there was by the mid-1960s a marked difference between the two groups in the proportion of public employment.

By 1971 both blacks and Puerto Ricans had expanded their representation: in the seven largest municipal agencies the minority labor force numbered one-third of the total, with the school, public health and housing systems employing the bulk of these workers.[53] These advances reverberated as well in the ranks of organized labor. The long-standing resistance of civil service unions to minority inroads began to give way in the period of insurgency, though these gains were due as much to growth in the public sector as to the improved political clout of the formerly excluded groups.[54] The rising government payroll during the 1960s brought about a surge in public employee unionism, and District 37 of the American Federation of State, County, and Municipal Employees (AFSCME) became the largest local in the United States, and the biggest union in the city. The leadership increasingly reflected the union's growing base of minority membership, and special programs were instituted to facilitate the union participation and career development, especially of black women.[55]

These signs of progress in the 1970s were a far cry from the situation in the 1950s when a movement of primarily Puerto Rican women faced entrenched opposition on the part of the leadership of the International Ladies Garment Workers Union. Stifling calls for greater democracy, ILGWU refused at that time to recognize a Spanish-language unit, even though Italian workers had been allowed to create their own locals. And in the early 1960s, when federal funds were being made available to upgrade the skills of workers in marginal industries, the top leadership of the union blocked legislation on the grounds that garment producers needed unskilled labor.[56]

Adjacent movements in the social and political sphere, exemplified by the militancy of the Black Power movement, provided equal impetus for testing the status quo. Unlike the antidiscrimination struggles of the 1930s, which were generally subsumed under class-based politics, these new movements tended to assert the primacy of race over class. Cold War affluence seemed to benefit the white working class but leave minorities in the lurch. If racial domination could proceed with apparently minimal discomfort to the average white American, to African Americans this implied a go-it-alone strategy. Thus Black Power came to mean community control, the idea that dominated groups had to rely on ethnicity-based strategies to take command of the important institutions in their communities: schools, health clinics, welfare bureaucracies, even the police. The full weight of the community's infrastructure would have to be deployed if these struggles were to achieve success.

This new orientation complemented the concern with employment issues by drawing attention to the importance of the consumption side of economic relations. In declaring direct authority over local structures of service delivery, these movements for community control were transcending the traditional demands of the workplace and positing a broader set of claims for citizenship.[57] Among key efforts symbolizing this new direction were the highly publicized conflicts in three demonstration districts of the school system (Intermediate School 201, Ocean Hill–Brownsville, and Two Bridges), the welfare rights movement, and strife over the Community Action programs that had been established to implement the federal government's War on Poverty.[58] In each instance, major segments of the black community were mobilized in search of far-reaching goals.

Puerto Ricans were also involved in these issues but usually as junior partners within coalitions of blacks and liberals. For the most part, when Puerto Ricans and other Latinos did take the lead, it was in language rights issues, especially the struggle over bilingual education policies. Since the early 1950s the fight for adequate education for the rapidly growing community had become a key rallying point for New York Puerto Ricans. The city's Board of Education responded to early concerns by issuing in 1953 its landmark *Puerto Rican Study*, which acknowledged that the school system was less than prepared to serve its hundreds of thousands of new students.[59] Many reforms were proposed—including the adoption of bilingual instruction, the hiring of Puerto Rican educators, and parent involvement programs—but few were realized. The community learned quickly that without political pressure their calls for innovation would remain unanswered.

Such experiences prodded community leaders to initiate a number of new efforts, covering a range of issues from housing to employment to civil rights. From the mid-1950s on a new generation of organizations emerged, products less of the community structures of the pre–World War II era, than of the postwar, first-generation migrant community. (Again, a significant ingredient in this new infrastructure was the New York branch of the Office of the Commonwealth of Puerto Rico.) Among the many new groups formed during the 1950s and early 1960s were the Puerto Rican Association for Community Affairs (PRACA), ASPIRA (an educational and advocacy agency), the Puerto Rican Forum, and the Puerto Rican Family Institute, all of which continue to this day.[60]

Nevertheless, a decade and more after the publication of the *Puerto Rican Study*, the educational plight of Puerto Rican youth continued unremedied. Of 21,000 academic high school diplomas awarded in 1963, only 331 went to Puerto Rican students. In 1969, though Puerto Ricans made up 20 percent of total student enrollment, less than 1 percent of all teaching and guidance positions were held by Puerto Ricans. As late as the mid-1970s the federal government found the New York City school system guilty of de facto discrimination in its personnel practices.[61] The community's response was a concerted, long-term effort that encompassed diverse aspects of the education problematic: the demand for bilingual education; participation in community control insurgencies; and—at the university level—movements for open admission, Puerto Rican Studies programs, and alternative schools such as Boricua College, founded in 1974.

In the public school struggles affecting blacks as well as Puerto Ricans, representatives of both communities—including parents and professionals—sought to reverse the top-down relationships prevalent in the school system. The objective was to decentralize power and resources so that the central bureaucracy would have to share control over the educational process. Unfortunately, the Central Board of Education, where the system's power was concentrated, was reluctant to concede any of its prerogatives. Even though the African American and Puerto Rican constituencies succeeded in garnering some support among liberal-minded politicians and such institutions as the Ford Foundation, these latter groups did not share the longer-range vision of the community activists. The concern of liberal supporters was to mitigate the disparities in educational quality by instituting some reforms in the schools and delegating some oversight functions to parents through elected school boards. But this agenda fell far short of the major overhaul of supervision, pedagogy, and resource allocation that minority groups pursued. Only a thorough revamping of public education, so parents argued, would enable the school system to prepare students adequately for the work force.

Further complicating the picture was the opposition of the United Federation of Teachers (UFT), which felt immediately threatened by the demands of the community groups. Teachers perceived the calls for major educational reform—including the controversial issue of parents' right to transfer teachers to another school—as incursions on their own professional sovereignty. Most white New Yorkers took the side of the union, fearing that a defeat in this instance would encourage minority movements in other domains. In 1970, after a three-year struggle, the first citywide elections for decentralized school boards were held. By then, however, the actual legislation had been so watered down and the opposition forces so well organized that only in a few newer school districts did reform-minded parents and activists achieve control. The established authorities were able to deflect and absorb the minority challenge. Marilyn Gittell's retrospective on the lessons of this episode provides a prophetic commentary on post-1960s race relations in the city. Referring to the entrenched power of the school bureaucracy, the teachers' union, and other "power sources" in the city and state, she says, "The[ir] complete insensitivity to the demands of the black and Puerto Rican communities and the[ir] unwillingness to compromise suggest a continuing and perhaps intensified struggle between these forces. Racial polarization has become more overt and more pronounced."[62]

A parallel conflict surrounded the antipoverty programs that emerged in New York. These initiatives were offshoots of President Lyndon Johnson's "War on Poverty" and came into being through the Economic Opportunity Act of 1964. As in the school decentralization controversy, according to Stephen M. David, supporters of change approached the problem from two standpoints. There were

> those intent on managing and controlling discontent and those involved with social reform. . . . The reformers tended to view these poverty groups as the organized base from which the poor could express discontent and press for change; the "elitists" viewed them as a means of promoting the inclusion of representatives of the black community in the ongoing political system.[63]

The principal thrust of the programs was to expand the provision of human services to distressed communities. The novelty consisted in the setting up of entirely new mechanisms of service delivery, agencies that would circumvent existing structures within local jurisdictions. To replace reliance on state employment agencies, local job training and referral centers were established in targeted communities. Family planning programs, legal service offices, day care centers were all established in local neighborhoods. Some of these programs were intended to replace already existing municipal agencies that were perceived as unresponsive to the needs of minorities; others (day care and legal services) amounted to totally new projects that filled a vacuum for inner-city populations. This extension of the public sector into new activities dictated an equally significant enlargement of public employment, because additional workers would be required to perform the new functions and staff the new offices. The ensuing growth in minority employment became a principal byproduct of the antipoverty programs.[64]

The more sophisticated community leaders maintained goals beyond this elementary level of service provision coupled with job creation. Why not broaden the compass of objectives toward politically empowering strategies, as suggested by the Economic Opportunity Act's language of "maximum feasible participation"?[65] Use the creation of parallel structures provided for by the federal community action programs to help institutionalize local clusters of minority power; include, as part of the service-delivery functions, components that would help to train and develop an insurgent political leadership based in minority communities. By shifting activities toward advocacy and political intervention in local issues (including school decentralization), black community leaders sought political goals much more ambitious than those envisioned by the politicians of the status quo.[66]

The effort to push the antipoverty programs beyond a simple call for more and better services brought minority activists into direct confrontation with the political elites and white ethnic constituencies. Several clashes erupted, spanning the mayoral administrations of Robert Wagner and John Lindsay, but by the early 1970s the implicit challenge to the traditional political structures had been deflated. Although the antipoverty drive seems to have contributed to the development of a generation of political leaders and to have helped mitigate some of the extreme manifestations of ghetto poverty, it never led to the transformation of the political and social order that the more militant contingents hoped for. Indeed, for some New Yorkers the principal accomplishment was that it prevented a recurrence of the mass riots that had plagued urban America during the late 1960s.[67] As in other areas of contention, the resiliency of the established structures thwarted fundamental social and political change.

Reaction and Backlash

By the early 1970s the intensity of social activism and insurgency had reached a plateau. This leveling off was occasioned both by negative trends in the economy and by the political and racial backlash of New Yorkers who resented and feared the demands of minority communities. Their resistance had already been evidenced in the outcomes of the various struggles and conflicts during the 1960s. In the many controversies involving housing, school decentralization, antipoverty programs, welfare rights, bilingual education, affirmative action, and political representation, the element of race was never absent.

On the economic front, the city was losing hundreds of thousands of manufacturing jobs as factory owners accelerated their migration from the area. In addition, the impact of a national recession in 1974–75 and a burgeoning fiscal crisis would bring the city to the verge of bankruptcy in 1975. In short, the share of the pie that New Yorkers were accustomed to receiving was shrinking. If concessions were to be offered to African Americans and Puerto Ricans who now insisted on receiving more than the morsels traditionally allowed them, where were these to come from? Whatever the extent of racial discrimination driving the opposition to minority social mobility, the deterioration of socioeconomic conditions facing all New Yorkers in the mid-1970s only worsened the prospects for a multiracial solution to the problems of poverty.

The conflict over community control in School District One provides a case in point. District One blankets most of the Lower East Side, the epitome of immigrant America. In the early 1970s the decentralization struggle pitted the school superintendent, a Puerto Rican, and a coalition of minority parents against an opposition composed of the teachers' union (UFT), the school bureaucracy, and white residents, few of whom sent their children to the local schools. After years of prolonged clashes and several elections, the minority coalition was defeated, and a new administration dismantled the programs associated with the decentralization initiatives: bilingual projects, black studies, and special reading classes—this in a district where enrollment was 73 percent Puerto Rican, 15 percent African American, and 8 percent Chinese.[68]

The resistance to racial equality seemed to be bitterest. In such matters as the 1971 scatter-site housing controversy in Forest Hills, where a minority victory would have forced whites to share social spaces on a daily basis. The proposal for creating low-income housing in white ethnic areas aroused so much opposition from the local communities, primarily Jewish and Italian, that it was abandoned and ultimately transformed into a plan for senior citizen residences.[69]

Conflicts over antipoverty programs took place primarily between the minority community and the established political institutions or bureaucracies. Here the more open manifestations of racial prejudice became muted, and the resistance was often based on fiscal grounds: namely, that the financial realities facing the city prohibited the funding of these initiatives. Yet the appeal to racial ideology also surfaced: the best way to fight poverty is to get up and find a job; or, all Americans should learn how to speak English on their own.

Once the more militant approaches were spent, minority political activity tended to converge once again on the electoral arena. The War on Poverty and the Wagner-Lindsay reform administrations helped move black political life closer to incorporation in the mainstream of civil society, although the *quality* of that incorporation still left much to be desired.[70] In Brooklyn, Al Vann and Major Owens, who had been leaders in many of the community struggles of the 1960s, challenged the regular Democratic organization, which had long excluded blacks from real decision-making processes within the party. Although their efforts were strenuously opposed for years, they finally prevailed when Vann was elected to the state assembly in 1974 and Owens to the U.S. Congress soon after.[71]

In 1977, citywide efforts centered on a run for the city's top office. Percy Sutton, the Manhattan borough president, was the first African American to aspire to the mayoralty. Although he was widely accepted by political bosses within the Democratic Party, with whom he had worked loyally for many years, the party organization and the incumbent mayor, Abraham Beame, reneged on their earlier promises of endorsement. And despite a campaign in which he explicitly toned down his racial identity, appealing to the broader white citizenry with a message of crime control and managerial excellence, white voters failed to respond. In the primary Sutton garnered only 14 percent of the vote, coming in fifth in a seven-candidate race. Herman Badillo, a Puerto Rican no less well credentialed than Sutton, ran in the same competition and received even fewer votes. For blacks and Puerto Ricans this dismal experience was indicative of the reluctance of white society to share political leadership with minorities. The subsequent victory of Edward Koch in the 1977 general election seemed to denote a postponement of the process of accommodation to minority political aspirations that had seemed promising in the early 1970s.[72] Not until the election in 1989 of David N. Dinkins as the first black mayor would African American New Yorkers see a more encouraging state of affairs.

Solidarity and Competition

With few exceptions, the struggles of blacks and Puerto Ricans were joint efforts, although leadership and participation varied according to circumstances. Perhaps the main departure from this pattern was in the area of bilingual education, which blacks, although more supportive than whites, did not take on as an issue. Also, by the 1980s the two groups increasingly found themselves in contention on the electoral front. But in general, they worked as allies for social mobility and political empowerment. Through most of the postwar period, their common socioeconomic standing and the shared position of "having nothing to lose" assured that the established authorities perceived the two communities as antagonists of a similar stripe.

Still, sharing an adversarial relation with the status quo did not always guarantee bonds of cooperation between the two groups. Within the overall context of unity, junctures of competition and sometimes of confrontation could threaten interethnic solidarity.

Differences in culture and history explain some potential causes of friction between the two groups. Along with their status as later arrivals, Puerto Ricans were frequently regarded by African Americans as sojourners, here only on a temporary basis, and thus perhaps less committed to long-term involvements in social movements. Language difference presented another obstacle often difficult to surmount. And when unity was sought between blacks and *all* Hispanics, the foreigner status of Dominicans and other Spanish-speaking immigrants posed extra complications for interethnic unity.[73]

Some members of each group retain unfavorable perceptions of the other. Puerto Ricans see African Americans receiving preferential treatment in the distribution of government jobs and human service funds, and believe that when black leaders are faced with situations of crisis management, they inevitably take care of their own community's interests first. In Chicago and Philadelphia, for instance, where Puerto Ricans and other Latinos have supported black candidates in successful mayoral campaigns, there has been concern that the change in regime has not benefited Latinos significantly.[74] Some sectors within the black community, on the other hand, contend that Puerto Ricans have played only a secondary role in civil rights movements and that Latinos and other groups have benefited disproportionately from black-led social struggles.[75] Within each community those least inclined toward interethnic unity trade accusations and barbs, often invoking stereotypes much like those voiced by whites with similarly narrow perspectives.

Whatever the sources of these cleavages, instances of conflict and turbulence have served only to reduce solidarity and the effectiveness of interethnic political action. Within the antipoverty programs, blacks and Puerto Ricans argued over budget allocations and personnel decisions. They often opposed each other when it came to seeking participation on advisory commissions set up by city agencies. Similarly, in the community control battles, disputes erupted among the partisans as mutual distrust led each group to question the motives and objectives of the other. In the heat of battle, as parents, community leaders, and sympathetic teachers in Washington Heights sought to build electoral slates, African Americans and Latinos heatedly disputed the numbers of school board candidates that each group should have. In other instances—as in the IS 201 case, involving a community takeover of a local school—the idealism and sacrifice typical of the early phases of the movement yielded to agitated dissension between blacks and

Puerto Ricans, especially when it appeared that the movement was headed for defeat.[76]

The failure to set aside group interests hampered interethnic unity again during the 1977 mayoral race, and even more gravely in 1985. If Sutton and Badillo had merged their campaigns into a single thrust in 1977, the African American–Puerto Rican vote would have won a plurality in the primary. Granted, the minority candidate would probably have lost in the general election, but a precedent would have been established for future contests. Instead, the quest for political power at the citywide level remained elusive. Even during the mid-1980s, when Mayor Koch had alienated minority communities and many other New Yorkers with his insensitivity on racial matters, blacks and Puerto Ricans were unable to field a unified platform. Divisions among black political leaders prevented them from supporting Herman Badillo in a new bid. The resulting stalemate led to the reelection of Ed Koch in 1985.[77]

Such were the dynamics internal to the two communities as they sought to establish themselves within the political economy of postwar New York. By the late 1970s the new economic realities required a lowering of expectations on the part of minority communities. Nationally, the politics of New Deal liberalism and militant radicalism came to defeat with the 1980 election of Ronald Reagan as president. Locally, the Koch administration increasingly took on the characteristics of a conservative regime, displaying greater sensitivity and concern for the white ethnic citizenry than had its predecessors. Even in a city as traditionally liberal as New York, racial prejudice and discrimination proved to be tenacious and resilient. It did not help that problems on the economic front threatened the security and living standards of most New Yorkers, white and minority. From the interminority perspective, these conditions appeared to chart an even more problematic course for Puerto Ricans than for African Americans.

The Differential Impact of Stagnation and Restructuring

By the mid-1970s the changes in the city's economic structure that had commenced two decades earlier were coming to a head. In Herbert Bienstock's assessment: "Job changes in the 1950's and 1960's led to significant changes in the source of job openings. . . . Between 1950 and 1970, the number of jobs in New York City increased by about 275,000, as the loss of close to 300,000 jobs in goods-producing industries was more than offset by an increase of 572,000 in the service sectors."[78] The rise of the service economy in the context of globalization reduced the traditional manufacturing sector to a shell of its former prominence. Between 1950 and 1976, manufacturing jobs declined from 1,038,900 to 527,000—more than a 50 percent loss—with half of the decline occurring between 1970 and 1975.[79]

The larger picture emerging from the data disguises certain distinctions between minority workers. For several reasons, the repercussions of these structural changes may have been more damaging for Puerto Ricans than African Americans. To begin with, Puerto Ricans were more heavily concentrated in the declining occupations. In 1950, 64.5 percent of all Puerto Rican workers held blue-collar jobs, compared with 42.4 percent of blacks.[80] Therefore, Puerto Ricans—and especially Puerto Rican women—had more to lose from the reduction of these occupations. Barring a successful transition to other types of employment, their overrepresentation in the shrinking blue-collar sector could only presage a difficult future.

Yet the two sources of employment for unskilled workers that did indeed expand significantly, the service and clerical occupations, were less accessible to Puerto Ricans than to African Americans because of the language factor. In retail sales and health industries, for example, workers whose job is to service the public would be expected to have facility in the English language. The same applies to persons in clerical occupations (such as receptionists and other office workers) that involve basic communication skills.

These circumstances appear to have been especially unfavorable for Puerto Rican *females*, who were heavily clustered in manufacturing jobs during the 1950s and 1960s. In 1960 and 1970, respectively, 72 and 41 percent of Puerto Rican female workers were located in blue-collar occupations.[81] Their relative disadvantage is demonstrated by trends in female labor force participation overall: between 1950 and 1980 the participation rate for black females increased slightly, from 48 to 51 percent (see Table 5), whereas for Puerto Rican females it dropped from 40 to 34 percent. Between 1960 and 1970 alone it fell from 38 to 27 percent, indicating that this was an especially damaging period.[82]

Finally, African American success in establishing an early foothold in the expanding government sector brought them a measure of protection against the decline in the goods-producing industries. Although some progress had been made in private industry, it was in the public sector that the importance of political power was most clearly registered. By 1980, 28.7 percent of all black workers were public employees, as were 18.8 percent of Puerto Rican workers; for white workers the proportion was 14.9 percent.[83] The advantage provided by public employment was manifested during the recession of the 1970s, when wages for public employees were largely shielded from the effects of economic contraction. In most clerical, skilled maintenance, and professional categories, municipal workers earned more than their counterparts in the private labor force.[84]

The city's fiscal crisis resulted in many layoffs, however, and these served to weaken the Puerto Rican position even further. Seniority provisions tended to protect more blacks—thanks to their earlier entry—than Puerto Ricans and other Hispanics. One study found that Hispanics were the minority group most disproportionately affected by municipal layoffs: during the period of July 1974 to November 1975, 51.2 percent of all Hispanic public employees lost their jobs. Before that they had made up 6.4 percent of the public work force. Black workers, who represented 25.4 percent, saw a 35 percent decline in public employment.[85]

In summary, during the crisis transition of the 1970s African Americans appeared to be somewhat better positioned than Puerto Ricans to withstand severe dislocations in the economic and political realms. The following decade brought new developments that would further shape the relative conditions of the two groups: a bifurcation in economic opportunities resulting from conscious restructuring policies, a sizable increase in immigrant labor and entrepreneurship, and the coexistence of increased political participation with continued economic exclusion for native minorities. But before turning to those issues, in the next chapter I probe empirically some of the themes already outlined.

CHAPTER FOUR

Patterns of Labor Market Mobility and Wages

This chapter evaluates some hypothesized relationships between segmentation, human capital, and political power, with special reference to their effect on the wages of African Americans and Puerto Ricans between 1960 and 1980. Briefly recapitulating the overall argument will help set these evaluations in the broader context of this study.

Capitalist economies depend on various systems of hegemony, based on class, race, and gender. The importance of each system in contributing to the self-reproducing capacity of the society varies according to the prevailing circumstances of place, culture, and history. In ethnically diverse societies, race plays an extremely important role in the stratification of the labor force: it gives economic elites additional advantages in the bargaining process by allowing them to use the time-honored strategy of "divide and conquer."

In twentieth-century America the system of class domination has generated a multiplicity of distinctions within the working class. Workers share a common exclusion from the ownership of productive resources; the need to sell their labor power is what distinguishes them from employers. Beyond this similarity, however, lie a host of differences: the occupation they hold, whether they belong to a union or not, the industry in which they work, their pay and benefit levels, and so forth. Between the teacher in an inner-city day care center and the sanitation worker in a middle-class suburb we find much less in common than their working-class status would suggest. It is these distinctions that labor segmentation theory attempts to capture, while at the same time pinpointing the fundamental dichotomy between worker and employer. The notion of labor segmentation describes the economic stratification that class domination has generated in the United States.

But hegemony also begets collective *responses*. Examples of responses to *class* domination include union organizing, employee ownership of enterprises, and full employment legislation. Responses to racial domination are often *ethnicity-based strategies* on the part of the oppressed groups. Both class- and race-based initiatives are shaped and constrained by the level of labor segmentation in the economy.

What are the implications of these ideas for the comparative study of racially oppressed groups—in this case, African Americans and Puerto Ricans in New York City? What is each group's distribution in the segmentation structure and its concentration in various segments, and how do these change over time? What is the role, if any, of political power in shaping the group's allocation throughout the segment structure? Finally, what connections are there between differences in labor market earnings and labor segmentation or political power or both? All of this presupposes that education—human capital—matters greatly in influencing socioeconomic status, independently of or interactively with labor segmentation and political power.

This chapter seeks to estimate empirically the extent of these relationships, using census data for the New York Standard Metropolitan Statistical Area (NYSMSA).[1] Table 9 summarizes the sample distribution by gender within racial/ethnic groups.

Patterns of Access and Mobility

Background Data: Wages and Personal Characteristics

During the 1960–80 period, according to census data for NYSMSA, the wage gap between African Americans and Puerto Ricans grew. Beyond the persistent conditions of black-white earnings inequality in the United States, the evidence discloses that Puerto Ricans remained even further removed from labor market parity than African Americans.

For example, in those two decades the *relative wage index* (which is computed by dividing the average wage for African Americans by the average Puerto Rican wage) rose from 1.18 to 1.23.[2] Other studies of the 1980s show that this trend is paralleled by continuing disparities in

Table 9
Sample Breakdown by Race/Ethnicity and Gender: 1960, 1970, 1980

	1960	1970	1980
Total sample (*N*)	4,338	4,364	4,577
Male	2,919	2,628	2,445
Female	1,419	1,736	2,132
Total white	3,910	3,539	3,590
Male	2,661	2,161	1,960
Female	1,249	1,378	1,630
Total black	302	610	790
Male	170	324	362
Female	132	286	428
Total Puerto Rican	126	215	197
Male	88	143	123
Female	38	72	74

Source: Andrés Torres, "Human Capital, Labor Segmentation and Inter-Minority Relative Status" (Ph.D. diss., New School for Social Research, 1988).

family income and poverty status between the two groups. Inside and outside the labor market, Puerto Ricans faced a lowered status relative to African Americans.[3]

A more focused look pinpoints female differences as the principal source of this divergence. From 1960 to 1980 the relative wage index for females rose uninterruptedly (1.24 to 1.42), while the corresponding ratio for males actually declined (1.20 to 1.12). Indeed by 1980, the wage differential between the two male groups was statistically insignificant. On balance, then, the growing divergence in wages between African American and Puerto Rican female labor outweighed the narrowing of the gap between male labor in the two groups.

Relative wage trends varied also with decennial period. During the 1960s, Puerto Ricans, male and female, reduced the wage gap; but the 1970s saw a reversal, with an increase in the relative wage favoring male and female blacks. Again, of course, one must take into account the gender components as well as the intertemporal dimensions of the differences in wages.

Background characteristics partially account for the wage differences and their pattern of change. Between the two male groups, the average levels of labor force experience, education, and residential stability in New York gradually converged between 1960 and 1980. In other words, as Puerto Rican males more closely approximated African American levels of work experience, schooling, and length of stay, these factors helped narrow the wage differential. Among females, however, the divergence in experience actually grew in the two decades, because of a significant decline in average years of experience for Puerto Rican females (from 21.3 in 1960 to 15.4 in 1980). This drop may reflect the retirement of the first cohort of Puerto Rican females, who arrived during the 1940s and 1950s. As these women aged out of the labor force, the group became dominated by younger females, including those born on the mainland.

Distinctions occurred also with respect to language, head-of-household position, marital condition, and public employee status. Blacks showed greater English-language proficiency. African American females had a consistently higher proportion of heads of household, and so did Puerto Rican males—except for 1980, when African American males reversed the pattern. While both groups increased their proportion of public employees, a substantially greater number of African Americans (33 percent to 23 percent) were located in the government sector by 1980.

These data offer an idea of the potential determinants of wage differences between the two groups. On the structural side, information on segment distribution provides further insights into the possible causes of wage disparities.

Segmentation Patterns: Distribution and Mobility

Trends for the total population of the New York metropolitan area (see Chapter Two and Table 3) show that for 1960–70 there was a growth of 7.7 percentage points in independent primary jobs, accompanied by a similarly significant decline of 8.6 points in the proportion of secondary jobs.

The subsequent decade witnessed a sizable increase in secondary jobs with a concomitant fall in the independent craft and subordinate primary sectors. Table 10, describing the segmentation structure by race and gender from 1960 to 1980, indicates that the bulk of this increase took place among white workers. Among minorities only black males experienced an expansion in secondary labor, their share rising from 50.3 to 56.4 percent.

A comparison of interminority differences in group segment distribution illustrates the correlation between segmentation patterns and labor market outcomes. Generally, we expect that those populations with larger proportions of workers in the primary segments (indepen-

Table 10
Segment Distribution within Groups: 1960, 1970, 1980 (percentage distribution)

Segment	1960	1970	1980
		White	
Male (*N*)	2,661	2,161	1,960
I	18.5	31.4	27.4
II	10.4	12.9	5.1
III	34.5	28.7	28.7
IV	36.5	27.1	38.8
Female (*N*)	1,249	1,378	1,630
I	11.0	17.6	20.8
II	1.6	1.3	1.9
III	51.5	57.5	43.7
IV	35.9	23.6	33.6
		Black	
Male (*N*)	170	324	362
I	7.1	8.0	11.0
II	7.6	10.8	5.8
III	30.0	30.9	26.8
IV	55.3	50.3	56.4
Female (*N*)	132	286	428
I	5.3	8.4	12.9
II	1.5	0.7	1.9
III	30.3	51.0	49.1
IV	62.9	39.9	36.2
		Puerto Rican	
Male (*N*)	88	143	123
I	2.3	9.7	17.9
II	9.1	10.4	6.5
III	21.6	25.2	21.1
IV	67.0	54.5	54.5
Female (*N*)	38	72	74
I	0.0	9.7	8.1
II	0.0	1.4	1.4
III	28.9	33.3	51.4
IV	71.1	55.6	39.2

Source: Andrés Torres, "Human Capital, Labor Segmentation and Inter-Minority Relative Status" (Ph.D. diss., New School for Social Research, 1988).
Note: Segments are represented by roman numerals: I—Independent Primary; II—Independent Primary Craft; III—Subordinate Primary; IV—Secondary. Percentages may not total 100% due to rounding.

dent, independent craft, and subordinate primary jobs) would manifest higher levels of mean wages.

In each year and for each gender comparison (except for males in 1980), African Americans displayed larger primary segment representation than did Puerto Ricans, and in each case the mean wage for black workers was higher. In two of the three cases in which the wage rate differential was statistically significant, the disparity in the proportion of primary-to-secondary labor was large. In 1960, 67 percent of Puerto Rican males and 55.3 percent of African American males were secondary workers. A decade later, considerably more Puerto Rican females were in the secondary segment than African American females: 55.6 percent to 39.9 percent. Compared with Puerto Ricans, African Americans had a higher portion of primary jobs. It is no surprise, then, that this relatively favorable profile contributed to a higher relative wage.

A group's segment distribution will change over time depending on its patterns of intersegment *mobility*. As groups gain experience, improve skill levels, or increase their use of political power, they enhance their chances of expanding their share of primary jobs and raising wages.

In the period 1960–70, Puerto Rican males enlarged their proportion in primary jobs (the aggregate of segments I–III in Table 10) from 33 to 45.3 percent. During the same period, the expansion of primary jobs among African American males trailed that of Puerto Ricans. Especially important for Puerto Rican males was the rise in employment within the independent primary segment, growing from 2.3 to 9.7 percent while increasing among black males only from 7.1 to 8.0. Notably, the male relative wage index declined during this decade.

In the following decade, 1970–80, the most salient trend occurred among females. For African American females, there was an appreciable growth in the number of independent primary jobs as a percentage of all jobs held, from 8.4 to 12.9 percent. During the same interval the proportion among Puerto Rican females actually dropped—from 9.7 to 8.1 percent—though this movement was partially offset by a sizable increase in the proportion of subordinate primary jobs held by Puerto Rican females.

These patterns offer some signs that the increase in the wage gap between minority females during 1970–80 bears a relation to the divergence in group segment distribution between African American and Puerto Rican females. Black females moved more rapidly into the primary segments than did their Puerto Rican counterparts.

Determinants of Minority Wages

The relationship of schooling, personal characteristics, and segment structure to variations in wages has been demonstrated more directly by using the multiple regression analysis discussed in the Appendixes to this book. Appendix A defines the variables used; Appendix B describes the data and methods; and Appendix C reports the results. The analysis examined the effect of various factors on hourly wages for each of four race and gender subgroups (African American males, African American females, Puerto Rican males, Puerto Rican females) for each decennial year (1960, 1970, 1980).

Human Capital, Labor Segmentation, and Wages

The results for 1960 show clearly that schooling was more important for African American females than for the other three subgroups. Being employed in the government sector significantly raised wages for black males only. African American workers benefited from their residential patterns; unlike Puerto Ricans, their wages were positively influenced by the length of time they had lived in the metropolitan area.

By 1970, education apparently ceased to make a difference in the relative wage levels of the two groups. The segmentation factor assumed greater importance: being located in the independent primary segment elevated earnings for African American females and Puerto Rican males. Government employment had a greater effect on wages for African American males than for Puerto Rican males.

Changes in some of these relationships took place in 1980. Human capital factors (see Appendix B) once again assumed significance as contributors to interminority wage status, especially for Puerto Rican males and black females. It was secondary and subordinate primary jobs that made a difference in comparative wages, favoring black females and males, respectively.

This cross-sectional perspective affirms the notion that labor segmentation (including government employment) contributed to differences in wages, even after taking into account such important elements as schooling, labor force experience, marital status, and other personal characteristics.

"Levels" and "Returns"

Decomposition analysis (Appendix D outlines methods and results) isolates the two aspects of a variable's influence on wages. The procedure distinguishes between the effects of change in the *level* of human capital endowments from the effects of change in the rate of *return* to these variables. Similarly, it separates changes in segmentation distribution from variations in the returns to location in specific segments.[4]

The results of this investigation confirm the importance of increasing returns to human capital for all groups between 1960 and 1980. Aside from the effects of demographic variables (see Appendix B), the results highlight two important patterns: (1) changes in the returns to human capital were proportionately greater for Puerto Ricans than for African Americans; (2) changes in group segmentation structure had a positive effect for African Americans, a negative one for Puerto Ricans.

The latter result is consistent with the discussion on the link between political power and changing segmentation structure. It appears that the two groups have experienced opposite effects from the segmentation process. African Americans were able to attain mobility across the segmentation structure, whereas Puerto Ricans, on balance, saw mobility slowed down by the segmentation process. As I argued in Chapter Three, this difference was due to the comparatively successful application of political power by African Americans.[5]

An alternative interpretation might be that increases in returns to human capital, which figured importantly for both groups, were also attributable to declines in discrimination resulting from politically based initiatives. That is, the use of political power to reduce discrimination opened up the possibilities for greater improvement in returns to education. Consequently, the political factor need not be linked exclusively to changes in the segmentation variable.[6] Additional controls need to be implemented before these interpretations can be treated with greater confidence.

An Intertemporal View

How important are human capital and segmentation when viewed from a longer-term perspective? There is no reason to suppose that the returns to these factors are constant over time, or that the relative weight of each is unchanging. Indeed, studies have shown that the benefits from higher education have been increasing in the recent past.[7] Perhaps they are related to changes in the nexus between job type and schooling level. A college degree may have greater monetary value to an employee in an expanding services industry than to one in a declining goods-producing sector; that is, the payback from education may have as much to do with the type of job one has as with the quality or years of one's schooling. Furthermore, although the reasons are not entirely clear, there is evidence that the return to human capital has risen for minorities, relative to whites.

The sample used for this study provides instances of variations in the return to human capital, over time and across groups.[8] When three comparisons were made—between (1) African Americans and Puerto Ricans, (2) white males and white females, (3) whites and minorities—the basic finding was that the importance of segmentation, compared with that of human capital, declined during the 1960–80 period.

1. In the interminority comparison, segmentation variables have had a greater effect on wages for Puerto Ricans than they had for blacks, and this was a *negative* effect because of Puerto Ricans' high concentration in the secondary segment. The relative importance of segmentation variables, however, declined to the point that by 1980 human capital variables predominated for both groups.

2. Human capital variables had a more consistently influential effect on the wages of white females, compared with white males, than did segmentation variables. That is, the relative importance of education and other human capital factors was more evident for white females than for white males. The labor segmentation process, as measured in this study, had less influence on wages than the accumulation of human capital.

3. As implied by the previous statements, human capital variables had a greater influence on wages for whites than for minority workers, regardless of gender. Segmentation processes appeared to be declining in impact but were still more important for African American and

Puerto Rican workers than for white workers. Structure matters for all workers, but it appears to matter more for minority workers.

Wage Patterns within Segments

Segmentation theory encourages a focus on the idea that structural features of the labor market may mediate the effect of *other* variables on wages. Are there differential returns to such variables as human capital, government employment, race, and gender, depending upon the segment under consideration? Stratifying the same samples for the same decennial periods by segment (instead of by race and gender, as in the earlier analysis) permitted an examination of the effects of segment location on these variables.

Several noteworthy findings came to light in the assessment of the returns to human capital variables by segment.[9] As anticipated, schooling delivered the greatest payback for primary workers in each decennial year. In 1970, the returns to education were insignificant for secondary workers; likewise, labor force experience failed to contribute to earnings in the secondary segment. In 1980, subordinate primary workers benefited least from schooling and experience; the relative advantage of being a worker in this segment apparently declined in the 1970–80 period.

A look at the income of public sector employees suggests further variations in within-segment returns. Government employment had a positive effect on earnings for primary workers in 1960 and 1980, but not 1970. In 1970, being a public employee was more important for secondary workers than for primary workers. It is perhaps a sign of the declining power of the public sector for secondary workers that from 1970 to 1980 they lost the unique advantage that holding a government job once offered.

Finally, racial earnings were found to differ by segment.[10] That is, even *within* a given segment, and after taking into account the effects of demographic and human capital variables (that is, controlling for differences unrelated to race), there were several instances in which minority workers received lower wages. In 1970 and 1980, wage disparities between whites and blacks were partially attributable to the race variable. Similar cases arose in the comparison between whites and Puerto Ricans. Although the wage differences between whites and Puerto Ricans were greater than between whites and African Americans, those differences derived less from racial discrimination than they did for African Americans.

The Changing Patterns and Importance of Segment Structure

The results of the analysis performed suggest that labor segmentation helps appreciably to explain interminority earnings differentials. How are the key findings of this chapter to be interpreted?

The Importance of Labor Segmentation

A correspondence was identified between a group's segment distribution and its relative wage status. This correspondence applies to interminority comparisons and also to gender distinctions within minority groups.

In each decennial year and for each gender comparison (except for males in 1980), African Americans showed a larger proportion of primary jobs than did Puerto Ricans, and in each case they received higher wages.

Comparisons for the periods 1960–70 and 1970–80 indicate too that changes in interminority differentials correspond to changes in internal segmentation structure. Specifically, increases in the proportion of primary labor coincided with improvements in relative wages.

Including segment location variables in the analysis enhanced the explanatory power of the human capital earnings functions. After controlling for the effects of human capital and demographic factors, segmentation variables (including government employment) affected the relative status of African Americans and Puerto Ricans in each year studied.

Changes in the importance of segmentation variables also contributed to the variation in relative earnings between blacks and Puerto Ricans. This was true for both periods, 1960–70 and 1970–80.

Further, between 1960 and 1980 the importance of segmentation variables *declined* for all groups, and human capital variables maintained a more significant influence on the earnings of whites than on the earnings of minorities.

All together, the three classes of variables examined—human capital, demographic, and segmentation (see Appendix B)—do not account for the total variation in earnings. In several instances a significant component of earnings differentials appears to be linked to racial factors. Overall, however, these results confirm the hypothesis that labor segmentation—statically and dynamically—contributes to interminority wage differentials.

The Changing Significance of Segmentation and Human Capital

Segmentation was clearly influential, but by 1980, education (human capital) seemed to have gained even more importance in the New York labor market. The declining influence of segmentation factors was a constant across each racial group of labor. Two possible interpretations for these findings come to mind.

First, the rising importance of human capital determinants for African Americans between 1960 and 1980 appeared to conform to William J. Wilson's 1978 finding that during the previous decades there was a national trend of upward mobility into primary jobs for African Americans.[11] This was generally true for African Americans in New York, though the bulk of this movement seemed to be happening among females. The increasing influence of human capital factors may therefore be viewed as a source of this upward mobility. Greater educational attainment enabled African Americans to qualify for higher-paying professional jobs. Whether the primary reason was *intergenerational* mobility (succeeding generations of African Americans obtaining higher levels of schooling) or *career-ladder* mobility (within-cohort progress from entry jobs to professional positions) is not deducible from the data examined.

Nor can these data definitely endorse the controversial element in Wilson's argument: that rising education and professional advancement meant that racial discrimination was on the wane. My research does show a decline in the "unexplained residual," offering prima facie evidence of a reduction in discrimination, but this measures only *direct* discrimination, as when an employer favors a white person over an equally qualified minority applicant.[12] Unaccounted for are extra-market, institutional forms of discrimination that can impede equal acquisition of labor market skills, since these indirect processes could not be incorporated in the regression model.

The second possible explanation is that the declining significance of segmentation for all groups may reflect the effects of the restructuring surge in the 1970s, whereby segmentation began to be replaced by *flexibilization* of labor markets. During the growth period, segmentation implied a certain stability in the structure of labor markets, because there was little mobility between segments and because large, core firms were not likely to make radical changes in the size of their primary labor force with changes in the business cycle.

The end of the growth era, however, ushered in a new period of "exploration": employers sought greater control over the production process in order to reduce vulnerability to globalization and intensified competition.[13] The resulting preference for nonunionized, part-time, and contingent labor all had a major impact on the segment structure: a reduction in the size of the primary segment.

With just a core of permanent employees retained, flexibilization offered management the "freedom" to vary work tasks and responsibilities and brought about a significant reshuffling of the boundaries between occupations even within the primary segment.

The scenario of a declining primary segment was indeed confirmed by the New York sample, in which the share of secondary jobs rose from 29.9 to 38.5 percent in the 1970s. This is evidence of the proliferation of low-wage jobs that is associated with flexibilization. Most of the increase came at the expense of independent primary craft jobs (–4.3 percentage points) and subordinate primary jobs (–3.4 percentage points); the "elite" independent primary jobs remained almost unchanged (see Table 3).

Exactly how this shifting or breaking down of segment structure may be related to the rise in returns to education is difficult to elucidate from the available data. With industry and the labor market undergoing such profound transformation, new ways of measuring structural variables appear to be in order. Until new methods are developed to reflect the "flexible" economy, human capital variables may be garnering undue credit for the determination of wage levels. Until new research is conducted on more recent data, however, this can be only a speculative comment.

In-Market Segmentation

Related to these findings is the question of "in-market segmentation," a source of contention between theorists of the labor segmentation and human capital camps.

One of the most trenchant critiques of labor segmentation theory is the claim that it fails to present an approach qualitatively distinct from mainstream theories of the labor market.[14] To be a distinct paradigm, segmentation theory would have to show that the labor market generates different outcomes for labor of *comparable* skill level. In this view, it is not enough simply to identify wage inequality that is associated with stratification or segmentation; the differentials discovered by segmentation theory often reflect inequalities in education, opportunities, and abilities, and these are products of *pre-market* experiences. One cannot find the market culpable, so the argument goes, for disadvantages created in childhood and adolescence, long before individuals seek employment. The market only reproduces differentials that arise from non-market processes and institutions.

In his response to this allegation, Paul Ryan agrees that labor segmentation theory needs to demonstrate the existence of "in-market segmentation" if it is to offer an alternative to neoclassical theory. He defines in-market segmentation as the case in which "individuals of similar achieved productive potential receive markedly different access to employment or job rewards, including both pay rates and opportunities for training, experience and pay increases."[15] In other words, in-market segmentation is demonstrated if one can show where equally qualified workers face different employment opportunities or receive unequal wages.

Neoclassical theory acknowledges the possibility that in-market discrimination may sometimes disrupt the correspondence between wages and labor quality but asserts that these instances are temporary aberrations and are subordinated to the tendency of wage equalization. Except perhaps in the short run, it does not pay employers to discriminate. For example, in the purely competitive case, an employer who has a preference or "taste" for "A" workers over "B" workers will offer the former a higher wage to attract them from other employers. But under conditions of equal productivity, the higher labor cost per unit will cause a decline in the firm's profit margin. Sooner or later, competition will drive this employer out of business or force a change in taste.

According to Ryan, "The dispute between the segmentationist and orthodox approaches hinges therefore upon their divergent assessments of the importance of in-market segmentation."[16] He acknowledges the difficulty of designing a rigorous test to show the existence of in-market segmentation, for it is practically impossible to disentangle non-market and market processes and measure them separately.[17]

Two tests conducted in my study provide indirect evidence of this form of market-generated divergence. The first is captured in the analysis of intrasegment differentials (the sample having been stratified by segment characteristics). That analysis identified other sources of differentials beyond supply-side characteristics and segment location. With individual characteristics and segment location—that is, pre-market segmentation—controlled for, the fact that race and, to a lesser extent, gender determinants partially accounted for differentials in several instances indicates the existence of in-market segmentation.

A second, less conclusive, test is embodied in the wage regression analyses conducted for each race and gender sub-group. A review of the results demonstrated numerous instances of greater returns for subordinate primary workers than for secondary workers, offering evidence of in-market segmentation.[18]

Segmentation and Race

Finally, what is the evidence of racial differentials within segments? Most labor analysts recognize the role of discrimination (whether individual or institutional) in the *allocation* of minority labor to inferior jobs and occupations. Many, however, would deny that the labor market itself generates and reproduces differential earnings by race and gender. I have argued that intrasegment differentials reflect patterns of in-market differentiation. To the extent that this is so, my results will not be comforting to those who hold such benign views of the labor market.

In sum, within the context of the labor market process—and not simply with regard to labor allocation mechanisms—segmentation appears to interact with race in the differentiation of outcomes for labor of a given quality.

The economic and political forces affecting the fortunes of New York's native minorities—primarily African Americans and Puerto Ricans—up through the 1970s led the two groups to generate various ethnicity-based strategies as they sought social mobility and access to power. Beginning with the 1980s a new set of conditions surfaced, presenting yet new challenges and opportunities.

CHAPTER FIVE

Native Minorities, Immigrant Minorities

Native Minorities: Political Participation, Economic Exclusion

For many years following the first term of John Lindsay in the mid-1960s, New York blacks and Puerto Ricans did not coalesce around an effective electoral strategy. From the late 1960s, when Herman Badillo became the first Puerto Rican to seek the mayoralty, through most of the 1980s, as various African American candidates sought to lead anti-Koch forces, the minority coalition failed to materialize. Times were not yet ripe for a transformation in the political structure whereby elected officialdom at the top would mirror the demographic changes in the city's population. But seeds were being sown for future victory.

Rainbow Decade

The impetus came from what at first appeared to many an improbable quarter. With his entry into the presidential race of 1984, Jesse Jackson made the 1980s the Rainbow decade. Campaigning with slender resources and ostracized by the political and media establishment, Jackson nevertheless won second place in New York City's Democratic primary. Everyone took for granted that he would gain the virtually unanimous support of black voters, and so he did. Even in a field including such liberals as Walter Mondale and Gary Hart, Jackson garnered four of every five African American votes.

At the other end of the racial/ethnic spectrum, only 8 percent of white voters supported him. New York, this bastion of American liberalism, sent a clear message: we are far from ready to select an African American president. Not that he was a typical establishment black liberal: Jackson's support of Palestinian self-determination, the insensitive reference to New York as "Hymietown," and his long track record as a charismatic mass leader within the civil rights movement made Jewish liberals and white conservatives uneasy. The overwhelming rejection by white voters became the center of media attention.

But something else had happened. Latino voters, mostly Puerto Rican, displayed surprising support for Jackson, by casting one of three votes for him. Indeed, in those districts where Latinos were a plurality, almost half of them sided with the Rainbow campaign.[1] Spurning exhortations from their entire leadership stratum, which had endorsed Mondale, Hispanics showed sufficient independence of mind to give Jackson a second-place standing in the city's polls, ahead of Gary Hart. Intermediate between black and white voters, Puerto Ricans sent a message too: we are far from discounting the viability of a black president. If we are yet unable to forge an electoral alliance locally, neither are we willing to participate in the wholesale denial of Jesse Jackson's legitimacy. A significant proportion of Hispanics in New York restated their bonds of affinity and struggle with blacks.

Equally important was the fact that both black and Puerto Rican voter participation showed a marked increase over that of the preceding presidential election. By providing a new vehicle for minority political participation, the Jackson campaign—in the face of Reaganomics, restructuring, and backlash—was laying the groundwork for a renewed insurgency.

The next chapter opened in 1988 with Jackson's re-entry into presidential politics. By then the city had endured two terms of federal neglect. Mayor Ed Koch's hold on the minority vote was nowhere near what it had been in the early 1980s, when the liberal opposition—white or minority—proved incapable of mounting a challenge.[2] Given his abrasive style and an ineffective record in dealing with the city's rising poverty, Koch's counsel to New Yorkers to reject Jackson failed to resonate as strongly as in 1984, even among whites.

Since the previous campaign, political trends had favored a broadening of Jackson's potential constituency. His evident commitment to a long-term strategy for empowerment brought together competing strands within African American politics, nationally and locally. Elected officials, civil rights and community activists, and nationalists could all unite behind a figure who had the potential to project an African American onto the center stage of the American political scene. Whereas Martin Luther King, Jr., in his call for social equality and economic justice, advocated a fair share in the American dream, Jackson's campaign challenged the United States to contemplate the possibility of black *leadership* for the nation. It was a challenge that raised aspirations and temporarily buried long-standing differences between various sectors within the black community.[3]

Among Puerto Ricans and other Latinos, a different kind of shift occurred. It consisted of an important split among elected officials, with a younger generation of politicians deciding to join the growing cohort of community activists and radicals who, galvanized by a "Latinos for Jackson" campaign, had backed Jackson the first time around, in 1984.[4] Even though realizing that the Rainbow campaign was only a symbolic crusade, the new wave of politicians saw an opportunity to begin building a base for an anti-Koch effort in 1989.

A bit further in the future lay the possibility of a major change in the way New York's electoral districts were drawn. Several lawsuits were winding their way through the judicial system, charging that the city's existing configuration violated the U.S. Constitution. Sooner or later a redistricting plan was bound to be approved, making it easier for Latinos and blacks to elect their own representatives to the city council. The moment seemed right for a new generation of Hispanic politicians to begin its ascendancy, and the Rainbow challenge offered the ideal vehicle.

In many districts, of course, Latino candidates would need black voter support and vice versa, and there was still some hesitancy among Latinos who were concerned that the Rainbow was too driven by African American issues and concerns. But many were convinced that Puerto Ricans and other Latinos had to reconstitute political unity with blacks. The Jackson drive offered both groups the chance to strengthen ties that had frayed during the 1980s and, just as important, to construct a political machinery for a new electoral push in the coming years. On primary day in 1988, Latino voters declared their endorsement of Jackson: they doubled their 1984 showing, with 63 percent voting for him.[5]

This historic shift was a principal factor in Jackson's slim victory over Michael Dukakis in New York City. In the 1988 presidential primary, New York's minority voters had staged a historic precedent: for the first time in the city's history, people of color delivered a victor—

one of their own—in a citywide electoral contest. It mattered little that at the state level Jackson trailed behind Dukakis, or that there was no actual office at stake. The stage had been set to meet future challenges.

Once again, as in 1984, the reactions of the media and political establishment ranged between worried disbelief and an interpretive "spin" that all but ignored the immense implications of the results. The public learned of the shortcomings of the Jackson effort: after all, Dukakis won the statewide vote; it was Koch's endorsement of Gore that weakened the front runner; Jackson had received only 17 percent of the white vote. The import of the Latino shift thus became a principal casualty of the way public discourse distorted the meaning of the campaign. Crucial changes in Latino politics were rendered invisible: the coming of age of a new generation of community and political leaders; the growth in political activity of non–Puerto Rican Latinos, especially Dominicans.

Perhaps the most fundamental development had to do with Puerto Rican/Latino–African American relations. Analysts failed to note the political maturity of the significant sector that had led in breaking from traditional Puerto Rican leadership in order to unite with Jackson. This insurgent stratum had to overcome resentments among Puerto Rican voters who felt that blacks had forsaken them during the debacle of 1985, when the Coalition for a Just New York (CJNY) backed off from Badillo. For years, activists had critiqued the veteran Puerto Rican figure as someone too beholden to establishment politics and lacking a strategic vision of grassroots organizing in the community. Still, for most Puerto Ricans and Latinos, Badillo had offered the best chance for a shot at political victory—and he was one of them. It was no easy decision, setting aside ethnic loyalties to support an African American maverick. But the media failed to capture this milestone in Latino politics. The overriding concern with black-white dynamics blinded many mainstream observers to the fact that other groups were undergoing important political transformations.

It was not long before a new opportunity arose for Rainbow politics to test its mettle. That moment surfaced with the mayoral campaign of 1989.

The Dinkins Primary

To become the city's first black mayor, David N. Dinkins would have to surmount two electoral hurdles: the Democratic Party's September 1989 primary to select a candidate, and the general election in November. But Ed Koch confronted a set of obstacles more formidable than past challenges to his reelection, and Dinkins seemed poised to take advantage of them.

To begin with, New Yorkers were fatigued by the antagonistic and quarrelsome manner in which Koch engaged his critics and adversaries. He was increasingly given to rebuking his critics, whether minority groups, labor unions, advocacy organizations, or the local press. After a twelve-year incumbency, his style was wearing thin even among New Yorkers, who are notably accustomed to cantankerous personalities. Indeed, many felt that his leadership style only aggravated the already frayed racial relations among citizens. His handling of a series of bias-related crimes that rocked the city during the late 1980s confirmed the feelings of many that he was ill suited to the role of conciliator.

Added to those problems were the failing economy and a rash of corruption scandals. Early in his tenure Koch could point with pride to a veritable explosion in jobs, especially within the financial and business services sector. His strategy of inducing a Manhattan-based development spurt gave the appearance that restructuring was successfully revitalizing the economic base. But much of this proved to be temporary, as the 1987 Wall Street crash revealed. Firms cut back on the number of employees as quickly as they had brought them in; vacancy rates in office towers rose; and manufacturing resumed its long-term fall. Unemployment shot up again, and poverty rates—never really improved by "trickle-down" economics—remained a stubborn reality for about a quarter of all New Yorkers.

To make matters worse, the city was plunged into one of its worst rounds of corruption. By his third term, Koch's regime had lost whatever innovative and energetic spirit it had had when he was elected in 1977. The promise of recovery and rejuvenation that had followed the 1975 fiscal crisis gave way to a stasis born of inbred political alliances and "old boy" networks. Behind the back of the outspoken and volatile mayor a series of scandals brewed, involving elected officials, governmental figures inside and outside his administration, city officials, and business connections.[6] Although not directly responsible for the instances of bribery that caught the public eye, the mayor found that New Yorkers had become less willing to tolerate his flaws and more open to the prospect of terminating his reign—even if the leading alternative was an African American.

It can be said that Koch's liabilities found their antithesis in the qualities that Dinkins offered. His greatest strength lay in his image as mediator and healer. African Americans, Puerto Ricans, and other minorities could identify with the challenger, seeing in him someone who would represent the interests of New York's dispossessed. To whites, he was a nonthreatening figure because they did not see him as closely linked to the militant wing of black politics.[7] They were assured further by his long association with the regular Democratic Party machinery. He was a classic Manhattan liberal who could move at ease among various ethnic and social circles. A Jesse Jackson he was not—a fact that relieved many Democrats.

Here was an effective politician, too, merging several constituencies behind his campaign. To the Rainbow Coalition that had accounted for Jackson's triumph in the 1988 primary, Dinkins added liberals, labor unions, and important elements of the business world. These last, including key figures such as Felix Rohatyn (chairman of the Municipal Assistance Corporation) and Arthur Levitt (former chairman of the New York Stock Exchange), surmised that Dinkins was best positioned to ease the potential racial and class conflicts of a post-crash New York.

After a long and often acrimonious campaign extending the better part of a year, Democratic voters had their say. For the first time ever, they nominated a black candidate for mayor, giving Dinkins half the votes, to Koch's 42 percent. The racial/ethnic breakdown revealed that Dinkins had successfully expanded on the Rainbow base of support: one-third of white Democrats had voted for the black candidate.[8] The first hurdle had been cleared.

Between Access and Power

The general election pitted Dinkins against Rudolph Giuliani, a Republican "law and order" candidate with strong support among white ethnics. Where the Democrat's message accentuated traditional liberal notions of civil rights and social programs for the needy, Giuliani stressed the need to control the violence and social unrest overtaking the city. Calling for a much tougher stand on crime than even Koch had countenanced, he appealed to middle-income homeowners and targeted Irish and Italian Catholics. These groups, along with many Jewish voters, felt that the defeat of Koch represented a throwback to the Lindsay era and, consequently, that the Democratic Party no longer represented their interests; worse still, the party's standard-bearer was an African American. Seeing a golden opportunity to win over to their side vast numbers of disaffected Democrats, Republicans spared no effort in their drive to pull off an upset victory.

On election day, Dinkins emerged victorious again, although not by much. Giuliani had at one point trailed by twenty points in the polls, but the final tally revealed that of 1.8 million votes cast, the Democrat had won by less than 50,000. Not quite three percentage points separated the contenders, the slimmest margin since the turn of the century. It was a historic moment for the city but by no means a resounding success for Dinkins. New York's first black mayor could not lay claim to a mandate—especially since over 30 percent of Democratic voters had abandoned their party to vote for Giuliani.

Despite both candidates' efforts to downplay racial issues, an atmosphere of racial mistrust and fear had pervaded the campaign. Survey data showed a strong feeling among African Americans and Latinos that Giuliani would favor whites if elected, and whites believed that Dinkins would favor blacks.[9] In addition to the normal divisions on policy issues to be expected between Republicans and Democrats, the election of 1989 exposed yet again the sharp racial cleavages that underlay New York politics.

Still, Dinkins was mayor, and his election signified, in part, a culmination of the ethnicity-based strategies propelling the minority challenge that had begun in the 1960s. During the 1970s and 1980s the insurgency had been stalled by fiscal crisis, racial backlash, and internal factionalism, but population changes and growing political experience produced the inevitable breakthrough. The new mayor could even point to a not insignificant sector of whites who endorsed him. One post-election assessment aptly summed up the final outcome:

> In conjunction with Dinkins's strong turnout in the black community and the Latino shift in his favor, the fact that a substantial minority of white Democrats and Independents trusted Dinkins, wanted him to reduce racial tensions, and address the legacy of social polarization from the Koch years provided Dinkins with the margin necessary for victory.[10]

Serious questions remained, however. Would having an African American mayor make a difference for blacks and other minorities? Could Dinkins win the general trust of white New Yorkers and begin the healing process that was so sorely needed? Just as important, could he reverse the city's economic misfortunes?

In his early pronouncements and actions Dinkins insisted that he would not sacrifice social priorities to fiscal constraints. His inaugural address promised listeners that his election meant more than just the elevation of another career politician: "I stand here before you today as the elected leader of the greatest city of a great nation, to which my ancestors were brought, chained and whipped, in the hold of a slave ship."[11] The mayor's followers hoped that his message signaled a new kind of leadership, one characterized by inclusiveness and tolerance and, especially, one that would defend the interests of the disadvantaged. This would not be politics as usual. President George Bush's call for a "kinder, gentler nation" had been greeted with incredulity, but Dinkins would be different.

Many gave the new mayor high grades in his first test: the selection of personnel to fill key positions in the new administration. Staying true to campaign promises, he fashioned a leadership team that reflected New York's population diversity. African Americans, Hispanics, and women were recruited to supervise major divisions and agencies throughout the city's government.

To those concerned about Mayor Dinkins's commitment to his social agenda—issues such as homelessness, AIDS, poverty, inadequate health services—there was hope in the fact that community activists and advocates were being brought into the sphere of municipal management. These included a cohort of loyal operatives from his previous role as borough president of Manhattan, where he had embellished his reputation as a champion of liberal causes. Others came from the grassroots campaign structure that had turned out voters in minority communities throughout the city. Finally, a significant number of progressive appointees were tapped from out-of-town locales for the giant social service and health agencies: Human Resources and the Health and Hospitals Corporation. In piecing together his administration the new mayor had compiled a management team that not only reflected the "mosaic" he often spoke of but also empowered a generation of veteran activists who had fought many battles against cutbacks during the Koch years.[12]

If the paucity of minorities in leadership had been a defect in past administrations, this seemed an ideal moment to test the notion that putting "outsiders" into the center of government could make a difference in the lives of the powerless. But it wasn't long before Dinkins had to face the limitations inherent in his professed mission. Two obstacles—one political, one economic—stood in his way.

On the political side, the fact of the matter is that Dinkins was not really a champion of insurgency. Although very much a leader of the black community, one whose election was a source of great pride to African Americans, he had always maintained personal and working relations with New York's political, business, and social elites. That he could move in those circles, as well as in liberal and even socialist networks, attested to his conscious strategy—apparently years in the making—to offer himself as a political figure acceptable to many factions. But harsh reality crystallized in the very first months of the new administration. After all, Dinkins had other political debts to clear up. For even as nervous voices and raised eyebrows greeted some of the mayor's early appointees, he had to acknowledge the support of those sectors within the regular Democratic Party machinery which had contributed to his victory over Giuliani. He could not ignore the fact that Koch himself had worked on his behalf to defeat the Republican.

Also to be reckoned with were representatives from the financial world, including Felix Rohaytn, who had persuaded colleagues that Dinkins was the better candidate.[13] Whatever his talents as administrator, it was apparent to Wall Street that Dinkins had a better chance to forestall a social breakdown in the city. The rejection of a Democratic Party candidate who happened to be the first African American could provoke racial tensions beyond the boiling point. This was not in Wall Street's interests. Indeed, Dinkins's background might make him uniquely qualified to cope with the looming fiscal crisis. Surely it must have occurred to some: who better than an African American to make the case for sacrifice and austerity?

The new administration, then, perforce reflected the contradictions and tensions embodied in the disparate forces that had elected the mayor. It contained elements of the old and new, outsiders and insiders, status quo and insurgency. On balance, though, it was clear that the administration was too beholden to the power elites to represent a qualitative break with the past.[14] Politically, Dinkins's grassroots constituency lacked the strength to pry him from the established interests to which he was partially indebted.

This was made patently obvious as soon as the mayor began tackling the severe economic problems of the city, foremost among them the fiscal deficit. Following his primary loss, Koch announced in October 1989 that the city faced an estimated shortfall of $500 million in a $27 billion operating budget for fiscal year 1990 (the year ending June 1990)—double the deficit estimates forecast just a few months earlier. It was becoming painfully clear that the worst-case scenario predicted in the aftermath of the Wall Street crash of October 1987 was indeed coming into play. Employment growth in both the services and manufacturing sectors had come to a halt, and in the two years since the fall of 1987 a total of 36,000 jobs had been lost.[15] Inevitably, a chain reaction was set off, hitting other areas of the economy, and the effect on tax revenues was not long in materializing.

The decline in economic activity, jobs, and incomes promptly threw city finances into a deep disequilibrium. A month after taking office, Dinkins was informed that the half-billion-dollar gap announced in October had grown to a billion. Although the city had been holding the line on expenditures, proceeds from taxes were plummeting as an all-out recession battered the economy. Before he could even contemplate the possibility of putting innovative social programs into place, the new mayor had to address the nuts and bolts of budget balancing. That neither the budget nor the recession was of his making appeared sadly ironic to many. Among his more progressive aides and supporters the fear grew that the larger political goals of the campaign would have to be shelved, perhaps indefinitely.

The Ongoing Fiscal Dilemma

The crash of 1987 symbolized the end of the first experiment with restructuring in New York City. It signified also that local politics would be driven increasingly by the exigencies of austerity and crisis management. Perhaps more clearly than ever before, the struggle over social priorities would mirror the contention over the budget process. Which expenditure items should be retained and which eliminated? Which revenue sources were to be mined for additional income? The outcomes of such decisions would partially shape the fate of individuals, families, and whole communities, as well as businesses small and large.

The battle lines of this policy struggle conformed fairly neatly to the expenditure-revenue choice inherent in the fiscal dilemma. The progressive contingent, made up of community activists, labor groups and Dinkins's progressive aides, argued for closing the gap by boosting revenues through increases in tax rates on corporations and wealthy individuals. The business community, especially financial powers on Wall Street, insisted on reductions in municipal expenditures. About the only point agreed upon by everyone was that there was no early prospect of "growing out" of the crisis. It would be some years before a revitalized economy, with an expanded job and tax base, could liberate budgetmakers from the hard choices that confronted them.

Since tax rates had been reduced during the 1980s, an upward readjustment seemed like cogent policy. (Indeed, the deficit would not have been so enormous had not rate reductions, starting in 1986, foreclosed hundreds of millions of dollars in income to the city.)[16] Add the idea of cutting back on tax abatements (exemption from future taxes) to corporations and real estate developers, and one could envision a solution to the budget gap. Tax breaks of this nature struck opponents as questionable because they were unrelated to any job-creation goals. Studies in New York and elsewhere raised doubts that abatements were the determining factor in luring or retaining employers.[17]

The corporate world, as expected, was diametrically opposed to these deficit-reduction schemes. Echoing views that had coalesced into powerful orthodoxy during the Reagan years, business interests scorned any attempt to tamper with the tax structure. Imposing new financial burdens, they argued, would only force companies to lay off workers or, worse, drive businesses out of the city. New taxes would be a drag on future growth and threaten a new out-migration of middle- and upper-income families. Ronald K. Shelp, president of the New York Chamber of Commerce, insisted on a precondition before business would even consider the idea of raising taxes. There would have to be evidence of cuts in city expenditures: "Then you can talk about taxes . . . not before."[18]

But which city expenditures? Dinkins had made it clear throughout the election contest that he was not about to abandon programs sorely needed by his minority constituencies. Now, with a much larger-than-anticipated abyss separating black from red ink, his commitments were being severely tested. Nevertheless, as push came to shove during the budget-balancing process, he held to his basic position. In the areas of education, social welfare, and health services he resolutely opposed the deep cuts that many hardliners urged.

True, his compromise in acceding to minimal cuts in programs for the needy was an insufficient response to the growing problems related to homelessness, the drug epidemic, AIDS, and child poverty. But in preserving the basic infrastructure of the social safety net, he was forcing policymakers inside and outside his administration to look elsewhere for answers to the budget dilemma. Since the late 1970s, social programs for the poor had been slashed to the bare bone. There was just no way to squeeze further "savings" there.

This left few other candidates for reduced spending, but one was quickly pinpointed by business interests: labor costs. While he could not undo previously negotiated contractual agreements, the mayor was encouraged to freeze wages for all but "essential" public employees (police) in the upcoming year. As Rohatyn argued in the fall of 1990, when the city was anticipating an estimated billion-dollar budget gap for fiscal year 1992: "There is no status quo in public life; either things get better or they get worse. In New York right now, they are getting worse. For things to get better, the city will have to make fundamental changes in the way it goes about its business. . . . We need to question the city's overall wage and personnel policy."[19] Applying pressure early for the next round of budget-balancing, Wall Street was targeting the municipal payroll. It was time again for retrenchment by holding down wages, increasing productivity, laying off employees, or some combination of the three.

Others sought to revisit the revenue side of the budget equation and redirect attention to a potentially important source of proceeds: homeowner property taxes. Whether by raising rates or reassessing market values, the city could put hundreds of millions of dollars in new income into its coffers. Besides, relative to other parts of the income stream, the taxes paid by homeowners had actually declined since the 1970s.[20]

To the dismay of his supporters in the business sector, Dinkins proved to be equally resistant to both these ideas. His stand on labor issues was particularly illuminating. He worked out a contract with the United Federation of Teachers, which—under the circumstances—appeared to be an adequate deal in the eyes of most UFT members. And he was ever mindful of the electoral endorsement he had received from the mammoth District Council 37 of the American Federation of State, County, and Municipal Employees. AFSCME boasted a membership of 100,000 and was headed by an African American, Stanley Hill. Hill had played an important role in local Rainbow politics throughout the 1980s and had ties with Dinkins from earlier campaigns. The mayor could hardly begin his administration by turning his back on these constituencies.

Still, he was not entirely motivated by future vote-getting. He understood that city services, including public education, constituted the safety net that remained after the federal abandonment of urban areas.

The caseworkers, teachers, hospital workers who toiled in the front lines of the war against poverty were the city's main defense against social disarray. His insistence on maintaining their morale, even in times of fiscal distress, was consistent with the progressive instincts that formed his outlook.

In the matter of property taxes, however, political considerations reigned; many of his allies in the regular Democratic Party in Queens and Brooklyn feared a voter revolt in their working-class base, mostly white, if he backed a homeowners' tax increase. Although most of Dinkins's white supporters were to be found among Manhattan-dwelling liberals, he could ill afford to alienate his allies' constituents. Moreover, he was not enthusiastic about giving middle-income families, of any color, further reason to leave the city.

In the final analysis, Dinkins stayed his course. The first budget gap was bridged with a hodgepodge of taxes, mostly corporate and sales, and selected reductions in service expenditures. When all was said and done, he struck a compromise that pleased few but at least, for the moment, stabilized the fiscal situation.

An Assessment

That Dinkins's first fifteen months left everyone, supporters and detractors, somewhat unhappy may be the greatest testimony to his capacity for conciliation. With his maneuverability extremely limited by the crunch on city resources, his success in temporarily appeasing the financial powers without drastically slashing city services was perhaps his greatest accomplishment. But this was not what progressives had had in mind as they worked to get him elected. They had set their sights on bold new programs, not just damage control and mere loss cutting. They recalled his campaign promises to bring about a fundamental realignment in social priorities, to attack old problems with new approaches. Their expectations had been raised by his oath to be an "agent of change," a "vehicle" for the advancement of the powerless. Now, they were forced into a strictly incrementalist, if not defensive, mode. Dinkins conceded that the budget crisis was forcing him to scale back his original goals, but reminded the public that things could have been worse. It was time for lowered expectations: "It may be that you affect things [only] at the margins . . . but when things get tight, the margins matter a hell of a lot."[21]

For those involved in the insurgency that had been evolving throughout the 1980s, this was meager consolation. Immersion in the political process had led to their tenuous existence as junior partners within what was basically a caretaker regime as crisis management rapidly became the chief function of the Dinkins administration. Cumulative pressures were stacking the deck against this fragile coalition just entering power: a decade of restructuring, nationally and locally; the intransigence of racial opposition to the city's first minority mayor; the difficulty of turning the tide against entrenched inequality and poverty.

There were few signs that Dinkins would break the national pattern that had afflicted African American mayors since the 1960s: the inability to parlay the gains from political access into socioeconomic progress for those most in need of it. New York, it appeared, would be added to the list of cities in which political participation coexisted with economic exclusion.

Kenneth Clark, long an observer and adviser in African American political life, voiced pessimism in this context.

> We do have more blacks in political professions. [But] I have been concerned about the fact that the increase in numbers of black political officials does not seem to me to be correlated with an increase in the ability of blacks in general [to advance]. . . . I do not see that there has been an association of blacks in political office and economic benefits to blacks in general.[22]

Immigrant Minorities: The Third World Settling In

While blacks and Puerto Ricans were working to build inroads into the city's power structure during the 1980s, the growing new immigrant minorities were concerned primarily with consolidating their economic presence. In 1990 their surging numbers pushed the share of European-origin New Yorkers below the halfway mark for the first time in the city's history. But still preoccupied with building the foundations of community infrastructure, they had not yet directed their energies toward city political processes.

Three fast-growing communities, each contributing its own set of experiences and challenges to the New York reality, illustrate social and economic developments within this immigrant populace and the implications for the political and cultural dynamics of the city as a whole.

Dominicans

Since the mid-1960s, immigrants from the Dominican Republic have gradually increased their presence in New York's labor market, small business world, and body politic. Today they constitute the third largest minority on the New York scene.[23] Official numbers fail to capture this growth because of the prevalence of undocumented persons within this community. Taking its full measure would easily raise the Dominican count beyond half a million.[24]

In certain respects the incorporation of this group resembles the early phase of the Puerto Rican experience. A largely rural and poverty-stricken population, Dominicans have come to fill those economic sectors most in need of low-wage labor: light manufacturing and personal services. By 1980 the occupational distribution of the Dominican labor force paralleled that of Puerto Ricans in 1960, with roughly equivalent proportions of blue-collar and manufacturing-based workers.

But as the Puerto Ricans found, it is one thing to establish a beachhead on the new terrain; it is another to convert the initial foothold into permanent niches in the economy. During the 1970s, as native minorities were grappling with high unemployment and low labor force participation, new immigrants such as Dominicans could find jobs only in low-wage sectors, both formal and informal. Like their predecessors, and like immigrants the world over, they struggled for a living, often sending their savings to relatives back home.

The 1970s, their period of initial settlement, was a decade of hardship. Between 1970 and 1980 earnings inequality among Dominican males and females remained constant. Male labor market incomes were only a third of those of white males. As with Puerto Rican workers, income distribution among Dominicans became polarized during the decade, the lower and upper groups expanded at the expense of the middle.[25] They discovered what all New Yorkers were learning: except for the well trained, the price to be paid for working in the restructured economy was acceptance of at best a constant, if not falling, wage level.

This truth was brought home again in the late 1980s. For just as the islanders appeared to be riding the crest of a wave of labor incorporation, the manufacturing sector was hit once more by a long-term slump. The October crash of 1987, followed by the recession of the early 1990s, dampened hopes that first-generation Dominicans could enjoy stable employment.

Much has been made of the entrepreneurial activity of the Dominican community.[26] It is visible in restaurants, "bodegas" (grocery stores), and light manufacturing. Although reliable comparative data are not available, this appears to be an area of contrast with the present Puerto Rican community. Puerto Rican neighborhoods no longer abound with the small businesses (bodegas, barber shops, beauty salons, travel agencies, and so on) that thrived in the barrios during the 1950s and 1960s. Many were driven out by the expansion of full-service chain stores and supermarkets; others closed down as the original owners retired and relocated to Puerto Rico.

In several areas, Dominican small businesses have filled the vacuum, but their markets are still limited to economically depressed ethnic enclaves. Competition from supermarkets and fast-food outlets, the practice of many owners who repatriate revenues to the Dominican Republic, and the narrow consumer market to which these businesses appeal limit the potential reach of this ethnicity-based strategy. Short of some dramatic turnaround in the conditions underlying these enclaves, these small enterprises are not likely to expand vigorously or to spur local reinvestment of capital. It remains to be seen whether neighborhood-based small businesses will flourish beyond the initial immigrant cohort.

The New York Dominican community has also entered an important phase of political activity at the local level.[27] This process will enable more effective action in the public sector, as it did for African Americans and, more recently, for Puerto Ricans. But the prospects for employment expansion in this sector are limited by the city's fiscal condition. The push toward reducing the size of city government will likely diminish employment opportunities for Dominicans and other recent immigrants.

As the larger context continues to be dominated by a politics of austerity and restricted state functions, the pressures sustaining competitive rather than coalitional interethnic relations will continue to operate. The government's role as employer and supplier of services will be increasingly strained as it seeks to manage the conflicting claims made upon it by the poorer racial/ethnic communities. In this competition, the more recent immigrant groups such as Dominicans will probably fare even less well than the native minorities.

Further, there are disturbing signs of extreme poverty and social stress within the Dominican community. Problems of housing, education, and health conditions are surfacing to an alarming degree. Washington Heights, the area of greatest Dominican concentration, has been consistently identified as one of the most depressed areas within the city and nation. In 1980 close to a quarter of families in the area lived below the poverty line; between 1980 and 1984 the percentage of households receiving welfare assistance increased from 19.1 percent to 24 percent.[28] Other symptoms of poverty plague this area: one of the highest rates of lead poisoning, a dangerous lack of prenatal care (28.5 percent of all births), more overcrowding than in any other school district, and the highest homicide rate in the city.[29]

In its first twenty-five years (1965–90) the community traversed a path toward relative deprivation similar to that followed by Puerto Ricans. Other factors may further impede Dominican social mobility. Unlike Puerto Ricans, Dominicans do not arrive as U.S. citizens and are thus less eligible early on for certain types of jobs and social support systems. Although numerically significant in a growing number of districts, their ability to convert residential concentration into voting power is subject to the time lag required by the naturalization process.[30] And as a people with a greater African heritage than Puerto Ricans, Dominicans may find their racial composition used as an additional barrier against them. The confluence of these factors may subject this community to even greater difficulties than those faced by Puerto Ricans.

West Indians

The same legislation which in 1965 enabled residents of the Dominican Republic to increase their presence in the United States opened the doors to the rest of the Caribbean.[31] Just a few years earlier, Great Britain had severely limited the entry of inhabitants from its former colonies in the West Indies. This de facto embargo encouraged English-speaking Caribbean people, overwhelmingly of African descent, to contemplate the United States as a new destination. Immigration reform at that time made it possible also for Haitians, once ruled by France, to look northward. Layered with variations in race, language, and culture, the post-1965 Caribbean immigration constituted a new chapter in population movements from a region where "migration" had once been virtually synonymous with "Puerto Rican."

The West Indies comprise more than two dozen nations, including several with very small populations. New York has become home to persons from all of these islands, but (aside from Puerto Rico and the Dominican Republic) Jamaica, Trinidad-Tobago, and Barbados have sent the largest numbers. Taken together, they make up a group almost a third the size of New York City's African American population.[32]

Patterns of labor market incorporation among these West Indians parallel those of Dominicans in several regards. Several low-wage categories have been occupied by women, who until recently dominated the gender composition of the immigrant flow: nursing aides, child care and private household workers, attendants for the elderly, workers in clerical sales and light manufacturing. Personal service and health industry jobs were identified as labor shortage areas during the 1960s and regarded in the United States as occupations desired among new immigrants. Males have moved into manufacturing, maintenance and security, health services, and the taxi industry.[33]

West Indian entrepreneurship is demonstrated in construction, travel agencies, beauty salons, and livery trades, including the so-called "gypsy cab" industry in which Dominicans are heavily involved. Most of these activities are concentrated in the principal neighborhoods of settlement within Brooklyn (Crown Heights, East Flatbush, and Flatbush). Other areas of West Indian growth include southeastern Queens and the northeastern Bronx.

Journalistic reports often dramatize the vibrancy and energy of West Indian commercial districts, contrasting them with African American areas.[34] And since the 1970s, scholars have extolled the socioeconomic advance of West Indians to illustrate that race need not be an obstruction to group progress. After all, it is said, Jamaicans and Barbadians endured slavery, just like American blacks. Yet when given a chance in a democratic environment, they have shown the ability to thrive. Like the Asian "model minority" (see below), West Indian "exceptionalism" has been used as a counterargument against the demands of native minorities.[35]

Often overlooked by outsiders is the fact that much of the progress identified among West Indians is an artifact of the selective nature of the *pre-1965* immigration. Hence, the West Indians who migrated northward during the first half of the century hailed from a background more professional and urban than was characteristic of blacks from the South. In the Caribbean a fairly significant elite had emerged, tracing back to the slave period.[36] Toward midcentury, as the prospect of nationhood became ever more real, the indigenous leadership on many of the islands gained further confidence in their political and economic dealings.[37] By 1960 there already were tens of thousands living in New York City, and their influence in the economic and political life of the city's blacks far exceeded their numbers. Indeed, the pre-1965 immigrants produced the crucial core of leadership of New York's African American community prior to World War II.

The evolution of this leadership sector, in both the political and economic realms, illustrates the dynamic relationship between race and ethnicity. In the early decades the small West Indian community amalgamated itself with the local black population, literally submerging ethnicity within race insofar as their relationship to the Euro-American society was concerned. Homeland traditions and customs often demarcated them from U.S. blacks, but when it came to the great black-white divide, West Indians were clear as to where their loyalties lay. And white New Yorkers, even though finding the black immigrants more to their liking, were clear as to what side of the divide the newcomers belonged on.

The story of how West Indians gradually assumed leadership over the African American community has been ably recounted.[38] In brief, before the 1930s, U.S. blacks were alienated from the national Democratic Party, which encouraged racial subjugation in the Deep South, whereas Caribbean immigrants—having little familiarity with Jim Crow—gravitated toward the Democrats who dominated New York City politics. In the 1930s, with Franklin D. Roosevelt and the New Deal, African Americans switched political allegiance en masse and infused the Democratic Party with their numbers. By then, Caribbean blacks had already established a power base within the local Democratic Party machinery and were recognized by the party as official spokespersons for the black community.

What is most noteworthy about this phenomenon is that leaders such as Herbert Bruce, Bertram Baker, and Hulan Jack acted as representatives of the entire black community, rarely accentuating their West Indian origins. For them, the problems of Jamaicans and others were basically inseparable from those of U.S. blacks. Besides, the growing numbers of migrants from the South promised to overwhelm the immigrant enclave. As long as they perceived themselves as African Americans, this was an opportunity, not a threat. Given their relatively small numbers, their already privileged status among blacks, and a crying need for talented leadership, there was no point in charting a path distinct from that of native blacks. Race took precedence over ethnic identity and continued to do so until the 1970s, when the *new* immigration began to take hold.

This prior history helps to explain the more independent orientation of political activity within the community during the 1980s. With a radically transformed population base and a newly emergent leadership stratum, relations with mainstream political structures and even with African Americans took a more complex form. West Indians imprinted their own variations on the racial and ethnic dilemmas of New York politics (see Chapter Six).

Chinese

Americans of Chinese descent trace their origins to the great immigrations of the mid-nineteenth century, when tens of thousands of contract laborers arrived in the American West to labor in gold mines and on the railroads. They were essentially a floating labor force, spreading throughout the West and untied to the land. From the start, they were treated differently from the Euro-Americans working the same domains. A xenophobic national government sanctioned discriminatory statutes that confined the immigrants to a social and political no-man's-land. Support for these restrictions came from a labor movement that feared competition from foreigners who were willing to work for much lower wages.[39]

In 1870, Asians were denied the right to become citizens; in 1882, Congress passed the Chinese Exclusion Act, which literally prohibited the entry of new immigrants—the first and only time that a specific nationality was denied admittance.[40] By this time there were some 100,000 Chinese in the United States, but only five of each one hundred were female; there seemed little likelihood of a "normal" assimilation process in the foreseeable future. Segregated from the broader society, devoid of property rights, they banded together in the cities of the West and, gradually, in places eastward: Chicago, New York, Boston, and Philadelphia. The Exclusion Act engendered the formation of the first urban enclaves of Chinese Americans—America's Chinatowns and, arguably, its first involuntary ghettos.

California, where Chinese made up one-fourth of all working males at the turn of the century, led the way in establishing legalized subjugation. Laws were passed prohibiting marriage between Caucasians and Asians. Asians were denied the right to testify in court and prevented from owning or leasing land. Unconstitutional as these measures were, they were tolerated by the national government, and most of them stayed on the books until 1940. And until the 1960s, Chinese-Americans continued to live quite removed from the booms and busts, the conflicts and crises raging in the nation. Like that of Native Americans, their presence was uneasily felt, publicly ignored. A legacy both of institutionalized ostracism and protective detachment, the urban Chinatowns—including the portion of lower Manhattan where New York's Chinese Americans had gathered for almost a century—evolved virtually in a world of their own.

This was all changed by revised immigration laws, the same changes that in 1965 opened the doors to Latin America, the Caribbean, and the rest of Asia. By 1990 the city's Chinese American population approximated a quarter-million persons, the largest component of the half-million Asians who made New York their home.[41]

Many would say that New York's new immigrant Chinese are the modern pioneers of urban economic development, as evidenced by Chinatown's boom of the 1970s and early 1980s. And indeed it is a story of the successful—some would argue serendipitous—combination of labor migration, foreign capital, and unparalleled locational advantage.[42] How equitable was the apportioning of the fruits of economic growth, how damaging the effects of intensive development—these questions are still debated. But the transformation of a quaint "city within a city" into an ultra-dense center of social and commercial activity says volumes about the promise and peril of community economic development.

Prior to the 1960s immigrant influx, the principal self-employment activity of Chinese American was in restaurants and hand laundries, concentrated in lower Manhattan but with outposts all over the city. These essentially family enterprises, however, appeared to have approached the limits of expansion. With changes in consumption patterns (the public's preference for dry cleaning services, coin laundries, or home washers) and the exhaustion of physical space in Chinatown (which put a constraint on expansion of the restaurant trade), development had reached a plateau.

The arrival of Chinatown-destined immigrants opened a new path of development: setting up the enclave as a center of garment manufacture. It would become an extension of the traditional midtown Manhattan factory district where Jews and Italians and Puerto Ricans in turn had concentrated. Making this strategy possible was a partnership among local leaders, small-time garment contractors, and—most important—the mainstream garment industry, which saw in this plan an alternative to closing down operations in the city altogether.

Garment producers had been taking a beating from foreign imports. Here was a way to put out products domestically, using a local labor force that would work for little more than Third World wages. The industry agreed to use subcontractors based in Chinatown who would select a work force from among their arriving compatriots. These operators would take production orders from the large manufacturers and retail firms, usually for last-minute orders, unique goods, and re-orders for staple items. The industry could exploit this new "spot market" because of the availability of low-wage labor.[43]

With a stable demand promised for their work, and modest start-up costs required to launch their business, many Chinese entered the field. From a few dozen in the mid-1960s, the number of Chinese-owned garment firms had zoomed to 247 by 1975 and to 480 ten years later.[44] The rising purchasing power of the workers, mostly female, helped to revive other sectors of the economy: food stores, restaurants, and various retail operations. The insulated community had its own banking institutions, which ensured that money spent or saved was recirculated within the confines of the Chinatown economy. And, although there is no public documentation available, it is evident that funds returned by workers to families back home were nowhere near the totals brought in by Far East investment.

The community became a pole of attraction for foreign capital, once it was apparent that the old Chinatown was being replaced by a new and economically vibrant one. Perhaps the key element in this appeal, differentiating it from other ethnic enclaves, was location. Its proximity to a huge cluster of government and business offices grants access to non-Chinese consumers. Its famed restaurants serve streams of workers at lunchtime. Abutting other points of interest such as Wall Street and Little Italy, Chinatown is a destination point for weekend visitors and tourists all year long.

By the late 1970s many signs were pointing to new prosperity: office towers and housing developments displacing some aging tenements, new bank offices cropping up, spiraling real estate prices forcing smaller and less profitable businesses to fold, the hustle and bustle of workers entering and exiting the loft factories. To an outsider, these may have seemed undeniable evidence of economic progress and of immigrant upward mobility.

But in the shadows behind the glitter and neon existed another Chinatown, a counterpart to the ghettos and barrios spread throughout the city. Here were the substandard housing units and sweatshops where most residents live and work. The price exacted for the boom was clear: uneven development—reminiscent of the slum areas of Hong Kong and Taiwan—tarnished the image of this economic "miracle." As of 1979, according to John Wang, "profits derived from foreign investment have contributed little to . . . the well-being of the community residents. Jobs . . . are generally low-paying and provide little or no upward mobility. Competition among businesses has threatened the job security of the workers and their families."[45]

Nevertheless, even more than West Indians, Asians have been depicted as "model minorities." At the high school level they consistently deliver outstanding performances in academic and scientific competitions; Asian students are overrepresented among enrollments in Ivy League universities; self-employment rates are well above the national average, as are labor market earnings.

Proponents of the model-minority thesis (themselves rarely of Asian origin) say that respect for tradition and a close-knit family structure uniquely prepare Asians for success in competitive societies such as the United States.[46] But that view belittles the significance of a simple historical fact: that in the 1970s two of every three previously employed Asian immigrants had a professional, technical, or managerial background.[47] The fact of this extremely skewed cohort goes a long way toward explaining the Asian "success" story.

Within the Chinese population the bifurcation in the migration flow was even sharper than for other subgroups. On the one hand, many women of peasant origin came to work in Chinatown factories; on the other, some 150,000 students from Taiwan entered the United States to pursue graduate studies, becoming the largest group of foreign-born students in the country. Almost all of these remained after completing their studies—and few of them live or work in Chinatown.[48]

Without fair comparisons, the case has not been made for a Chinese or Asian—or West Indian—model of assimilation, much less for one that can be replicated by other immigrants or native minorities. What is clear is that the New York region has been the beneficiary of a "brain drain" from developing countries. This serves as testimony to the continuing ability of the United States to attract elites from abroad, but it is hardly proof of its fabled capacity to engender upward mobility for the poor. The tens of thousands of Chinese Americans who barely eke out a decent living are evidence of another reality.

CHAPTER SIX

Politics and Culture in the New New York: An Expanding Foundation

At the heart of current speculations about the role and impact of new immigrants is one of the great unknowns facing the United States in the twenty-first century. What will be the social and political trajectory of the new Americans? Will their adaptation process remind us of the Euro-American model of assimilation, in which socioeconomic mobility facilitates inclusion and a cultural metamorphosis that gradually eradicates the traces of their country of origin? Or do the new arrivals encounter qualitatively distinct conditions in late twentieth-century America that will alter the traditional process of immigrant incorporation?

What will be the effect of heightening racial tensions on the reception accorded Third World newcomers? Already the pressures to slow down further immigration are growing, with congressional leaders and even representatives of African American and Latino constituencies calling for a closing of the borders. Will immigrants gravitate socially and politically toward the end of the racial-ethnic spectrum occupied by native minorities? A complex interplay of economic, political, and cultural forces makes it difficult to predict the paths of immigrant settlement. Current trends show that competing forces simultaneously promote and thwart accommodation within the dominant Euro-American society.

For decades, although scholars have disputed the sources and ends of "assimilation," it has generally been seen as a positive force, helping to homogenize numerous ethnicities into a stable, self-reproducing

American identity. Characteristics of successful membership in U.S. society include penetration into the economic mainstream, emergence of a significant middle class, monolingualism in the second generation, allegiance to European cultural traditions, suburbanization, and participation in established political structures.

In recent decades, however, that model has been severely tested. First, native minorities fall outside several of the specified parameters. Earlier in the century, because of their relatively small numbers and because racial hegemony kept them impoverished and invisible, these groups posed no fundamental threat to the assimilationist model. But as the postwar years brought about their population growth, migration to urban centers, and political insurgency, the racial and cultural backgrounds of groups such as African Americans, Mexican Americans, and Puerto Ricans challenged the country to broaden its definition of "American."

Immigrant minorities are providing the second major test of the assimilation model. This chapter compares their historical experiences with those of the native minorities and assesses the evidence for the view—quite prominent among mainstream social scientists—that these new groups will validate the "melting pot" capacity of U.S society.

Barriers to Incorporation

Breaking into the Economic Mainstream

Many foreigners, driven to migrate by deprivation or political persecution, voice a genuine enthusiasm about the "American dream." In light of the poverty and social strife so prevalent in their home terrain, U.S. economic vibrancy and political stability seem like something out of a dream. Part reality, part cultivated mythology, this view is particularly appealing to the world's poor, who envision a chance to prosper in the "promised land." Many go so far as to seize the opportunity by unconventional means, as in the case of undocumented aliens.

Legal or undocumented, the bulk of these potential citizens are initially grateful and disposed positively toward U.S. customs and institutions. And since the immigration process seems to be quite self-selective, with the most ambitious and risk-taking individuals taking the leap, the nation tends to attract those willing to endure the hardships and rigors of the immigrant life. When it comes to following through on the "work ethic," few native-born citizens can outdo the newcomers.

These facts precipitate optimism in some long-time observers of New York's immigration history, such as Emmanuel Tobier:

> The people who come here are the most ambitious of . . . [their] groups. They may sometimes look like poorly educated people to us, but they are more educated than those who don't leave. And they have a higher sense of self-esteem, of what they can do in the world. They have more of an incentive to work hard and have less to fall back on, in the sense of the welfare system. They come here and feel they have to rely on themselves, and their own effort.[1]

Economic outcomes act as a feedback mechanism in the immigration process. Very simply, if individuals fail to find work, they will return to their homeland. The mere fact of large-scale population inflows during the post-1965 years, however, demonstrates that foreigners are having little difficulty in being absorbed into the economy. As noted previously, small business entrepreneurship and secondary labor opportunities serve as reinforcing agents for their growing presence. On the positive side, they have allowed foreigners to establish tentative moorings in the labor economy. Whether working for their own compatriots in a small business or employed as laborers in garment manufacturing, retail stores or the health industry, they at least have a job. On the negative side, what all these jobs have in common is their inferior pay and working conditions.

Steady employment is conducive to assimilation if it integrates workers into the larger social context—for example, by placing them in contact with workers of diverse backgrounds. But the growth of the underground economy, typified by the resurgence of sweatshops during the 1980s, means that many immigrant workers are disconnected from the mainstream economy.

By the early 1980s, local estimates of the number of illegal factories within the garment industry stood at around 3,000, employing some 50,000 workers—a tenfold increase over the figures of a decade earlier.[2] Foreign competitors had forced local contractors in the apparel field to seek cost-cutting measures to keep their businesses afloat. Nationally, their share of the U.S. market in women's and children's clothes had fallen from 95 to 50 percent since the 1960s. Many entrepreneurs responded by relaxing standards: paying subminimum wages, ignoring overtime pay rates, hiring child labor, permitting unsanitary and hazardous working conditions.

Interviews with undocumented workers, in garmentmaking and other industries, reveal the alienation that pervades their lives: "I went to work in a factory making hair curlers, the type you heat up. . . . All I did seven hours a day was sit with a toy pistol going tic, tic, tic, painting one little red spot on each curler. Imagine that. . . . I did that for eight months."[3] A person living this daily experience can begin to lose enthusiasm for the American dream. For beyond the tedium described by the maker of beauty products, the greater tragedy is that life in the underground economy isolates workers from the larger society and creates yet another strand in the web of divisions that plagues the city and nation. Most immigrants appear to accept these limitations; given the options available to them, this should not be surprising. But unless this is a transitory phase, something like a rite of passage to a better world, the dream can end in a nightmare. Economic isolation functions as a deterrent to social assimilation.[4]

There are nuances to the simple causality just described, however. Recent surveys indicate that rather than being helpless victims of exclusionary processes, immigrants pursuing economic mobility are consciously choosing to maintain their own culture, even to the point of waiving U.S. citizenship. Compared with the New York foreign-born of the 1940s, today's immigrant population has only half the naturalization rate.[5]

This pattern is thought to result in part from the ease with which Caribbean people and Latin Americans can travel back and forth, and in part from resilient nationalism. Even second-generation immigrant youth are evincing a sturdy resistance to assimilation (replicating a pattern prominent among native minority youth). Examining social relations among offspring of Cuban, Haitian, Mexican, Filipino and Vietnamese parents in Miami and San Diego, Alejandro Portes and Min Zhou found that most youth associate with other children of immigrants, usually of the same nationality. Ironically, even those who are overwhelmingly English-dominant feel it unnecessary to abandon their cultural heritage to achieve success in life.[6]

Racism's Reach

As non-Europeans, Third World immigrants become subject to the prevailing system of racial hegemony. They learn quickly that differences in skin color, language, and cultural traditions serve to demarcate them from the dominant standards and values of the society.

Increasingly, language difference has become a focal point of discriminatory practices and attitudes. In New York's suburban areas in the late 1980s, forces arraigned on the side of making English the official language narrowly failed to legislate monolinguism.[7] Throughout the country, English-only movements have become an integral part of the racial and political backlash.[8]

In attempting to eliminate other tongues from workplaces, schools, courts, and public documents, conservatives insist on a uniformity that can only make new Americans wonder about this country's supposed tolerance. If these measures were to become the law of the land, they no doubt would drive immigrant communities further away from assimilation. Enforcement would be practically impossible, given the large number of people involved, and immigrant ties to cultures of origin are simply too deep for them to abandon their primary language.

The same racial backlash that targeted native minorities envelops their immigrant counterparts, regardless of language. Notwithstanding all the efforts to end employment discrimination, access to job opportunities is still shown to be weighted in favor of white applicants. For example, the practice of "race steering"—whereby employment agencies sift out African American and Latino job candidates before referring them to clients for interviews—continues to be exposed by antidiscrimination agencies.[9]

Immigration policies have fed discriminatory practices by encouraging employers to avoid hiring persons who are perceived as foreigners. Because provisions of the Immigration Reform and Control Act of 1986 (IRCA) impose penalties on businesses that employ undocumented workers, employers in many industries react by turning away any person who speaks English with an accent. In New York a 1989 government-sponsored study uncovered numerous instances in which immigrants with proper documentation were nevertheless denied employment.[10]

As long as prejudicial practices thrive in the labor market, the prospects for assimilation are diminished, for both native and immigrant minorities.

The Political Dimension

Two further deterrents to conventional adaptation have become more apparent: the fragile condition of society's assimilative institutions, and renewed political militancy within certain sectors of immigrant communities.

A glaring example of the first problem is the failure of urban public schools to equip today's youth for gainful employment. New York City's schools can barely keep up with the ever growing needs of their students for bilingual teaching, sex education, disease and drug prevention. Teachers are asked to deliver a range of services and information that surpasses anything expected of their predecessors. With school crime and violence common and a bureaucracy that staggers the imagination, it is no wonder that the ideal of imparting a basic liberal education to all is very rarely attained.

Yet historically, the New York City public school system came into being precisely to standardize instruction for the masses. From its founding, its mission was to prepare the citizens and workers of the future, and it performed this function quite adequately for most Euro-Americans.[11] Now, given the new makeup of its student population, the system faces its most severe test ever. The continuing inability of schools to replicate their traditional role raises serious questions about exactly how native and immigrant minorities are to be "processed" for assimilation.

Political parties and established religions are other institutions that were once reliable integrators of new groups. But among minorities today, although their electoral involvement has expanded, voter participation is still perilously low. And each year brings more announcements of churches and parochial schools closing down and relocating to the suburbs. Even divine authority is subject to budgetary constraints, it seems.

The erosion in assimilative institutions is creating a vacuum. How it will be filled is anyone's guess, but what seems less and less likely is that replacements will effectively transmit Euro-American traditions and values. To the extent that minority political activity, for example, takes on forms that question basic social priorities and power relations, it represents a break from standard politics. The urban insurgency of the 1960s united economic and cultural issues in an overarching strategy of protest against class and racial domination. Workplace and community were seen as interrelated aspects of the human condition, and the struggles corresponding to each domain as complementary. Electoral politics had a subordinate place within the total picture.[12] The Black Power movement directly engaged racial hegemony through mass mobilization and ideological denunciation. Puerto Rican radicalism challenged U.S. colonialism in its own back yard.

Although these movements fell short of achieving predominance within their respective contexts, their influence cannot be measured in numbers of partisans. Indeed, their legacy continues to the present; today's disputes over affirmative action and multiculturalism resonate with the debates of yesteryear. Insofar as this legacy endures and feeds new social struggles, the assimilative process is obstructed.

In recent times, immigrant minorities too have shown an inclination to draw upon the traditions of radical protest. The student strikes of 1990–92 affecting the City University of New York (CUNY) were remarkable for the prevalence of immigrant youth in both the leadership and the rank and file. Dominican, other West Indian, and Asian youth were prominent members of the citywide coordinating committee of this movement. The immediate cause of the conflict was the threat of raised tuition and the elimination of programs and services. But it was becoming clear to many students that a larger change was afoot.

For decades, CUNY's mission was to offer a college education to any city resident who applied. Historically, it had benefited working-class New Yorkers bent on sending their children to college. In the early 1970s an open enrollment policy widened the doors even further, largely as the result of activism led by African American and Puerto Rican students which culminated in the takeover of several campuses throughout the system. In the early 1990s, however, the university administration promulgated new admission standards and fee increases, effectively permitting the withering away of open enrollment. In the words of a veteran faculty member: "It's just going to be a closed door for anyone except those with money. . . . I think the . . . vision is a smaller, middle-class university."[13]

This "vision" had become obvious to students as well. Many immigrants and children of immigrants feared that the door to educational progress was being closed just as they were coming of age. Anger and desperation led to one of the most militant mass movements the city had seen in years. In 1990 there were some victories to celebrate as tuition increases were canceled. But by 1992 the restructuring of the university was under way, and the student insurgency had petered out. Open enrollment became another casualty of New York in decline.

Despite the setback, something had been gained. In a trial by fire a new generation of immigrant youth had staked a claim to their rights in a way that worried conventional politicians and observers. The platform of the new student movement directly engaged the debate over multiculturalism, arguing for a new curriculum in which Eurocentric ideas would share the platform with other world views. It was not purely a fight over admissions policy and tuition; the new generation was arguing for a new vision of the United States as a nation with multiple roots and identities.[14]

This is decidedly *not* what the sociologists have in mind when they talk about "immigrant adaptation" or "assimilation." Will the political strategies adopted by the new immigrants enhance or hinder their integration into civil society? It seems that the jury is still out on this question.

Identities of Culture, Language, and Race

Arguably, the greatest challenge to assimilation is the cultural one posed by racial/ethnic minorities themselves. Whatever the outcomes of their economic and political ambitions, they are unlikely to trade in their traditional customs and language as the price of admission to the new society. Even Puerto Ricans, who have been U.S. citizens since 1918, display a remarkable resistance to relinquishing their heritage: "We still maintain and speak Spanish despite the second- and third-generation youths. No other [European-origin] cultures preserve that here. It's a sore point because they [Americans] say we want to be different. To this I say, 'Vive la difference.' "[15]

The enormous cultural transformation wrought by the new immigrants in New York is evidenced in widespread changes in patterns of language and citizenship. For example, by 1990 the proportion of New Yorkers speaking a language other than English at home increased to 41 percent (a decade earlier it was 35.5 percent). Half of these indicated that they did not speak English well. Of slightly more than two million immigrants, seven of ten had come to the United States since 1970. And only a minority of the foreign-born (41.5 percent) had become naturalized; a decade earlier, the majority (52.1 percent) were citizens.[16]

These figures do not take into account the hundreds of thousands of undocumented persons. If we accept the common estimate that there are at least a half-million undocumented immigrants in the city, then it can be said that almost one of every four persons living in New York is a non-citizen.[17] And for the roughly two and a half million native minorities (primarily African Americans and Puerto Ricans), citizenship status is a poor indicator of cultural incorporation, as this book has already argued.

The factor more likely than anything else to confound traditional patterns of assimilation is racial self-identification. For decades (despite the chiding of Latino scholars) official census practice was to pigeonhole all persons in one of four "races": white, black, Native American/Indian, and Asian/Pacific Islander. But the 1990 census brought to light an astounding fact: asked to list their racial origin, ten million Americans declined to categorize themselves within any of the four groups and defined themselves instead as "other." Most of these turned out to be of Hispanic origin.[18]

Since the early part of the century, the question of race had been an issue for Puerto Ricans, here and on the island. In the days when census takers unilaterally determined the racial characteristics of Puerto Ricans, government reports persisted in declaring that upward of 90 percent were "white." Was the island officials' depiction of the populace as basically of European origin a stratagem to gain congressional concessions? The historical record is not clear. It is uncontested, however, that throughout the island's history there has been extensive intermingling of African and European population sources. Even the remnants of indigenous peoples (Tainos) were swallowed up in a blending that continued for four centuries. As is true throughout much of Latin America, Puerto Rican racial identity transcends the strictures developed by racial hegemony in the United States.[19]

Since the 1960s, movements for civil rights and cultural affirmation among native minorities have instigated a turnaround in racial identification. This, along with revised rules permitting census interviewees to designate their own classification, led to a radical realignment. Each decade an increased number of Puerto Ricans defined themselves as neither white nor black. In 1980 the proportion reached 48 percent, compared with 44 percent who defined themselves as white, 4 percent as black.[20] A similar pattern has been observed among Hispanics in general: the 1990 census showed that of 1.8 million Latinos, the largest group (47 percent) termed themselves "other." Another 37 percent said white, and 14 percent said black; the remainder classified themselves as Asian or Native American.[21]

It appears that a wholesale shift is taking place as Latin American, Caribbean, and other Third World racial identities enter the U.S. scene in full force. The outcome of this increasingly polymorphous culture on the system of racial hegemony cannot be predicted. One possible consequence is the attenuation of white-black differences as the central tension in our society. Whether this will be replaced by a realignment along other lines—class, for example—is anyone's guess.

At the heart of this refusal to be bound by dichotomies of color is really a plea for acceptance of broader notions of humanity. An impulse to obliterate rigid categorizations drives the work of many minority artists and writers: "I refuse to have any identity. In reality we are so mixed up—not only Latinos or blacks but Russians, Italians, Irish—that to have an identity is like to have a fake passport. It's an absurdity."[22] Is it possible that the United States—especially its urban core—is moving toward a society of blurred racial and ethnic identities, perhaps even reviving the melting pot image? Or will increased cultural interaction make it comfortable for individuals to sustain multiple identities?

Ethnic and racial loyalties are now subject to greater alteration. For native minorities, the dilemma of identity was to define oneself vis-à-vis the dominant culture: what it meant to be the "Other" in the context of Euro-America. For the most part, among African Americans and Puerto Ricans, race and ethnicity were merged into a single identity, though this is somewhat less the case for Puerto Ricans. For them, racial categories—white and black—may retain a certain gravitational pull, but the power of cultural identity among them is so deeply felt that even after nearly eight decades of citizenship, they decline the use of hyphenated terminology. They see themselves as Puerto Ricans, not "Puerto Rican Americans."

Today's immigrants encounter, and engender, still more complexity and variation in the range of potential identities. They are less likely to overlap the categories of race and ethnicity. Besides the long-standing dichotomy between "other" and "Euro-American," they have choices vis-à-vis native minorities as a whole and with respect to the ethnic identity with which they feel the greatest affinity. Dominicans, for example, in their cultural and political activities, are faced with a configuration of options that encompasses blacks, whites, Latinos/Hispanics, various Caribbean nationals, and Puerto Ricans. They may choose an "identity" from among these categories, depending upon circumstances and exigencies. The same applies to Koreans and Cambodians in their relationship to the larger Asian-American picture.

Trends in the West Indian community during the 1980s exemplified permeability and variation in the nexus between race and ethnicity. In contrast to earlier decades when their numbers were much smaller, Jamaicans, Trinidadians, and Barbadians began to assert greater independence from the African American civic leadership. Growing immigration from their homelands revived sentiments that they should project themselves as distinct entities in local politics.[23]

Long-standing attitudes nourished this new impulse. Although respectful of the struggle for social equality, Jamaicans express a feeling of ethnic superiority over African Americans. Their social life tends to center on relations with other Jamaicans, and they feel that by emphasizing their ethnicity they encourage whites to treat them more favorably than black Americans.[24] Consequently, a growing perception of having to subordinate aspirations to the political agenda of African Americans led to ruptured relations in several contests for political office in Brooklyn and Queens. In one case two minority candidates—one Caribbean, the other African American—split the vote in a heavily black district and thereby handed victory to a third contestant, who was white. West Indians felt that the entire black community should have endorsed the Caribbean candidate, who had a stronger base of support in the community.[25]

African Americans have something to fear in a resurgence of ethnic nationalism among West Indians, because it may dissipate the potency of racial identity as a source of unity among blacks. Yet it seems more likely that the enduring character of racial hegemony will restrict the potential for ethnic assertiveness among immigrant minorities. If the West Indian experience is a fair indicator of this thesis, it instructs us that in the United States, loyalty based on national origin is ultimately responsive to status within the racial order. The experience of racism will override many of the tensions and fissures between racial minority groups. In the dialectic of West Indian–African American relations, this has been attested to by the observations of veteran observers and in polls cited by Charles Green and Basil Wilson:

> These [polls] appear to corroborate the opinion expressed by a number of persons that African Americans and Caribbeans are firm allies in a struggle that would seek to improve their mutual depressed social, economic, and political situation in the city. It is understandable that foreign blacks from the Caribbean and native black Americans would find common ground in pursuing the objective of political empowerment."[26]

The resiliency of racism as a bonding agent among blacks of all ethnicities was made patent in the middle and late 1980s. A rash of violent attacks, including several instances of police brutality, drove the city's racial climate to the boiling point. Among the victims were Jamaican and Trinidadian newcomers and second-generation immigrants. The resulting campaigns for racial and social justice amassed West Indians and African Americans in militant movements that, for the duration, submerged ethnic differences. Once again, the connection between race and ethnicity proved to be variable, subject to the whirlwind of daily events.[27]

A New Alternative?

No discussion of the obstacles to assimilation should be taken to mean that irresistible forces are directing newcomers on a course of separation. Indeed, many studies argue that the newer immigrants are in fact undergoing incorporation into U.S. society. Trends relating to language use, economic mobility, intermarriage, and political participation hint at various degrees of immersion.[28] But the weight of evidence I have examined seems to favor the view that rather than becoming absorbed, these groups are transforming U.S. urban society in ways that change traditional understandings of the immigrant adaptation process.

Immigrants today are hardly embarked on a path toward assimilation. Neither are they merely expanding the family of ethnicities that make up the American experience, as cultural pluralists believe. The repercussions of their presence go further and deeper, for two reasons.

First, in their sheer diversity and complexity, they shatter beyond recognition the previous racial-ethnic balance and arrangements. In many New York school districts, especially in Queens and Brooklyn, there are no less than ten linguistic minorities; the demand for adult instruction in English as a second language far outfaces supply, because social service agencies and health care institutions lack personnel who can speak to a variegated clientele. Today's Third World influx brings Dominicans, Colombians, Jamaicans, Haitians, Guyanese, Taiwanese, Koreans, Cambodians, Vietnamese, Indians, Pakistanis, Arabs, and a dozen other groups. To equate this phenomenon with the earlier immigration movement of Europeans—bound together by race and Judeo-Christian tradition—is to mix apples with oranges.

Second, it is no less significant that their arrival comes on the heel of political insurgency by native minorities beginning in the 1960s. With its fundamental challenge to some of the central tenets of U.S. culture—especially, faith in individualism and competition—that insurgency predicated a new basis for social relations, one likely to find many adherents among the new immigrants. The ideals of social equality and multicultural tolerance will strike a chord appealing to foreigners.

In summary, the newcomers represent a qualitatively different chapter in U.S. history—because of the great diversity they introduce and because their presence overlies an already existing foundation of non-European elements. Up to now the choice offered to immigrants was assimilation or cultural pluralism—but a cultural pluralism that meant ethnic diversity within strictly *European* traditions. Native minorities that demurred were threatened with exclusion. The new immigrants in effect help to recast the range of options and raise another alternative, a *third* path, reflecting the global character of populations in urban centers.

It would be premature to announce the definitive emergence of a global alternative to immigrant adaptation, and an analysis of its implications for social relations in multiethnic, multiracial America is well beyond the scope of this book. Suffice it to say that in New York and in other cities throughout the country an important new drama is being enacted, and as in the past, newcomers are among the leading actors.

CHAPTER SEVEN

Policy Wars 2000

Lessons from the Underclass Debate

During the 1980s and 1990s few issues have been as emblematic of public frustration (or, for many, fear and anger) as the so-called "underclass." Despite puzzlement over prevalence and causes, it is generally agreed that something new and pernicious has been happening in the inner cities. A cluster of worsening conditions, including long-term joblessness, social isolation, teenage parenthood, substance abuse, and criminality, seem to signal that existence in the ghetto has become qualitatively harsher than ever before. There have always been pockets of deep poverty, but, in the words of William J. Wilson, the current period is witness to a marked "rise of social pathologies in the ghetto."[1]

The present concern recalls an earlier exchange in the 1960s, in which Oscar Lewis's notion of a "culture of poverty" provided the impetus for a new generation of studies on inner-city life.[2] Unfortunately, Lewis's *La Vida,* recounting the story of a single family, set the context in which all Puerto Ricans were to be viewed for the next twenty years. Still, notwithstanding the negative imagery it elicited by following the daily comings and goings of an impoverished, marginalized family, the work at least had the virtue of being embedded in a larger social analysis of inequality and structural dislocation.

The current round of discussion and research, prompted initially by neoliberal journalists and conservative social scientists, offers little pretense of evaluating the effects of economic and structural constraints on individual behavior. Studies by Charles Murray and Lawrence Mead in the mid-1980s clearly established the intellectual terrain that conservatives would cultivate.[3] For them, the problem was one of social deviancy, incited by government policies that rewarded poor labor force attachment and failed to penalize aberrant activity.

Liberal analysts, unpersuaded by an *exclusive* reliance on behavioral approaches, nevertheless conceded that this time around it was important to examine ghetto family life for signs of deficient norms or values. The way to engage the conservative incursion, Wilson reasoned, was to acknowledge that ghetto residents were living in an increasingly hostile environment, leading to a severe deterioration in personal conduct. Yes, structural economic change, out-migration to the suburbs, and discrimination each contributed to the rise of the underclass, but the new research had to be directed at family and community dynamics.

Foundations, universities, and government bodies entered the fray by funding several rounds of research on the "underclass problem." A plethora of conferences, books, and journal articles resulted, begetting a new generation of literature on poverty.[4] Much of the work was characterized by rigorous theorizing and modeling, as well as quantitative analysis, importing techniques and methods from new strands of social science research. Models of rational choice were adapted from economics to show that persons who remain on welfare for long periods are actually acting in a logical way: recipients intuitively calculate the relative costs and benefits of low-wage work (the only real alternative for most) and conclude that it pays for them to continue on the welfare rolls. Extensive use of census data and specialized surveys spawned a corpus of quantitative studies unparalleled in prior generations of poverty research.

Shifts in the Discourse

Beyond methodological changes, important shifts marked the modern wave of poverty research. The first was an emphasis on analyzing individual behavior. Antisocial attitudes, cultural deficiencies, and departures from purported middle-class values—such as delayed marriage and childbearing, single-worker households, and appreciation for educational pursuits—all became objects of keen interest. The emphasis on personal behavior was underscored in Christopher Jencks's description of the underclass literature:

> It soon became clear . . . that those who talked about the underclass had something more in mind than just persistent poverty. The term under-

> class, with its echoes of the underworld, conjures up sin, or at least unorthodox behavior. Low income may be a necessary condition for membership in such a class, but it is not sufficient.[5]

His own effort to categorize types of underclass behaviors led Jencks to identify several underclass contingents—economic, moral, criminal, reproductive, and educational—yet the focus remained on the individual. Only for the "economic underclass" did he acknowledge a structural component: the decline in demand for low-skilled workers. But he added that "native born workers may . . . have grown choosier about the jobs at which they are willing to work steadily."[6]

A second shift in focus was that whereas Michael Harrington's *Other America* and Lewis's *La Vida* had pictured a heterogenous poverty population, the 1980s discourse was almost exclusively devoted to African Americans. And whereas an earlier generation looked often to black-white comparisons to place in relief the racial divide in America, the later research put a lens on class differences *within* the black community.[7] The modern discussion of persistent poverty became associated mainly with black America, and continuing deprivation among Latinos, Native Americans, new immigrants, and whites was lost sight of. Was it because blacks became a more effective scapegoat, politically, for the conservative backlash? Was it because of sheer numbers? Or was there governmental resistance to acknowledging that poverty-creation transcends the African American case? Perhaps the existence of a new generation of black researchers and analysts, eager to shape the discourse, drew even greater attention to their concerns. In any event, the result has been to encourage other groups to develop research programs largely in isolation from one another.

Because conservative and neoliberal writers have spearheaded much of the underclass discussion, and because the principal unit of analysis has been the black inner-city family, institutional racism has largely disappeared as an explanatory variable for the rise of poverty—even in the work of leading African American scholars. An example is William J. Wilson's critique of affirmative action and other targeted programs, for which he would substitute an agenda of structural economic reform. "Race-specific" strategies are unwarranted, in his eyes, since the vestiges of slavery and segregation are no longer the driving forces of black deprivation. From a political standpoint, he adds, such strategies weaken the political possibilities for broad, multiracial alliances of working and poor people.

Outcomes of the Debate?

Despite the enormous energies and resources committed to modern debates, most objective participants concur that we are not much closer to agreement on either the magnitude or the determinants of "underclass" behavior or—worse still—on what to do about it. One federal official, a senior policy analyst in the U.S. Department of Health and Human Services, has expressed skepticism that the time is yet ripe even to discuss policy options. In 1991, summarizing several studies commissioned by his agency, William R. Prosser declared:

> Given the lack of agreement on the definition of the underclass or its causes and the complex nature of the issue, it seems to me that research on the underclass *throughout this decade* [emphasis added] will continue to be positive social science rather than policy analysis. . . . Any serious discussion of the policy implications from underclass research that I have reviewed is, in my opinion, very premature.[8]

Why has there been so little payback to all the effort? One important limitation on the fruitfulness of the underclass discussion may be its politically charged nature. After more than thirty years of intense debate over the poverty question, the lines seem to have been drawn, the camps formed.

Much of the impetus for the new outlook on poverty comes from government agencies and think tanks with conservative leanings. Groups such as the American Enterprise Institute, the Heritage Foundation, and the Manhattan Institute are in the forefront of questioning existing social programs. Liberal intellectuals, many of whom have accepted aspects of the conservative critique, gain sustenance from organizations like the Urban Institute, the Joint Center For Political and Policy Studies, and the Rockefeller Foundation. Although some academics and researchers enter the dispute with an open mind and seek truth for truth's sake, most observers—including politicians, policy advocates, and lobbying groups—seem more concerned with "bottom line" policy conclusions than with the production of new knowledge. In this environment, the notion that the investigation of underclass behavior should be accepted as a legitimate part of the social science research agenda has been called into question.

From the beginning, use of the expression "underclass" contaminated the possibility of reasoned discussion. A throwback to the sociological notion of "lower class" and to such concepts as *lumpenproletariat* and "culture of poverty," the new label provoked a counterliterature that condemned the pejorative and ideological character of the term.[9] Its definition commingled too many disparate subpopulations: mothers struggling alone to raise infants, school dropouts, the unemployed, criminals. Why the need to attach an all-encompassing term to such a varied population? No wonder the debate quickly passed from scientific research to political haranguing. Even William J. Wilson recanted his previous acceptance of the word; he came to believe that it stigmatized all the poor, and especially blacks.[10]

The term nevertheless maintains wide currency and contributes to the difficulty of generating a policy consensus. It distorts the discourse by prompting progressives to devise an ideological defense of the disadvantaged, often overlooking the real possibility that inner-city conditions *are* substantially worse than they were a generation ago.[11] In short, the 1980s effort produced remarkably little in the way of new understanding about the causes of sustained poverty (most explanations were derivative, reworkings of older debates) and even less consensus on policy recommendations. Historians may very well look back upon the "underclass" debate as a strange episode in the development of social welfare theory.

Indeed, in the early 1990s, the principal impetus for revisiting America's urban crisis came neither from volumes of research and analysis nor from a paridigmatic shift in theory. Rather it ensued from the Los Angeles uprising of May 1992, in the wake of a jury verdict absolving the police in the beating of Rodney King.

That outburst of rage and destruction, leading to fifty-two deaths, 1,500 arrests, and more than a billion dollars' worth of damage, did more to draw attention to our urban ills than any other event in the previous two decades. Polls suddenly showed Americans favoring more spending for our inner cities, more recognition of the dangers of our racial divide.[12] At this writing the ravaged areas are still in recovery, and the original promises of relief and assistance are far from realized. Is it an exaggeration to say that this singular event rendered meaningless the efforts of mainstream scholars and policymakers to understand our urban crisis?

The Conservative Agenda: Toward the Market Society

With the underclass debate, the new generation of neo-liberal and conservative social thinkers scored an important victory. Riding public anger over rising taxation, budget deficits, and economic stagnation, they prevailed in presenting a coherent framework that pinpointed culprits for the country's malaise.

Reagan's victory in 1980 shifted dramatically the terms of policy debates. A new conservative agenda was articulated, based on a simple but far-reaching imperative: unleash the forces of market competition across the entire range of public policy areas. Joined to this idea was an important but often unspoken corollary: relegate to the back burner an explicit policy goal of poverty elimination. Ideas and programs that were viewed as punitive or unrealistic during the heyday of 1960s liberalism—such as "workfare" and educational vouchers—now became staples of the public discourse.

Part of the attraction in this new conservative thrust was the argument for the efficiency of market processes. According to its logic, the key is to allow the price of a good or service to be discovered. This can be achieved only by letting competition prevail in as many markets as possible. Prices mirror the cost of producing goods and services, and ensure that the economy allocates its human and material resources to the most desired ends. Competition, by allowing many players in the economic game, prevents prices from being artificially set by the monopolistic power of a few producers. Consumers are protected by competition because the sellers' scramble to outwit one another in the search for buyers keeps prices low. The twin mechanisms of price and competition guarantee that society's true choices are offered by the economy, and in the most efficient way available.[13]

Any system promising maximum choice and efficiency is bound to have great appeal, and during the 1980s conservatives scored a political breakthrough by successfully arguing for the penetration of market processes throughout the public sector. The role of government, in this view, should be to let all goods and services find their real price, to implement market principles even in those spheres of activity—education, housing, social services—where government had long assumed a significant role. To get out of the business of providing such services, to stop subsidizing special-case industries and consumers, and to eradicate controls or unreasonable regulation: these were seen as appropriate policy goals for government. Only in the areas of national defense and law enforcement should government remain the prime actor.[14]

Across a wide spectrum of issues, these ideas took root. In the realm of economics, government was counseled to refrain from pursuing an activist fiscal policy. Rather than using tax revenues to stimulate public works programs, it should reduce tax rates for corporations and individuals; provide tax incentives for employers to locate business in depressed areas. This advice held doubly for local government.[15]

Housing for low- and moderate-income families was among the items targeted by the conservative backlash. In big cities such as New York, a freely functioning housing market had successfully increased the production of housing stock for upper-income families and would do the same for the entire populace, it was argued, if permitted to do so. But prospective builders glimpsed little potential for profitability in the lower end of the market, because current restrictions made it too costly to produce new low-priced housing stock. Prescription: (a) end rent control, which keeps the price of housing artificially low; (b) abolish public housing projects and sell each unit to its resident; (c) eliminate zoning and construction restrictions that inflate the cost of bringing new housing to the market. In short, make it profitable to produce shelter for families at each income level.

Nowhere did the notion of maximizing consumer choice resonate so emphatically as in education. Conservatives maintained that the only effective way to reform inner-city schools was to subject them to competition with one another and with private schools. Instead of using tax revenues to finance public education, local government should offer education "vouchers" to parents, who could then shop around for the school of their preference, public or private. Parents would become more involved in their children's schooling and students more enthusiastic about learning, given the opportunity to select their school.

Carrying the consumer analogy further, proponents claimed that educational choice would induce innovation and creativity on the part of individual schools, which would have to prove the value of their "product" in the marketplace. Substandard schools would be forced to close down for lack of students as parents sent their children elsewhere; new schools would emerge where there was an unmet demand. Schools would be ultimately accountable to economic criteria, instead of to centralized bureaucracies, and could exploit this new autonomy to develop specialized missions and creative programs. Advocates argued that voucher-based systems offered the best chance to transform education in America.[16]

The drive to introduce market processes was not limited to the foregoing examples. In many other areas the case was forcefully made to replace sociopolitical with market criteria: urban development, criminal justice, health, social services and welfare, sanitation, and so on.

Whether by competitive mechanisms such as vouchers, tax credits, and deregulatory measures or by wholesale transference of public functions through privatization schemes, the conservative design was clear: let laissez-faire principles dictate the allocation of resources to meet citizen needs.

For all its logical consistency and appeal to the ideology of choice, the resurgent conservative agenda was distressingly silent on the issue of poverty. Indeed, for those concerned about the state of urban America, the absence of an explicit reference to the goal of poverty elimination struck a worrisome note. Something seemed to have been lost in the bargain offered.

The 1980s agenda reflected the "trickle-down" premise of traditional economic theory, which asserts that the best antidote to joblessness and stagnant incomes is private entrepreneurial activity. We can spur the economy on, it is said, by providing incentives to producers in the way of tax reductions and subsidies. Employers will hire more workers, who, in their role as consumers, will increase purchases of output and trigger a new round of expansion. Eventually, if all goes well and the cycle is repeated to bring in more and more of the unemployed, the benefits resulting from the initial incentives will filter downward to all members of society.

It is clear in this theory, however, that bringing an end to unemployment is only a hoped-for outcome of the drive for profits. Indeed, for the individual entrepreneur, success is attainable without satisfying the larger social goal. Eradicating joblessness is not a targeted objective. Similarly, for the conservative policy agenda ending poverty was not a goal per se, in the sense of the 1960s War on Poverty. Rather, the oblique approach to facing this critical issue sounded a not-so-roundabout message to the poor: "These are the conditions you must meet if you wish to reenter the mainstream of society; if you decide not to accept them, society can only assume that you choose to remain poor; but understand that the programs and supports you have come to rely on will no longer be available to you; you are on your own."

Examples of this hardening of attitudes continue to abound especially in the approach to dealing with individuals on welfare. Several states, including California, New Jersey, and Wisconsin, have introduced proposals to limit support for additional children born to women on welfare. Other ideas include forcing women to work at low-wage jobs without provision for child care assistance or health benefits. Wisconsin considered a proposal in which a second child would receive only half the level of support provided for its older sibling; a third child would do without any. In Michigan's experiment with "learnfare" regulations, families with a truancy problem among their children would have their allotments reduced.[17]

Similarly, "workfare" proposals barely disguise an impatience with AFDC (Aid to Families with Dependent Children) clients. Disheartened that past strategies showed only faint success in getting recipients permanent jobs in the labor force, such plans now promote a "final offer" strategy. A composite picture of this ultimatum, gleaned from several state proposals, reveals the basic contours of the conservative-influenced plan to deal with welfare poverty.[18] All persons deemed "job ready"—those without disabilities and with no children under three years old—will be notified of a time limit on their benefits, perhaps a two-year period. During this interval the state refers recipients to job opportunities, any earnings from which they will be allowed to keep, along with their normal benefits. This incentive ends after the two years. If a recipient has been unsuccessful in the job search by the deadline, benefits are terminated anyway, and the person is assigned work in a community service program at a salary equivalent to their former benefit level. Hence the transition from welfare to "workfare."

Augmenting this "incentive" to work are a spate of recommendations increasing the "disincentive" (cost) to remain on welfare. General reductions in benefit levels, counting the value of Medicaid and food stamps as part of the allotment awarded, "learnfare" (see above), cutting grant levels for additional children, and so on. This approach follows a long line of punitive social policies dating back to the English Poor Laws of the nineteeth century, wherein the guiding principle was to make public relief programs less desirable than the most menial, low-paying job.[19] The conservative agenda revives this strategy with a vengeance.

Given an endemic shortage of jobs with decent pay, designs for encouraging welfare mothers into the labor market are doomed to failure. The system of incentives embedded within public assistance makes it irrational for individuals to cease participation when the employment alternative would result in reducing their already meager standard of living. As Christopher Jencks, who exhaustively examined welfare reform programs instituted throughout the 1980s, said of federal legislation introduced during the Bush presidency:

> Judging by the experience of states that have already established compulsory training programs and work requirements, [the Family Support Act

> of 1988] . . . will not move many single welfare mothers off the welfare rolls. The reason is simple: single mothers do not turn to welfare because they are pathologically dependent on handouts or unusually reluctant to work—they do so because they cannot get jobs that pay better than welfare. The new law will not do much to change this fact.[20]

Despite flaws in these and other aspects of the new agenda, the conservative policy juggernaut continued undeterred until Bill Clinton gained the presidency in 1992. Even then, most experts predicted, it would be years before progressive policy would regain center stage.

A Communitarian Agenda of Community Development

In the meantime, it is not impossible to conceive of an urban development program that would approach social problems from a collective sense of responsibility and sharing. Philosophically, the guiding principle would be to set social priorities first, then use a flexible mix of *market* and *planning* approaches to attain these goals. Planning mechanisms might be based in government, community, or workplace. Various kinds of proposals are consistent with such an outlook.[21]

The following strategy outlines the elements of a restorative program for urban areas with a focus on economic development and job training. It is a partial program, obviously, since a larger scope of action is needed to deal with the broader social ills. The focus is on economic regeneration, because without work that sustains a decent livelihood, families and individuals lack the wherewithal and self-esteem to be active and productive participants in the society. Although incomplete, the "communitarian" agenda presented here presupposes a complementary set of initiatives across the many dimensions of daily life: health services, education, housing, public safety, and so on. Realization of this general program would also require certain political and cultural conditions (considered below).

Community Economic Development

What should be done with the inner city: the actual land, facilities, and neighborhoods where the bulk of minority poor people live? Earlier talk of "busting up the ghetto" and encouraging residents to disperse into suburban communities ignored the realities of housing and real estate discrimination and cost. Except for a small number of middle-income minority families, homeownership is out of the question. In the United States today, the immense racial and class divide obstructs the ideal of residential integration.

Setting aside the illusory notion of massively decentralizing minority populations, the remaining option is to invest in the economic and social renewal of the inner city, with the expectation that internal progress over a period of decades can bring these depressed areas into parity with the rest of the country. This will require a commitment similar to the Marshall Plan, through which the United States underwrote the rebuilding of a devastated Europe. As with postwar reconstruction, success will depend on furnishing local populations with the resources to generate their own paths to self-sufficiency. But it will need to be done in a way that is not predicated on the exploitation of local people and resources. Success hinges on breaking the pattern of looking for quick solutions to deep problems.

Here are three ideas for the economic renovation of poor communities, their central characteristic being the socially conscious application of market processes to reducing blight and deprivation.

1. Support "community development collaboratives" to work with government and the business sector. These collaboratives, comprising neighborhood groups, religious institutions, and schools, would serve as the principal local agents for brokering public and private resources for economic development projects. They would survey local residents on consumption patterns; assess local needs in housing, health, and other services; provide technical assistance to small businesses; help negotiate regulatory requirements and licenses; monitor affirmative action and community benefits agreements; advertise the advantages of doing business in the area. Whether development is driven primarily by local entrepreneurship or external enterprises, these collaboratives could be important mechanisms in ensuring that the community truly benefits.

2. Encourage small business development by local entrepreneurs and cooperatives. Significant infusions of capital are needed if community economic development is to make a dent in poverty and unemployment. Banks need to expand commercial loans to community entrepreneurs who lack traditional conditions for credit and loan approval.[22]

Government must radically alter the way it funnels investment opportunities into the ghetto and barrio. Federally funded urban enterprise zones (EZs), though an attractive idea at first sight, often fall prey to outside firms with little attachment to the designated area. Wages are frequently kept at a minimum, and only a small fraction of area residents are brought onto the payroll.[23]

A reformed strategy would grant the inside track to existing and prospective businesses in the community. New construction projects, public and private, should meet criteria that enhance the community's capacity for self-development: hiring area residents, subcontracting with local businesses for products and services, and contributing to community capital formation through "linkage" agreements that set aside funds out of the proceeds of their operations.[24]

3. Endorse and subsidize cooperative enterprises. Although often frowned upon or simply ignored, co-ops offer a unique opportunity to employ workers in labor-intensive projects. By involving participants in the various phases of planning and management, they offer a promising means of empowering activities that need to be nurtured in depressed communities.

Because a distinctively new community economic development strategy requires a radical departure from past practices these ideas hinge on two attendant propositions.

1. Make the most of indigenous resources. Offer communities the means to organize their self-reliance. Use local institutions—schools, churches, community-based organizations (CBOs), social groups—as key instruments for negotiating agreements with governmental agencies and business groups. Recruit local youth to serve as peer counselors and educators in dropout prevention and health awareness campaigns. Involve religious and civic groups in efforts to promote local businesses.

A program to engender community-based activities and enterprises is preferable to one that simply attracts factory relocation to the area. Although both approaches can create jobs, the latter only indirectly feeds into the larger goal of community regrowth, through the wages of its employees. There must be a conscious design to use the community's own assets and strengths, both physical and cultural.

2. Maximize coordination among service areas. In most communities, service delivery takes place in a fragmented, often duplicative manner. Establish key "nodal points" in each community where several activities are synchronized. Two indispensable hubs of operation are schools and neighborhood health centers.

Schools need to be kept operational all day, all year, for all residents—not just students. They should service a range of community ventures: educational, recreational, and civic. They are ideal locations for centralizing basic health care and counseling services, the places where professional staff may most effectively reach youngsters. With teenage pregnancy and sexually transmitted disease so prevalent among inner-city youth, the schools are the first line of resistance to their spread. Similar advantages accrue to local health centers as places where public services should be offered in a coordinated fashion.

Job Training

The challenge for our inner cities is dual. The first challenge, to make them viable places for the production of goods and services, is the intent of the community economic development outlined above. The second is to equip residents with skills that are valued in the labor market, whether locally or beyond. Since local economic regeneration is not likely to provide work opportunities for *all* neighborhood residents, people must be prepared for jobs in the regional market. Job training strategies must be designed to complement economic development activities, and to enable individuals to calibrate their human capital with the rapidly changing labor market. There are at least five essential components to such a program.

1. Modernize public school curricula so that students will be prepared for the work force of the future. In New York and elsewhere, high school youngsters in commercial and business programs are still being taught typing at a time when computer literacy is minimally required for clerical and secretarial jobs in most companies. Teachers need to be offered incentives for their own retraining so that their pupils may be provided knowledge relevant to the labor market needs of the coming century.

2. Promote hiring and training alliances between businesses and the community. Businesses know what kind of employees they want, and neighborhood groups are familiar with the strengths and deficiencies of unemployed residents. A direct method for reducing joblessness is to establish formal agreements between employers and CBOs that bind both sides to support the transition of the unemployed into entry-level work. For these jobs, employers generally look for personnel who are punctual and reliable, who dress conventionally, and who are—most

important—highly motivated. In fact, few insist on job-specific skills or even high school diplomas if the prospective worker appears sufficiently motivated.

CBOs and neighborhood schools are often in the best position to reach out to the unemployed and draw them into "job readiness" programs that promote self-esteem, impart a sense of hope and aspiration, and inculcate the traits and habits appropriate to the work environment. Given role models with whom they can identify, and a culturally sensitive training component that respects their potential, youth can acquire the rudimentary life and work skills that are necessary to successful employment.

The training and hiring alliance would commit participating organizations to "sponsor" unemployed persons referred to them by social service agencies, school programs, or community organizations. By the terms of this sponsorship, a local training group would provide basic job readiness skills to unemployed persons, who would then be hired by an associate company. A participating firm would enroll a new recruit in an internal training plan for its entry-level workers and provide the skills specific to the job for which he or she was hired. The employer would thus commit to assisting the jobless in a controlled transition into the labor force, understanding that progress will be uneven and that individual attention is required.

Such an arrangement would also help business management to become aware of the various backgrounds and heritages of the increasingly diversified labor force. To date, the minority poor have been the main casualties of the "culture shock" taking place in corporate America. Unless they conform to traditional standards of dress, speech, and bearing, the newcomers are often excluded from or ostracized in the workplace. A more tolerant middle ground must be established which values elements of both the standard and the new. This requires not only job training for recruits but "sensitivity training" for management as well, a service best performed by community organizations.

Corporate America has long reserved most of its training for management and professional employees, leaving lower-tier workers to fend for themselves, on their own time, and with whatever meager resources they can garner. By encouraging employers to assume greater responsibility and have more say in preparing unskilled workers for specific jobs, business-community alliances could involve the private sector in the problems of providing labor force access for the urban poor. These training-hiring alliances, properly organized and financed, could bring about a new consortium of job placement activities and strategies.

3. Revive occupational mobility through workplace upgrading programs. Entry-level jobs are dead-end jobs unless they serve as feeders into a long-term process of upgrading and retraining. Too often new workers lose hope as they see the confining nature of their first few jobs. It dawns on them soon enough that without a plan of continued education and training they cannot expect much upward mobility. Yet for those with family responsibilities it is becoming more and more difficult to leave their work careers to resume schooling—especially if there is no guarantee that employers will reserve their jobs.

In several industries, unions and businesses could coalesce around a program to provide workplace training and education in the form of subsidized apprenticeships. Following the European experience in this area, workers would be given released time (financed mutually by unions and industry) to take classes in an officially accredited program of higher education. Courses would be given at the employer's location—rather than at a college—so that personnel could resume work with minimal disruption. The curricula, tailored to the firm's labor needs in areas of actual or projected skill shortages, would be designed to prepare entry-level workers for promotion to specifically targeted higher-level positions.

In effect, this approach calls for rejuvenating the system of career ladders that once formed the core of internal labor markets in large firms.

4. Establish a national training system. Existing training institutions—Joint Training Partnership Act (JTPA), vocational education, community colleges, and proprietary schools—are too dispersed and powerless.[25] As currently configured, they have neither the unity of purpose nor the political clout to handle the immense challenge of preparing the U.S. labor force for the future. Compared with their counterparts in other industrialized nations, they are weak actors in the economic drama.

JTPA provides a case in point. Successor to the Comprehensive Employment and Training Act (CETA), the national training program of the 1970s, JTPA was intended as a corrective to CETA's reliance on public sector jobs. Unfortunately, JTPA has been even less effective, given its sparse funding and a misguided infatuation with rigid performance standards. By expecting training providers (both proprietary organizations and CBOs) to operate like profitmaking enterprises, the

JTPA system has weeded out the most needy applicants. Severe budgetary limitations make for brief and superficial training courses; demands for high job placement rates result in an extremely selective recruitment process, with those perceived as most likely to succeed generally being signed up for participation. Finally, with most trainees getting jobs that pay barely above the poverty level, the program has offered little hope to those yearning for long-term economic security.

This approach needs to be reformed, first by replacing the current practice of performance-based contracting, which compels training providers into a "penny wise, pound foolish" mentality in dealing with clients. Like many other social programs, JTPA has become obsessively cost-conscious: providers, both governmental and private, are more concerned about getting reimbursements for their expenditures than with the quality of their mission and program. Smaller providers, especially community-based organizations, have been gradually squeezed out of the system; the main survivors are the old-line, large training organizations. Not surprisingly, few of these have roots in the communities. Rather than helping build local training capacity, the government's handling of JTPA has served mainly to consolidate the power and influence of traditional providers.

Reforming JTPA means offering trainees intensive instruction in specific skills and continuing to assist them after they have been placed in a company. It means expanding the role of CBOs so that they can be principal actors in the training system, especially within the context of the hiring and training alliances described above. A revitalized JTPA must also improve the agency's dismal performance in the recruiting and preparation of unemployed persons whose primary language is not English.

Federal training programs, however, make up only a fraction of the nation's potential training capacity. Unfortunately, the level of coordination among the remaining entities—public school vocational education, community colleges, proprietary trainers, and corporate human resource departments—is insufficient to handle the challenge of upgrading the U.S. labor force.

Note, for example, the enormous asymmetry that characterizes the discourse on industrial and job training policies. On the one hand, many, if not most, analysts are coming to the view that America simply cannot permit its producers to compete in the world economy without some sort of planned coordination with government. In Japan and western Europe the state sector works closely with business to develop strategies in key products and markets; and firms receive incentives, sometimes protections, to pursue their ambitions. While a comprehensive industrial policy has yet to crystallize in the United States, there is growing bipartisan pressure to bring it about.

Yet on the other hand, as far as skills development in nonprofessional areas is concerned, we have hardly even reached the discussion stage. How can we bring together the various institutions involved in job training? Vocational education programs are mired in outdated equipment and training that is largely irrelevant to the modern economy. Often, educators and parents scorn traditional "vo-tech" programs, which too frequently track poor and minority youth into dead-end careers. Community colleges face declining enrollment pools, partly because the postwar "baby boom" cohort has peaked in size and also because skyrocketing tuition is pricing out many potential students. Yet the largest pool of potential students is made up of adult workers who are in real need of upgrading their skills. The two-year colleges, whose decentralized locations and technically oriented curricula place them in an ideal setting to serve those in the labor force, have yet to tap this growing population successfully.

Failure to understand the importance of our human resources threatens to undercut the effectiveness of the emerging consensus on industrial policy.

5. Finally, assuming that our community recovery agenda includes a public works component (a key feature of CETA), take advantage of this opportunity to tap into the underutilized human resource waiting to be brought into the renovative process. The rebuilding of our inner cities—streets, parks, schools, recreational facilities—requires all kinds of labor. Again, however, without firm direction from the national government, the economic revival of our inner cities is unattainable; that much should be clear, however ingenious and creative local strategies are, however forthcoming is community enthusiasm.

A federal commitment is essential for two reasons. First, government can induce the private sector to channel capital to the most distressed areas; second, as the country's single largest economic agent, government has an unrivaled power to create jobs and stimulate business activity. No combination of community-based initiatives, tailored either to human capital or economic development ideas, will suffice on its own. Such initiatives must be included within the context of a comprehensive program of national revitalization: public investment in roads, highways, and parks; research and development in new technologies.[26]

Class Agendas, Racial/Ethnic Agendas

The proposals outlined here are characterized by a concern with the problems facing all the poor, regardless of racial/ethnic origin. Can a universalist agenda adequately deal with the special needs of populations that have been subject to the added burdens of racial domination? Does pragmatism require that the demands of minorities be subsumed into a broader progressive program, downplaying the issue of racism? Likewise, does the communitarian agenda belie the specificity of individual group needs? Previous chapters have dwelt on the differential paths to poverty for African Americans and Puerto Ricans. Does a universalist program imply a "boilerplate" approach to poverty elimination, a singular model to be applied across the board to all underprivileged groups?

This certainly is not the intention or spirit of the communitarian agenda. Improving service delivery and promoting economic rejuvenation in our nation's depressed inner cities requires a political will on the macro level, which can be summoned only when the citizenry comes to terms with its history and recognizes the second-class status that has been accorded to the "other" Americans. Differences in language, cultural traditions, political practices, and community assets suggest that targeting mechanisms will vary, depending on the group in question. Strategies for community organizing, for instilling self-esteem, and for raising aspirations will differ. Taking the historical and cultural endowments of each group into consideration will enhance the implementation of universalist strategies.

Toward a Socially Useful Research Agenda

At a time when assemblies of social scientists routinely deplore the diminishing commitment to scholarly investigations, it is a less than enviable task to argue on behalf of an agenda of research that is oriented toward practical needs. Yet if we have been taught anything by the growth industry of "underclass" research, it is that ideology and politics drive much current inquiry. Is it not better to face up to this fact and direct our efforts toward work that is socially useful?

What are the criteria for a research agenda that is complementary to a communitarian outlook?[27] Central is the idea of a collaborative relationship between researchers and community groups. The latter should have a say in the goals of the investigation, in determining the objects of analysis, and in shaping the research design. Community and advocacy representatives may lack the technical expertise to specify in detail the content of a research plan, but they can often provide access to the populations or institutions about which studies are being conducted. They can also help the professional academic be more sensitive to the human factor involved in the subject-researcher relationship.

Too often, outsiders with their survey instruments and computers intrude in the lives of their subjects and then depart, never to be seen again. Results are reported, articles and books are published, but the information and interpretation fail to complete the circle back to the subjects. The involvement of community groups is essential to bring the research process to closure.

Creating such a partnership is not easy. Academics, pressed for time and resources, know that on the professional side there is little reward for a collective approach. Being able to boast of association with community groups ranks low in the faculty prestige system; it is normally viewed as less important than teaching and scholarly publication. Moreover, local groups and researchers operate within different time constraints. If a project's findings are intended to be of practical use to community residents or an advocacy campaign, researchers may feel coerced to accelerate their efforts. Such pressure conflicts with attention to methodological rigor and other demands typical of scholarly activity, which tend to prolong the effort.

Finally, whereas convention dictates that researchers conduct their work without preconceived notions of the findings or conclusions to be derived, community groups are less agnostic in their expectations. They may be interested in a needs assessment that will provide the rationale for a particular type of program or service, or in a critique of specific policies or legislation. The presumption that a given conclusion will be "confirmed" by the expert alienates the expert, and legitimately so.

Scholars concerned with understanding issues of poverty and race as we approach the twenty-first century must maintain a sensitivity to these intricacies. What might such a research agenda look like?

Basic Research on Socioeconomic Conditions and Structural Context

A priority item on any social science research agenda is investigation into the enormous changes in population composition during the recent past. Household structure, levels and sources of family and individual income, human capital attainment, labor force and employment data, immigration status, race and ancestry: these and other items are the standard variables that analysts examine to get a sense of socioeconomic patterns within and across population groups. A new generation of studies is under way as scholars process results from the 1990 census.[28]

At the same time, it behooves researchers to continue the work on structural change that has had an equally prodigious output. Working with data on employer establishments, they should pursue new lines of inquiry into the effects of flexibilization and industry location. Particularly, they need to evaluate the degree to which urban centers are still having to cope with capital flight, a polarized job structure, and the growth of informal sectors. Related topics include the suburbanization of jobs and politics, government policies in the area of social welfare, expenditure patterns, and urban aid.

By contextualizing individual-level data with information on the broader economic and political picture, social scientists can avoid the pitfall of one-sided analysis.

"Best Practices" Research

Why not train our analytical sights more systematically on *successful* experiences and models, especially those instances of positive relationships within multiracial, multiclass environments. Here are two possible approaches.

1. What are the characteristics of urban neighborhoods or suburban districts with a history of racial-ethnic integration? Clues to the origin and reproduction of settings in which differences in background are secondary to a sense of community might be found by exploring the stability of residential patterns, homeownership versus rental housing, income levels and distribution, political structures, economic base, type of school system, community infrastructure (religious institutions, social networks), social relations, mechanisms for conflict resolution. All

these would be examined to determine the ingredients most likely to account for social harmony.

A corollary area of work would deal with attitudes toward racial minorities. For example, it might be instructive to survey racial attitudes among white ethnics in an integrated area and to compare these with the views of their counterparts in a segregated region: are there differences in life experiences, class, personal values, political and religious beliefs, and so on?

2. What generalizations can be made about successful practices in multicultural political action? There might be great value in conducting in-depth studies of multiracial coalitions, particularly those with a progressive empowerment agenda. Several dimensions would come under scrutiny: leadership style and governance structure, the process used for setting goals and defining mission, methods for resolving disputes, strategies for dealing with elected officials and established political structures, sources of financial support, principal accomplishments.

A similar agenda could be constructed to look at agencies involved in service delivery, especially those known to be efficient and having strong ties to a local community.

The overriding purpose of both kinds of investigation would be to document the characteristics and experiences of organizations that consciously strive to build bridges between disparate components of the community. We are taught that "nothing succeeds like success," yet rarely do we try to learn about what works. Race relations research could benefit by turning some of its energies to case studies of successful multiracial activities. Perhaps these are only oases in a wasteland of conflict and failure, but should we not be utilizing whatever replicability they may offer?

Evolving Identities

The changing nature of racial-ethnic identity is an issue that not only has significance for the study of race relations but also carries implications for the feasibility of coalition-building and even for the promotion of effective social service programs.

Little research has been done on the evolution of self-identity over the life cycle, yet we do know that group loyalty and identity vary with age. Toddlers and elementary school children seem remarkably oblivious to differences in race and language, but the "ignorance is bliss" mind set rarely survives the transition to young adulthood. And *within* groups, self-identification constantly transforms and adapts, depending heavily on the milieu in which individuals are operating.

And now, the presence of millions of foreign-born persons interjects new complexities into race relations. The days of racial bifurcation, and the corresponding cultural divide between black and white, are passing. The *other* "Others"—Native Americans, Mexican Americans, Chinese Americans, and Puerto Ricans—have been joined by a dizzying constellation of ethnicities, languages, and cultures. What does all this mean for the process of identity formation and for race relations? Until substantive research is carried out to get a new fix on these changing interactions, it is hard to go beyond speculation.

That this is more than a trivial pursuit is brought home clearly by past experience in designing effective public health strategies. Too often, programs dealing with immunization, infant mortality, sex education, teenage pregnancy, and AIDS prevention envision a typical individual. We must learn to communicate a public message in a way that takes account of the varied generational and cultural characteristics of our population. To that end, it is critical to discover how each segment perceives itself along the various dimensions of identity.

The proliferation of new immigrant communities calls attention also to the need for intensive study of the settlement process. The following topics, some alluded to in earlier chapters, should be examined in greater depth for each of the relevant groups: the history and characteristics of the community formation process; factors affecting naturalization rates; modes of incorporation in the local economy; utilization of social services; attitudes toward assimilation; analysis of community infrastructure in general; informal networks; scope and methods of political intervention in the broader society.

Supporters and funders of all the proposed branches of research should encourage the development of social scientists who are indigenous to the respective communities under study. Let us not permit a whole generation to elapse before voices from those communities are heard.

CONCLUSION

This book started by noting irony in the emergence of the "gorgeous mosaic" metaphor: oddly, it is the powerless who are advancing a concept of broadest unity and inclusion. One might think that after being kept on the outside for so long, desperation would drive racial minorities to narrow-minded nationalism or even withdrawal. To find excluded groups still capable of adopting a vision that invites participation is a sign of hope in a despairing world.

I have been at pains since the beginning, however, to show that this ideal is subject to the power of a system of class and race hegemony, a system that divides people precisely in order to maintain the stable reproduction of the status quo. As long as society continues to tolerate political and economic disparity, the hoped-for reality behind whatever symbols we conjure up—melting pot, plural society, grand mosaic—will fail to materialize. In their place will remain the dualistic images that have competed equally for our acceptance: rich and poor, white and nonwhite, Wall Street and ghetto, condo and shelter.

Implicit in these pages is an argument for the importance of accenting the joint experience of African Americans and Puerto Ricans, of recognizing how factors external and internal to the two communities have conditioned their mutual history and their status relative to other New Yorkers. I have tried to show how they have fared through phases of economic growth and stagnation, through periods of insurgency, backlash, and renewed insurgency; how, in comparative perspective, African Americans seemed better positioned to use political power as an instrument for negotiating a highly segmented labor market and achieving a measure of upward mobility, while Puerto Ricans found their progress constrained by the same rigidities in the labor market; how both groups having attained a modicum of political power, remain on the margin of the economy.

It is a story of how New York's first wave of native minorities evolved from outsiders to key players in the city's life, a fifty-year episode in political maturation. The two communities were drawn together by many unifying elements, positive and negative. These include common bonds of culture, music, and residential proximity, as well as shared experiences in the school system, the workplace, labor unions, and in social, political, and professional groups. Having to contend with racial discrimination and political and economic exclusion, they engaged in a decades-long joint struggle for empowerment. Perhaps the greatest force joining them was the sense of being ostracized citizens in the very home of the Statue of Liberty. For African Americans it may have been knowing that they were not alone in their striving for equality, and among Puerto Ricans there may be a similar sentiment, poignantly expressed by the renowned musician Charlie Palmieri: "Three-quarters of our thinking they [whites] don't understand. Only a black American seems to come closest to understanding us."[1]

In the process of asserting their identity and rights, the two groups created movements, organizations, and institutions—often with shared participation—many of which survive to this day and continue to work together. Yet this common experience, this important episode in New York's history, also reveals the limits to ethnicity-based political strategies.

For it is one thing to gain access to levers of power; it is another to ensure that doing so benefits more than a circle of upwardly mobile professionals. As the old adage proclaims, "New York City: democratic in its politics, elitist in its economics." Given the changed economic context of the end-of-century United States, and the lasting potency of racial and class divisions, one suspects that what has been accomplished to date is just the easiest part. One would like to imagine, with some hopefulness, a future consensus of unity, with African Americans and Puerto Ricans as key protagonists helping to guide a new politics of inclusion. This would imply a remarkable political maturity. But it means overcoming a number of potential traps and pitfalls.

New Challenges

Not the least of these dangers is the totally revised political picture resulting from David Dinkins's defeat in 1993. The election of Rudolph Giuliani presents a new test of the historic bonds forged between

African Americans and Puerto Ricans. First, the two groups must once again deal with each other as outsiders, as they were during the Koch years, and revert to defending programs and resources against a hostile, budget-cutting regime—not the preferred set of circumstances for a coalition that had matured only after decades of joint struggle.

Second, there is potential tension in the role of a small but highly visible group of Latino leaders who broke with the Democratic Party. In joining Rudolph Giuliani's election slate, Herman Badillo helped legitimize the challenger's claim to speak for all New Yorkers, usurping Dinkins's mantle. Even though he failed to dislodge Dinkins's Latino support (the percentage of Latinos voting for the Democrat in 1993 was identical to that in 1989), Badillo provided Giuliani with a veneer of "diversity."

Whether his motivation was to revive his flagging political career or to avenge past slights by the African American political leadership, his candidacy for city comptroller contributed importantly to the defeat of Dinkins by enabling ambivalent white voters to shift their support from the incumbent. Whether blacks interpret this as a sign of Latino disengagement remains to be seen. A small group of Latino disciples were awarded posts in the new administration, but—isolated from the Latino electorate and political organizations—they are hardly in a position to influence policy making within the new conservative regime.

Leadership of the "mosaic" will be tested also in its handling of relations with white ethnics, still the largest voting bloc. There is one fairly simple explanation for the intransigence of racism in recent history: white Americans have seen a decline in their standard of living. In New York, as average earnings stagnated for working families during the 1980s, poverty rose more for whites than for any other group. Sadly, they accept the dogma that the culprits are those less fortunate than they. Volumes have been written about this problem.[2] Is racism—especially against blacks—simply too ingrained to be rooted out of the American psyche? Does it serve some need for self-esteem among European Americans? How important are the economic benefits of racial hegemony for working-class and middle-class whites? Are nonwealthy whites the victim of some vast conspiracy that prevents them from strategically allying with their class brothers and sisters?

Unless minority leadership transcends the inherently limited scope of ethnicity-based politics by forging class-based alliances, the economic basis for racism will remain uncontested. By the same token, new leadership must emerge from Jewish, Italian, Irish, and other communities traditionally progressive on economic issues; leadership willing to challenge the prerogative of racial hegemony.

Immigrant minorities present yet another challenge to the possibility of a minority-led consensus. In a sense they are a wild card in the city's political game. Many signs point to the potential departure from traditional notions of immigrant incorporation. Reliance on ethnic enclaves and informal economic activity only furthers the chances of isolation. Differences in culture and citizenship status leave them susceptible to the workings of racial domination.

Yet it does not necessarily follow that the newcomers will be absorbed by default into the native minority sphere of influence. African Americans and Puerto Ricans both face a test in dealing with West Indians and Haitians, with Dominicans and other Latinos, who will increasingly intervene in the political and economic struggle. Will Pan-African and Hispanic loyalties disturb the alliance between African Americans and Puerto Ricans?

And then there is the fastest-growing group of all: Asian American New Yorkers, internally diverse and, as a group, greatly distanced from this country's cultural legacy. Whether they will find a common identity and act as a unified force is a question that will inspire reams of research and analysis, no doubt. How they are received by native minorities and Euro-Americans, in both the political and the economic realm, will greatly determine their path of adaptation.

It is unlikely that native minorities can count upon the uncritical support of any of these newcomers. Indeed, the new immigrants, whose citizen *children* are already becoming part of the native minority world, will more likely transform the cultural and political outlook of African Americans and Puerto Ricans.

A New Leadership on the Horizon?

If a new consensus is to be constructed, rooted in a tolerant multiculturalism yet capable of appealing to the economic concerns of all New Yorkers, a new leadership will have to emerge, a leadership willing to contest some basic tenets of conventional thinking about the urban crisis. At least four approaches to guiding the city into the next century can be gleaned from views hinted at in this book.

1. Encourage the idea that community and labor are indispensable

to the formation of a new social pact, which until now has been primarily conceived of as a partnership between government and business. The two new partners need to be conceptualized broadly: both neighborhood and environmental community; both unionized and unorganized labor.

2. Challenge the usurping of everyday life by market-driven criteria and principles. Center the revitalization of urban areas in locally based initiatives, drawing upon a philosophy of "empowerment from below." Defeating the cynicism and despair so prevalent in poor neighborhoods will require liberating the energies of community groups for their self-development.

3. Transcend the idea that antipoverty strategies should be centered on enlarging the middle class among minority communities. Too many affirmative action programs, it seems, benefit only the children of professionals. Enormous resources are expended by employers and educational institutions recruiting minorities to satisfy "diversity" criteria, but many of those who gain are persons with few roots in and even less commitment to the communities they supposedly represent. Moreover, similar resources are sorely lacking when it comes to the unemployed or average working people, minority or white. The consequent stresses on racial and class harmony should be obvious. To question these practices and priorities has to be a main task.

4. Promulgate a notion of diversity that reveres democratic principles. Finding ways to enlarge the American tradition so that it treats equally the heritages of other civilizations and surmounts its European bias is a fundamental aspect of the challenge of multiculturalism. This means deepening, not abandoning, the democratic impulse evident in the human experience. The new leadership must be concerned with taking democracy *seriously*.

These are but a handful of the ideas that may help orient the new social movements and leadership needed in the Great Metropolis. Together with the communitarian and research agendas described in Chapter Seven, they constitute a rudimentary design of renewal. If African Americans and Puerto Ricans are to assist in New York's rebirth, their greatest contribution may be along these lines. To follow the well-trodden paths of earlier groups is to pursue business as usual in the game of ethnic politics. To embark on a program of inclusion from below is to begin mustering up the forces for a broad challenge to economic privilege.

APPENDIX A

Definitions of Variables

BLACK	Person is African American.
CHILDREN	Number of children ever born.
EDUC	Schooling: highest grade completed.
EDUC*LFEX	Schooling and labor force experience interaction term.
EDUC*LFSQ	Schooling and labor force experience squared interaction term.
ENG*EDUC	English-speaking ability and schooling interaction term.
ENG*EXP	English-speaking ability and labor force experience interaction term.
ENG*EXPSQ	English-speaking ability and labor force experience squared interaction term.
ENGLISH	English-speaking ability. For 1960: "Mother tongue is English" (asked of foreign-born); for 1970: "Mother tongue is English" (asked of all persons); for 1980, "Speaks English well."
GOVT	Person is government employee; includes all levels of government as well as public schools, hospitals, etc.
HH	Person is head of household.
INDPRM	Located in independent primary segment.
INDPRMCR	Located in independent primary craft segment.
LFEXP	Labor force experience. Calculated as age–EDUC–5.

LFEXPSQ	Labor force experience squared. Calculated as (LFEXP) × (LFEXP).
LNHOURS	Log of hours worked.
LNINCOME1	Log of wage and salary income. For 1960/1970 income was reported in intervals, and converted to continuous variable. For 1980 income was reported as a continuous variable.
LNWAGERT	Log of wage rate. Wage rate calculated as wage = total earnings from wage and salary/(hours worked x weeks worked).
LNWKSW	Log of weeks worked.
MALE	Person is male.
MARPRE	Previously married (widowed, divorced, or separated).
MARSP	Married with spouse present.
MIGNONE	Person resided in same house five years earlier.
MIGNY	Person resided in different house, same state, five years earlier.
PUBAST	Recipient of public assistance.
PUERTO	Person is Puerto Rican.
SECOND	Located in secondary segment.
SINGLE	Single, never married.
SUBPRM	Located in subordinate primary segment.
VETERAN	Person is a veteran.
WORKDIS1	Person has disability that limits possibility of work; applies only to 1980.
YOTHER	Person had other source of income in addition to wage or salary; includes social security and public assistance; applies only to 1960.

APPENDIX B

Wage Regressions: Data and Methods

The empirical analysis discussed in Chapter Four is centered on a series of multiple regression procedures exploring the determinants of wages. The basic equation upon which the analysis builds is the standard human capital earnings function, in which the dependent variable, earnings, is regressed on a vector of human capital variables.[1] For this study, the model includes demographic and segmentation variables, reflecting other potential determinants of earnings.

Methodology

Estimates of the augmented human capital earnings function are made for each of the four race/gender groups in the sample African American males, African American females, Puerto Rican males, Puerto Rican females and are conducted on 1960, 1970, and 1980 data.

The object of this procedure is to allow for full interactions between the race/gender classifications and the various independent variables. This permits an examination of the extent to which differences in the coefficients of human capital variables—differential human capital effects—contribute to variations in relative levels of the dependent variable. For example, the coefficient on schooling can be evaluated to determine whether it is significantly different in the African American male equation from its corresponding value in the Puerto Rican male equation. An affirmative finding would indicate the existence of differential returns to schooling for the two groups in a given year. If no difference in the coefficients is ascertained, the implication is that dissimilarities in educational attainment do not contribute to the differential status of the two groups.

These regressions also enable a determination of the degree to which differences in the coefficients of the segment location variables influence the variations in levels of the dependent variable. Conducting regressions for each decennial point permits an extention of the analysis to intertemporal comparisons. Results can be noted with regard to changes in the explanatory power over time.

Variables

The dependent variable is the wage rate (LNWAGERT). Following convention, the natural logarithm of the wage rate is entered as the value for the dependent variable.[2]

The independent variables are classified into three areas. First, the human capital vector encompasses schooling, work experience, language, and their interaction terms. Second, the demographic vector includes residential stability, marital status, head of household status, number of children, veteran status, public assistance, and disability status. Third, the set of segmentation variables incorporates government employment as well as the various segment locations.

Human Capital Variables

Schooling (EDUC), expressed as years of education completed, is a principal factor presumed to influence earnings.[3]

LFEXP captures the effect of general labor force experience. Since no direct data are reported in the census on labor force experience, this variable is calculated—following standard practice—as the difference between age and years of schooling completed, with a further deduction covering the five preschool years.[4] This variable is simultaneously expressed in a geometric specification, as a squared term LFEXPSQ, to allow for a nonlinear effect of labor force experience.[5] The expectation is that earnings increase with respect to labor force experience (positive coefficient of LFEXP) but at a decreasing rate (negative coefficient of LFEXPSQ).

The language variable (ENGLISH) presents several complications because of the inconsistent manner in which this information was collected in the three census surveys (see Appendix A). Indeed, it is not possible to interpret this effect in a consistent fashion across the various decennial results. Aside from these difficulties, the measure of language ability would be expected to be a significant factor influencing interminority differentials.[6] It is argued that insufficient English-language proficiency limits the performance of certain job functions, especially in higher-skilled occupations. In the results for 1980 (the year in which this variable has the most relevant meaning) the language variable carries the interpretation "ability to speak English well" and therefore implies a positive coefficient. For the 1970 data this variable signifies "English is the mother tongue," also implying an expected positive sign. But a question asking for the respondent's "mother tongue" refers to the language spoken at home when the person was a child and is therefore not a direct measure of an individual's English-language proficiency; for Puerto Ricans born or raised in New York, for instance, the answers elicited would underestimate English-speaking ability. In 1960 the ENGLISH variable refers only to the foreign-born and thus has little application to the two groups considered here.[7]

A number of interactive effects are considered, including, for example, the relationship between schooling and experience.[8] Returns to labor force experience are partially dependent on workers' intellectual or cognitive skills, measured by level of schooling. The theory would therefore hypothesize a positive coefficient on the interaction term EDUC*LFEX. The coefficient term on the nonlinear expression of the experience variable (EDUC*LFSQ) would carry a negative sign because this positive effect would occur at a decreasing rate over time; that is, the enhancing effects of education on the returns to experience will decline over the course of the work history of the individual.

It is also postulated that language ability interacts with the cognitive process and thus mediates the effectiveness of the schooling variable. An analysis of the potential differences between African Americans and Puerto Ricans would take into account this language and education interdependency. For the 1980 data this term (ENG*EDUC) is expected to display a negative sign on the coefficient, since workers with low English-speaking ability will derive relatively lower returns to their education than their counterparts exhibiting higher English language proficiency. Opposite relations would hold for the 1970 data, because of the more limited meaning of the language variable.

A final pair of interaction effects that might reasonably be posited relates to the connection between language ability and labor force experience. Positive returns to experience (LFEXP) reflect improved skills or seniority benefits that accrue over time and are translated into higher wages. A high level of English-language ability might presumably enhance returns to experience for a worker (ENG*EXP) compared with another worker with less English-language ability. This would apply, for example, in the case of workers who undertake job training programs or career advancement strategies with a significant educational or cognitive component. The expected signs on the coefficients for these interaction terms (ENG*EXPSQ) would parallel those for the language-schooling variables, again with contrasting interpretations for the 1980 and 1970 data.

Demographic Variables

One might expect that among lower-income families (as typified in African American and Puerto Rican communities) residential stability (MIGNONE) would be positively associated with wages. Changes in residence imply changes in employers, thus eroding seniority benefits and other advantages of job tenure. This is not the case, however, where job changes (and residential moves) result from occupational mobility.

Among the marital status variables are included "married, spouse present" (MARSP), referring to married persons who are principal income earners. Geoffrey Carliner's idea that family responsibilities may act as a motivation to work harder leads to a positive association with wages.[9] Other marital status possibilities are "previously married" (MARPRE), which includes the divorced, widowed, or separated; and "single" (SINGLE).

One would anticipate head of household status (HH) to be positively associated with labor market earnings, for the same reason as that elucidated in the case of MARSP. Number of children (CHILDREN) also raises earnings, resembling the influence of HH.

Other demographic variables include veteran status (VETERAN), recipient of public assistance (PUBAST), recipient of transfer funds (YOTHER, used only in 1960, which includes all forms of government funds), and limited work disability status (WORKDIS1, representing a disability that restricts a person's capacity to work).

Segmentation Variables

Four segment location variables are constructed: INDPRM (independent primary segment), INDPRMCR (independent primary craft segment), SUBPRM (subordinate primary segment) and SECOND (secondary segment).

In the first series of regressions, INDPRM is excluded. The constant in these regressions includes this dummy variable, and the coefficients on the other segment variables are to be interpreted as differences from this segment.

Government employment (GOVT) is treated as part of the vector of segmentation variables because it provides additional structural determinations of labor market earnings which are not directly captured by the segment location variables. On the one hand, the public versus private sector distinction has had a changing influence on labor market conditions over time. Relative shares have varied, suggesting that the significance of public employee status may vary in different periods. Also, the algorithm assigning workers to segments ignores industry characteristics of workers who are in the non-goods-producing industries.[10] The segment location of these workers is based strictly on occupational status. Thus inclusion of industry information for public employees, who are a subset of the non-goods-manufacturing labor force, supplies additional information.

APPENDIX C

Wage Regressions by Race and Gender

Results for 1960

Full reporting of regression results for all wage equations, including parameter estimates and significance tests, are in Andrés Torres, "Labor Segmentation: African American and Puerto Rican Labor in New York City, 1960–1980," *Review of Black Political Economy* 20, no. 1 (1991): Table 3.

In the equations for the race/gender classification of the sample, the results indicate that among the four minority subpopulations, only for black females do human capital variables appear to exert a consistent influence. African American females' returns to education in 1960 were equal to those of white males.

Contrary to expectations, returns to INDPRM location are less for both African American and Puerto Rican males than for the other subgroups. The difference is greater among Puerto Rican males. Also, GOVT is statistically significant for black males but not for Puerto Rican males.

The residential stability proxies (MIGNY, MIGNONE) have a greater effect on mean black wage (male and female) than on mean Puerto Rican wage.

Results for 1970

Only EDUC*LFEX among the human capital factors is significant for African American and Puerto Rican females. The positive sign on the coefficient suggests that minority women derive an increasing rate of return to schooling over the course of their work history. In 1970 Puerto Rican females receive greater returns than black females. For black males there is no differential among the various segment effects. At the same time, male Puerto Ricans located in SECOND receive returns significantly less than those in INDPRM. This means that there is differential significance of the INDPRM dummy for the two groups, contributing to the narrowing of the male wage differential in 1970. The opposite relationship prevailed between the two groups of minority females. For African American females, returns to INDPRM has a greater effect than for Puerto Rican females. As in 1960, GOVT has a positive effect for black males, and shows no influence for Puerto Rican males. Among minority females, GOVT exhibits a greater effect for Puerto Ricans than for blacks.

Results for 1980

For the first time in this study, EDUC and LFEXP are important determinants of minority workers' earnings. Puerto Rican males and African American females derive greater returns to schooling and experience than do their respective gender counterparts. For females, this distinction correlates with the observed differentials in wages. Among minority females, the difference in returns to INDPRM versus SECOND is substantially greater for Puerto Ricans than for blacks. Location in SECOND garners significantly smaller returns for Puerto Ricans females than for African American females. Location in SUBPRM has a greater (positive) effect for black males than for Puerto Rican males. GOVT is significant for Puerto Rican males and negative for Puerto Rican females.

Among demographic variables, only head of household status is conspicuous in demonstrating a differential affect across the samples. This result indicates that HH, which is consistently significant for African American males, contributes to the male differential. This is not the case for minority women.

In the 1980 sample—the only one for which there is a reliable specification of the English-language proficiency variable (ENGLISH)—the ability to speak English well is a significant determinant of wages among Puerto Ricans males.

Intertemporal Comparisons: 1960–1970

Synthesizing the results from different years draws attention to changing patterns of differential effects over time. Recall that during 1960–70, the wage level for African American males decreases compared with that for Puerto Rican males, and increases for African American females.

GOVT has a declining importance for black males during this period, although it maintains a statistical significance that is lacking in the case of Puerto Rican males.

For Puerto Rican males in 1970, returns to INDPRM exceed those to the other segments, representing a reversal of the unexpected pattern that prevails in 1960, in which returns to INDPRM are less for both male subgroups than for the other segments. This may have contributed to the observed narrowing of relative status between the two groups.

For both African American and Puerto Rican males, there is a decline in the importance of residential stability (as measured by MIGNONE and MIGNY). Since this is a much more important factor for black males in 1960, the attenuation of this influence appears to contribute to the relative decline in the black wage.

For black females, head of household status shows increasing importance, in contrast to Puerto Rican females.

Among minority males, schooling and labor force experience exert no influence on changes in relative wages during 1960–70. Differential returns to these variables therefore cannot account for any of the decline in the relative wage of African Americans.

Intertemporal Comparisons: 1970–1980

The data show a decline in the relative wage for African American men during this decade, accompanied by an increase in relative wage for African American females. Several factors appear to account for these trends:

For black females, there is an increase in the importance of labor force experience—in contrast to Puerto Rican females, for whom this variable is not significant in 1970 or 1980.

There is a decline in the importance of GOVT for Puerto Rican females. In 1980, GOVT actually has a negative effect on Puerto Rican females' wages, whereas in 1970 it has a positive effect.

Education increases in importance for both female groups during the period. Additionally, in 1980 the schooling effect has a greater impact for black females than for Puerto Rican females.

Among males, GOVT increases in importance for Puerto Ricans.

APPENDIX D

Decomposition Analysis

Method

The decomposition analysis reported in Chapter Four is performed on the results of the multiple regressions by race and gender to ascertain the relative importance of changes in coefficients and stocks of variables.

The objective is to separate intertemporal changes in the dependent variable, logged wage rate (LNWAGERT), into two components: that portion due to changes in the levels of the independent variables, and that portion due to changes in the regression coefficients.[1] The former captures the effects of compositional changes in human capital endowments and group segmentation structure. The latter measures the impact of changes in returns to human capital and segment location. For each race/gender group the results indicate (1) the comparative influence of compositional effects versus changes in returns to variables; (2) the relative importance of human capital and segmentation variables.

The specific issue addressed here is the presumed relationship between political power and the segmentation process in the determination of wages. Given a more developed base of political power for African Americans, one would expect to find that compared to Puerto Ricans this group derived greater positive effects from (1) changes in segment distribution and (2) changes in returns to segment location. These two component sources of change reflect two distinct processes. The first component measures the extent to which the political factor may have facilitated a proportionately larger concentration in primary jobs for African Americans than for Puerto Ricans; it is therefore a measure of the effect on wages of group occupational mobility.[2] The second component measures the changes in returns to location in given labor segments, the structural counterpart to changes in returns to human capital.

Since no attempt is made to measure directly the level of each group's political power, the regression equation does not explicitly include this variable. The procedures used indirectly test for the impact of this variable by attributing to it some of the expected difference in segmentation effects.

Also, data limitations and resource constraints prevented the introduction of controls for other potential determinants of earnings differentials. First, although one would normally expect compensating payments for undesirable working conditions, labor market segmentation may alter this relation. The job structure will be characterized by segments with low wages and poor working conditions versus those with high wages and favorable working conditions. If these conditions are accompanied by intersegment immobility, the existence of negative compensating payments can be found. Thus some of the earnings differences in the sample may be due to this process.[3] Second, differential allocation across the occupational structure may arise from the optimizing behavior of individual workers who invest in training activities to enhance opportunities for promotions and career advancement.[4] Independent of any collective political efforts, this may partially account for the relatively favorable segment distribution of African Americans. Finally, the level of union membership may vary significantly between the two groups, leading to another source of earnings differences.[5]

Given these issues, results tending to confirm my hypothesis are to be construed as suggestive rather than conclusive.[6]

1960–70

Changes in the levels of independent variables are much more important for females than males. For females, changes in segment distribution have a greater positive impact than do increases in the levels of human capital skills. This is especially so for black females, who exhibit a sizable exodus from the secondary segment between 1960 and 1970. Changes in segment distribution have a negative impact for Puerto Rican males and are slightly positive for black males. Changes in segment returns have a negative effect on predicted wage for both male groups, but much more negative for Puerto Ricans than African Americans. This result is in keeping with the reasoning that the political factor helped to shelter black males somewhat from the declining importance of segment returns in the 1960–70 period. Changes in segment returns have a negative impact on wages for African American females, a slightly positive one for Puerto Rican females.

With regard to changes in the human capital regression coefficients, the data suggest that for all groups except African American females, increases in the returns to human capital have greater positive influence than do changes in returns to segment location.

1970–80

Only in the case of Puerto Rican females do changes in variable levels register a greater positive impact than changes in regression coefficients. For all groups except Puerto Rican males, stocks of human capital levels contribute more to the increase in wages than do changes in the segmentation structure. For Puerto Rican males, changes in segment allocation have a slightly less negative effect than do changes in human capital levels.

Increases in returns to human capital variables are more important for most groups, especially Puerto Rican males, than are changes to segment location returns. Puerto Rican females are an exception to this pattern.

1960–80

Two broad conclusions emerge in an assessment of the entire period. First, changes in regression coefficients are more important for all groups. Second, within the component of changing regression coefficients, the vector of human capital variables is consistently greater in importance for all groups. With regard to variations in the levels of independent variables, changes in segment allocation are more important for blacks, whereas the reverse holds for Puerto Rican females. For Puerto Rican males, neither component appears to exhibit much importance.

From the perspective of intergroup comparisons, the decomposition analysis highlights further important distinctions.[7] Changes in returns to human capital variables are proportionately greater for Puerto Ricans than for African Americans. Changes in the levels of human capital variables are proportionately more important for Puerto Rican females than for African American females. Changes in the levels of the segmentation variables have a positive effect for African Americans, a negative one for Puerto Ricans.

NOTES

Introduction

1. Among white New Yorkers, the poverty rate was 12.3 percent. *Nationally,* 13.1 percent of U.S. residents lived in poverty. Port Authority of New York and New Jersey, *Demographic Trends—Income Distribution and Poverty,* (New York: Port Authority of New York and New Jersey, 1994), Tables 11–12.

Chapter One

1. Some readers may be put off by terms like "capitalist" and "class conflict," thinking them vestiges of outdated theories. Nothing could be further from the truth: political candidates routinely trade charges of promoting "class warfare" (some are accused of "bashing the rich," others of "squeezing the poor"); the dissolution of the Soviet Union is celebrated as a victory for the system of capitalist free enterprise. This book attempts to apply concepts within the historical materialist tradition to contemporary issues.

2. George Frederickson, *White Supremacy* (New York: Oxford University Press, 1982); Winthrop D. Jordan, *White over Black: American Attitudes toward the Negro, 1550–1812* (1968; New York: Norton, 1977); Michael Omi and Howard Winant, *Racial Formation in the United States* (New York: Routledge, 1986); Benjamin Ringer, *"We, the People" and Others: Duality and America's Treatment of Its Racial Minorities* (New York: Tavistock, 1983); Ronald Sanders, *Lost Tribes and Promised Lands: The Origins of American Racism* (New York: Harper, 1978). For recent scholarship on the emergence of the "Euro-American," see Richard D. Alba, *Ethnic Identity: The Transformation of White America* (New Haven, Conn.: Yale University Press, 1990).

3. The system of racial hegemony encompasses the entire set of institutions, ideologies, and practices that serve to reproduce racial dominance under capitalism. Prejudice, which anyone can harbor, is an attitude of hostility toward persons of a different race, ethnicity, gender, or religion. Of late there has been a tendency to define all expressions of individual bias as racism. But equating the prejudice of racial or ethnic minorities with the prejudice of whites

ignores the fact that the latter feeds the system of racial domination. Needless to say, this point is of little import to the white person who has been offended or abused by a minority person's expression of hatred.

4. Jordan, *White over Black.*

5. This discussion follows the radical political economy tradition of segmentation theory, first stated in Michael Reich, David M. Gordon, and Richard C, Edwards, "A Theory of Labor Market Segmentation," *American Economic Review* 63, no. 2 (1973): 359–65; reprinted in David M. Gordon, ed., *Problems in Politial Economy* (Lexington, Mass.: Heath, 1977). For differences between institutionalist (or "dual labor market") and radical labor segmentation views, see Jill Rubery, "Structured Labor Markets, Worker Organization, and Low Pay," *Cambridge Journal of Economics* 2 (1978): 19–23; Richard C. Edwards, *Contested Terrain* (New York: Basic Books, 1979); and David M. Gordon, Richard C. Edwards, and Michael Reich, *Segmented Work, Divided Workers* (Cambridge: Cambridge University Press, 1982), pp. 7–8.

6. Edwards, *Contested Terrain;* Gordon, Edwards, and Reich, *Segmented Work, Divided Workers*; David M. Gordon, *The Working Poor: Towards a State Agenda* (Washington, D.C.: Council of State Planning Agencies, 1979). Because of its emphasis on historical and qualitative study, segmentation theory relies less on mathematical formalization and empirical testing than do neoclassical theories of labor economics. This leads to a certain imprecision when it comes to estimating the actual extent of stratification in the economy. Studies of various regional and national economies have generated models comprising anywhere from two to twenty segments. The important point is that these numbers are offered as approximations of real-world divisions in the labor market.

7. Gordon, *The Working Poor,* p. 46.

8. Edwards, *Contested Terrain,* chap. 9; Russell Rumberger and Martin Carnoy, "Segmentation in the U.S. Labor Market: Its Effects on the Mobility and Earnings of Whites and Blacks," *Cambridge Journal of Economics* 4 (1980): 130.

9. Gordon, Edwards, and Reich, *Segmented Work, Divided Workers,* pp. 213–15.

10. Harold M. Baron, "Racial Domination in Advanced Capitalism: A Theory of Nationalism and Divisions in the Labor Market," in *Labor Market Segmentation* ed. Richard C. Edwards, Michael Reich, and David M. Gordon (Lexington, Mass.: Heath, 1975); and Baron, "Racism Transformed: The Implications of the 1960's," *Review of Radical Political Economics* 17, no. 3 (1985).

11. Edwards (*Contested Terrain,* chap. 9) believes that labor segmentation began during the early part of the twentieth century, with the rise of bureaucratic control systems in large firms and the organization of mass industrial unions. Before that time the bulk of white American workers (excluding racial/ethnic and female labor, which were still isolated from the capitalist

labor market) were fairly "homogeneous" with respect to their skill levels and wages.

12. Baron, "Racism Transformed," p. 206.

13. Mario Barrera, *Race and Class in the Southwest* (Notre Dame, Ind.: Notre Dame University Press, 1977), chap. 2. Other histories of the Mexican American experience include Vernon Briggs, *Chicanos and Rural Poverty* (Baltimore, Md.: Johns Hopkin University Press, 1973); Mario Garcia, "Racial Dualism in the El Paso Labor Market: 1880–1920," *Aztlan*, Summer 1975, pp. 197–218; Carey McWilliams, *North from Mexico* (New York: Greenwood Press, 1968).

14. African Americans gained citizenship with the Emancipation Proclamation in 1863. In contrast, Puerto Ricans did not seek out U.S. citizenship when it was extended to them in 1917; in fact, Puerto Rico's elected legislative assembly and the majority party (the Unionists) opposed citizenship, but it was assigned unilaterally by the U.S. Congress. At the time, many island residents were holding out for the possibility of national independence and felt that accepting U.S. citizenship would derail their strategy. See Ringer, *"We, the People" and Others*, chaps. 19–20; and Kal Wagenheim, *Puerto Rico: A Profile* (New York: Praeger, 1970), pp. 67–70.

15. Clearly, however, moral claims do not guarantee results. Native Americans, perhaps the group to whom the United States is preeminently obligated, have been unable to extract more than the barest support for their livelihood and cultural autonomy.

16. Admission of colonial domination would also strengthen the demand for monetary compensation, were national independence to be conceded to the island at a later time.

17. Cuban Americans provide a fascinating episode in the history of immigration to New York. Little has been written about their transformation of Washington Heights during the 1960s and 1970s, prior to Dominican settlement of the area. Arriving primarily as refugees, they established a major economic enclave but have since out-migrated to other parts. For a political-economic analysis of the Cuban enclave in Miami, see Marifeli Pérez-Stable and Miren Uriarte, "Cubans and the Changing Economy of Miami," in *Latinos in a Changing U.S. Economy*, ed. Rebecca Morales and Frank Bonilla (Newbury Park, Calif.: Sage, 1993).

Chapter Two

1. Three geographic entities need to be distinguished. The New York Region includes more than twenty counties in the tristate area of New York, New Jersey, and Connecticut. This is the unit of analysis developed by the Regional Plan Association in its studies since the 1920s. The New York Standard Metropolitan Statistical Area (NYSMSA), developed by the U.S. Bu-

reau of the Census, refers to a smaller set of counties that excludes the more distant areas of New Jersey and Connecticut. Although the composition of NYSMSA has varied over time, the core remains New York City, Long Island, and Westchester County. New York City encompasses the five boroughs of Staten Island, Queens, Manhattan, Brooklyn, and the Bronx.

2. James Heilbrun, *Urban Economics and Public Policy* (New York: St. Martin's Press, 1974), p. 138.

3. Raymond Vernon, *Metropolis* 1985 (Cambridge, Mass.: Harvard University Press, 1960), pp. 4–5.

4. "New York's economic cycles were always less volatile than those of the rest of the country, primarily because of the diversity of our industries. In 1960, however, there was a break in that pattern" (Louis Winnick, comments at a roundtable discussion sponsored by the Manhattan Institute, published in *Manhattan Report* 5, no. 4 [1985]: 15).

5. Wilbur R. Thompson, *A Preface to Urban Economics* (Baltimore, Md.: Johns Hopkins University Press, 1965).

6. Vernon, *Metropolis* 1985, pp. 68–78.

7. Ibid., p. 120.

8. In the 1950s the majority of industries dominated by single-plant firms had a large (more than 30 percent) portion of their total employment located in the New York Region. Vernon (*Metropolis 1985*, p. 72) points out that these enterprises generally employ the fewest number of workers. Dale L. Hiestand and Dean W. Morse report that in 1973 the average number of employees per establishment was much lower in the New York area (12), than in other major cities (about 20) such as Los Angeles, Houston, Atlanta, and Chicago (*Comparative Metropolitan Employment Complexes* [Montclair, N.J.: Allanheld Osmun, 1979], p. 53).

9. In 1957 New York hosted more corporate headquarters than the next five largest cities combined; see Robert B. Cohen, "The New International Division of Labor, Multinational Corporations, and the Urban Hierarchy," in *Urbanization and Urban Planning in Capitalist Society*, ed. Michael Dear and Allen J. Scott (New York: Metheun, 1981), Table 12.2, p. 305.

10. George Sternlieb and James W. Hughes, "Metropolitan Decline and Inter-Regional Job Shifts," in *The Fiscal Crisis of American Cities*, ed. Roger E. Alcaly and David Mermelstein (New York: Vintage Books, 1977), pp. 152–53.

11. The radio and ladies apparel industries are given fuller discussion in Vernon, *Metropolis* 1985, chap. 4.

12. Sternlieb and Hughes, "Metropolitan Decline and Inter-Regional Job Shifts," p. 153.

13. Herbert Bienstock, "New York City's Labor Market: Past Trends, Current Conditions, Future Prospects," *City Almanac* 12, no. 4 (1977): 5, fig. 3.

14. Vernon, *Metropolis 1985;* Dick Netzer, "New York City's Mixed Economy: Ten Years Later," *Public Interest*, no. 16 (Summer 1969): 195–96.

15. Dick Netzer, "The Cloudy Prospects for the City's Economy," *New York Affairs* 1, no. 4 (1974): 28, 29.

16. Raymond D. Horton, "People, Jobs, and Public Finance in New York City," *City Almanac* 12, no. 2 (1977): 8.

17. Jon C. Teaford, *The Twentieth-Century American City: Problem, Promise and Reality* (Baltimore, Md.: Johns Hopkins University Press, 1986), p. 142.

18. Abraham Beame, *Economic Recovery: New York City's Program for 1977–1981* (New York: Department of City Planning, 1976), p. 9.

19. Regional Plan Association, *Outlook for the Tri-State Region through 2000* (New York: Regional Plan Association, 1986), p. 3.

20. Samuel M. Ehrenhalt, "Changing Configurations in the Regional Labor Market," in *Proceedings of the 17th Annual Institute of the New York City Council on Economic Education* (New York: Council on Economic Education, 1984) p. 18, Table 15.

21. David M. Kotz, *Bank Control of Large Corporations in the United States* (Berkeley: University of California Press, 1978).

22. Beame, *Economic Recovery*, p. 12.

23. Matthew Edel, "The New York Crisis as Economic History," in Alcaly and Mermelstein, *Fiscal Crisis*, pp. 238–39.

24. Bennett Harrison and Barry Bluestone, *The Great U-Turn* (New York: Basic Books, 1988).

25. Cohen, "The New International Division of Labor," pp. 297–300.

26. Bienstock, "New York City's Labor Market," p. 13.

27. Roger Waldinger reports that New York City attracted over a million legal immigrants between 1966 and 1979 ("Immigration and Urban Change," *American Review of Sociology* 15 [1989]: 53). Nathan Glazer notes a study that estimated a flow of 1.68 million immigrants between 1970 and 1986 ("The New New Yorkers," in *New York Unbound*, ed. Peter D. Salins [New York: Basil Blackwell, 1988], p. 56).

28. Emanuel Tobier, "Foreign Immigration," in *Setting Municipal Priorities 1983*, ed. Charles Brecher and Raymond D. Horton (New York: Russell Sage Foundation, 1983); Marcia Freedman, "Urban Labor Markets and Ethnicity: Segments and Shelters Reexamined," in *Urban Ethnicity in the United States*, ed. Lionel Maldonado and Joan Moore (Beverly Hills: Sage, 1985); Saskia Sassen-Koob, *The Mobility of Labor and Capital* (New York: Cambridge University Press, 1988).

29. In contrast, the rest of the metropolitan area, including Long Island and northeastern New Jersey, saw population grow by 65 percent between 1950 and 1970 (Bienstock, "New York City's Labor Market," p. 9).

30. Netzer, "The Cloudy Prospects for the City's Economy," p. 30.

31. Kal Waghenheim, *A Survey of Puerto Ricans on the U.S. Mainland in the 1970's* (New York: Praeger, 1975), p. 74, Table 6.

32. The five cities containing the largest number of blacks (New York,

Chicago, Detroit, Philadelphia, and Washington, D.C.) saw declines in the total employed labor force; of the fifteen next largest cities, eight experienced declines (Richard C. Hill, "State Capitalism and the Urban Fiscal Crisis in the U.S.," *International Journal of Urban and Regional Research* 1 (1977): 37–43.

33. "The history of the New York area suggests that there have always been significant discrepancies between the number of people which the area generated and the number of job opportunities it generated—discrepancies bridged by streams of in-migration" (Vernon, *Metropolis 1985*, p. 192).

34. As U.S. citizens, Puerto Ricans are entitled to unrestricted entry and movement; they must therefore be classified as internal migrants. Most observers would agree that, economically, the Commonwealth of Puerto Rico is a de facto region of the U.S. much like Hawaii or Alaska. There is considerable contentiousness over Puerto Rico's political status, however, and culturally, most Puerto Ricans resist complete assimilation into U.S. society. A change in political status could very well alter the economic relationship of the island to the United States. For discussion of the political, economic, and cultural aspects, consult Raymond Carr, *Puerto Rico: A Colonial Experiment* (New York: Vintage Books, 1984); Edgardo Meléndez, *Puerto Rico's Statehood Movement* (Westport, Conn.: Greenwood Press, 1988); and Arturo Morales Carrión, *Puerto Rico: A Political and Cultural History*, (New York: Norton, 1983).

35. Hiestand and Morse, *Comparative Metropolitan Employment Complexes*, p. 93.

36. Horton, "People, Jobs, and Public Finance in New York City," p. 3.

37. Bienstock, "New York City's Labor Market," p. 17.

38. Tobier reports that in 1971, 66.5 percent of all immigrants arriving in New York City came from these regions; by 1979, the proportion was 77.8 percent ("Foreign Immigration," pp. 180–81, Table 5.11). These data exclude undocumented immigrants and do not indicate what number may have left the city for other points in the United States.

39. Hiestand and Morse, *Comparative Metropolitan Employment Complexes*, chaps. 3–5.

40. Ibid., p. 33.

41. The method for defining the segment categories is described in David M. Gordon, "Procedures for Allocating Jobs into Labor Segments" (unpublished paper, New School for Social Research, 1986). In keeping with the emphasis on structural determinants of labor market outcomes, Gordon stresses that segment categories should rely primarily on *job* characteristics, as opposed to worker traits. Additionally, information on market outcomes (such as wages) should *not* be incorporated in the definition of segments, because this introduces circularity into the methodology: since the theory hypothesizes that segmentation leads to income differences, one cannot use earnings data to characterize or define labor segments in the first place. For further discussion of the rationale underlying Gordon's classification system, see David M. Gordon,

Richard Edwards, and Michael Reich, *Segmented Work, Divided Workers* (Cambridge: Cambridge University Press, 1982), chap. 5.

42. Andrés Torres, "Human Capital, Labor Segmentation and Inter-Minority Relative Status" (Ph.D. diss. New School for Social Research, 1988), app. A.

43. Whereas mass industrial unions were able to reduce regional wage differentials in industries like mining, steel, and automaking, the leaders of large New York unions such as apparel and printing apparently colluded with employers to restrict wage increases, hoping to keep the businesses in the city (Vernon, *Metropolis 1985*, p. 50).

44. Altagracia Ortíz, "Puerto Rican Workers in the Garment Industry of New York City, 1920–1960," in *Labor Divided: Race and Ethnicity in U.S. Labor Struggles, 1835–1960*, ed. Robert Asher and Charles Stevenson (Albany: State University of New York Press, 1990).

45. Hiestand and Morse, *Comparative Metropolitan Empolyment Complexes*, p. 84.

46. Seymour Z. Mann and Edward Handman, "The Role of Municipal Unions," *City Almanac* 12, no. 1 (1977): 8.

47. Tobier, "Foreign Immigration," p. 195.

48. Hiestand and Morse, *Comparative Metropolitan Employment Complexes*, p. 74.

49. Matthew Drennan, "The Decline and Rise of the New York Economy," in *Dual City: Restructuring New York*, ed. John H. Mollenkopf and Manuel Castells (New York: Russell Sage Foundation, 1991), Table 1.4.

50. Ibid.

51. Hugh O'Neill and Mitchell L. Moss, *Reinventing New York* (New York: Urban Research Center, New York University, 1991), pp. 53–54.

52. Harrison and Bluestone, *The Great U-Turn;* Anthony P. Carnavale, *America and the New Economy* (Washington, D.C.: American Society for Training and Development, 1991).

53. *Time*, April 9, 1990; *New York Times*, March 22 and April 1, 1991.

54. New York City Department of City Planning, Population Division, "Components of Population Change by Race and Hispanic Origin or Descent: 1980–1990" (May 1991), Tables 1A–1E, 2, 2A–2E.

55. Bienstock, "New York City's Labor Market," p. 11. Illustrating the downward trend: by 1976 the employment-population ratio for all city residents, regardless of age, had descended to a historic low of 48 percent; ten years earlier it had been 55 percent (Samuel M. Ehrenhalt, *Looking to the 90's: Continuity and Change* [New York: Bureau of Labor Statistics, Middle Atlantic Region, 1987], p. 13, Table 6).

56. Netzer, "The Cloudy Prospects for the City's Economy," p. 30.

57. Samuel M. Ehrenhalt, "Insight and Outlook: The New York Experience as a Service Economy" (paper presented to the New York City Council on Economic Education, May 14, 1986), Table 27, p. 45.

58. Hiestand and Morse, *Comparative Metropolitan Employment Complexes*, p. 93.

59. Robert Wagner, Jr., comments at a roundtable discussion published in *Manhattan Report* 5, no. 4 (1985): 16.

60. Netzer, "The Cloudy Prospects for the City's Economy," p. 30.

61. Samuel M. Ehrenhalt, "New York City's Changing Role in the Regional Economy," in *Proceedings of the 18th Annual Institute of the New York City Council on Economic Education* (New York: Council on Economic Education, (May 1985), p. 4.

62. Walter Stafford, *Closed Labor Markets: The Underrepresentation of Blacks, Hispanics, and Women in New York's Core Industries* (New York: Community Service Society, 1985), pp. viii–x.

63. Some writers consider it erroneous to associate the mismatch with economic restructuring, either because most minorities were not concentrated in traditional manufacturing in the first place (Thomas Bailey and Roger Waldinger, "The Changing Ethnic/Racial Division of Labor," in Mollenkopf and Castells, *Dual City*,) or because the driving force behind falling participation rates among the young are rising school dropout rates (Daniel Chall, "New York City's 'Skills Mismatch,'" *Federal Reserve Board of New York Quarterly*, Spring 1985, pp. 20–26).

Chapter Three

1. Nathan Glazer and Daniel P. Moynihan, *Beyond the Melting Pot* (Cambridge, Mass.: MIT Press, 1963), pp. 299–300.

2. These tables rely on the principal indicators that can be derived from *published sources* for the period 1950–80. Other measures such as wage rates and labor earnings (explored in Chapter Four) were not available for each decennial year for African American and Puerto Rican workers.

3. An exception is found in the case of African American females, whose participation rate increased from 48 percent (1960) to 51 percent (1980).

4. This is the topic of Chapter Four.

5. Oscar Handlin, *The Newcomers: Negroes and Puerto Ricans in a Changing Metropolis* (New York: Anchor Press, 1959); Milton Gordon, *Assimilation in American Life* (New York: Oxford University Press, 1961); Daniel P. Moynihan, "Patterns of Ethnic Succession: Blacks and Hispanics in New York City," *Political Science Quarterly* 94 (Spring 1979): 1–14; Thomas Sowell, *Ethnic America* (New York: Basic Books, 1981).

6. Roi Ottley and William J. Weatherby, *The Negro in New York* (Dobbs Ferry, N.Y.: Oceania, 1967); Herman Block, *The Circle of Discrimination: An Economic and Social Study of the Black Man in New York* (New York: New York University Press, 1969).

7. Glazer and Moynihan, *Beyond the Melting Pot*, pp. 26–27; Ira Katznelson, *Black Men, White Cities* (London: Oxford University Press, 1973), p. 79.

8. Virginia Sánchez-Korrol, "The Survival of Puerto Rican Women in New York before World War II," in *The Puerto Rican Struggle: Essays on Survival in the U.S.*, ed. Clara E. Rodriguez, Virginia Sanchez-Korrol, and Jose Oscar Alers, (Maplewood, N.J.: Waterfront Press, 1984), pp. 47–57.

9. Joseph Fitzpatrick, *Puerto Rican Americans* (Engelwood Cliffs, N.J.: Prentice-Hall, 1971), p. 61.

10. U.S. Commission on Civil Rights, *Puerto Ricans in the Continental United States: An Uncertain Future* (Washington, D.C.: Government Printing Office, 1976), Table 8.

11. Katznelson, *Black Men, White Cities*, p. 78.

12. During Walker's incumbency (1917–29) the number of city jobs going to blacks rose from 247 to 2,275 (Sterling D. Spero and Abram L. Harris, *The Black Worker* [New York: Atheneum, 1974], p. 412).

13. Mark Naison, *Communists in Harlem during the Depression* (Urbana: University of Illinois Press, 1983), chap. 10.

14. Jervis Anderson, *This Was Harlem: 1900–1950* (New York: Farrar, Straus & Giroux, 1981), p. 244; Spero and Harris, *The Black Worker*, chap. 20; Naison, *Communists in Harlem*, p. 263.

15. Carlos Sanabria, "Patriotism and Class Conflict," *Latino Studies Journal*, Spring 1991; Altagracia Ortíz, "Puerto Rican Workers in the Garment Industry of New York City: 1920–1960," in *Labor Divided: Race and Ethnicity in U.S. Labor Struggles, 1935–1960*, ed. Robert Asher and Charles Stephenson (Albany: State University of New York Press, 1990).

16. Angelo Falcón cites a decline in political activism during the late 1940s and 1950s, attributing it in part to the imbalance between the size of the arriving population and the established community ("A History of Puerto Rican Politics in New York City," in *Puerto Rican Politics in Urban America*, ed. James Jennings and Monte Rivera [Westport, Conn.: Greenwood Press, 1984], p. 39).

17. Gilbert Osofsky, *Harlem: The Making of a Ghetto* (New York: Harper & Row, 1971), p. 177.

18. Glazer and Moynihan, *Beyond the Melting Pot*, p. 54.

19. José Sánchez, "Residual Work and Residual Shelter," in *Critical Perspectives on Housing*, ed. Rachel G. Bratt, Chester Hartmann, and Ann Meyerson (Philadelphia: Temple University Press, 1983), p. 217.

20. Terry J. Rosenberg and R. W. Lake found housing segregation to be greater among blacks than Puerto Ricans ("Toward a Racial Model of Residential Segregation and Succession: Puerto Ricans in N.Y.C., 1960–1970," *American Journal of Sociology* 81 [1976]: 1148). For a description of critical housing shortages during these years, see P. Jackson, "Paradoxes of Puerto Rican Segregation

in New York," in *Ethnic Segregation in Cities*, ed. C. Peach, V. Robinson, and S. Smith (London: Croom Helm, 1981).

21. See Ronald Calitri and Angelo Falcón, *Latino Voter Registration in New York City* (New York: Institute for Puerto Rican Policy, 1982), for a demographic analysis of fourteen voting districts with significant Puerto Rican populations; only five had Hispanic majorities. This study also points out that because of a younger median age and lower voter registration levels, the actual voting population was disproportionately low. As a veteran political analyst had remarked earlier, "Despite having some 300,000 registered voters, the Hispanic votes are scattered throughout the city, which diffuses their strength. . . . Hispanic voters are notorious for poor turnouts, often as low as 5%" (Frank Lombardi, "It's a Tough Town," *Daily News*, March 31, 1977, p. 62.

22. Fitzpatrick, *Puerto Rican Americans*, p. 57.

23. Glazer and Moynihan, *Beyond the Melting Pot*, p. 94.

24. Clara E. Rodríguez, *Puerto Ricans: Born in the U.S.A.* (Boston: Unwin Hyman, 1989), chap. 5.

25. Anderson, *This Was Harlem*, p. 252. See also Robert Weisbrot's *Father Divine* (Boston: Beacon Press, 1983), which details the life and times of the legendary religious leader (born George Baker), emphasizing his role as social activist.

26. Anderson, *This Was Harlem*, pp. 256, 258.

27. Glazer and Moynihan, *Beyond The Melting Pot*, p. 80.

28. Charles Green and Basil Wilson, *The Struggle for Black Empowerment in New York City* (New York: Praeger, 1989).

29. Ibid., p. 81.

30. "[The Church's] impact on the people, in guiding their lives and molding their ideas, and in serving as a vessel for their social life, is relatively small" (Glazer and Moynihan, *Beyond the Melting Pot*, p. 103).

31. For the Church's role in earlier immigrant communities, see, e.g., Richard M. Linkh, *American Catholicism and European Immigrants, 1900–1924* (Staten Island, N.Y.: Center for Migration Studies, 1975); and Silvano Tomasi, *Piety and Power: The Role of Italian Parishes in the New York Metropolitan Area (1889–1930)* (Staten Island, N.Y.: Center for Migration Studies, 1975). Antonio Stevens-Arroyo traces the internal contention over "pastoral" vs. "social action" philosophies, arguing that the Church failed to develop "ethnic catholicism" among Puerto Ricans ("Puerto Rican Struggles in the Catholic Church," in Rodríguez, Sánchez-Korrol, and Alers, *The Puerto Rican Struggle*).

32. On the rise of pentecostal groups, see Fitzpatrick, *Puerto Rican Americans*, pp. 127–29. Green and Wilson, *Struggle for Black Empowerment*, recounts the community activities of Protestant churches in the South Bronx (p. 80) and of Catholic involvement in the North Bronx (pp. 75–77), where African Americans and Latinos live.

33. For the impact of these institutions on black community development and on New York City, see Kenneth Clark, *Dark Ghetto* (New York: Harper & Row, 1965); Seth M. Scheiner, *Negro Mecca: A History of the Negro in New York City, 1865–1920* (New York: New York University Press, 1965); Ottley and Weatherby, *The Negro in New York.*

34. Ottley and Weatherby, *The Negro in New York,* p. 245.

35. See Richard E. Rubinstein and Robert M. Fogelson, *The Harlem Riot of 1935* (New York: Arno Press, 1969).

36. James Q. Wilson, *Negro Politics: A Search for Leadership* (Glencoe, Ill.: Free Press, 1960), pp. 98–99.

37. Puerto Rico, a Spanish colony until the Spanish-American War, was ceded to the United States (along with the Philippines and other smaller territories) in 1898. Made U.S. citizens in 1917, island residents remain ineligible to vote in presidential elections, although they are obliged to serve in the armed forces. Not until 1948 were Puerto Ricans allowed to elect a native governor. For the historical background, consult Raymond Carr, *Puerto Rico: A Colonial Experiment* (New York: Vintage Books, 1984); James Dietz, *Economic History of Puerto Rico: Institutionalist Change and Capitalist Development* (Princeton, N.J.: Princeton University Press, 1986); Loida Figuora, *History of Puerto Rico* (New York: Anaya, 1974); Arturo Morales Carrión, *Puerto Rico: A Political and Cultural History* (New York: Norton, 1983).

38. Fitzpatrick, *Puerto Rican Americans,* p. 64; James Jennings, *Puerto Rican Politics in New York City* (Washington, D.C.: University Press of America, 1977), pp. 75–85.

39. Jennings, *Puerto Rican Politics,* 76–77.

40. Oscar Lewis, *La Vida: A Puerto Rican Family in the Culture of Poverty* (New York: Random House, 1966), p. x.

41. Frank Bonilla and Ricardo Campos, "Ethnic Orbits: The Circulation of Capitals and Peoples," and "Exclusion from Work: Race, Ethnicity, and Sex in the Formation of U.S. Labor Reserves," both in Bonilla and Campos, *Industry and Idleness* (New York: Center for Puerto Rican Studies, 1986).

42. Jackson, "Paradoxes of Puerto Rican Segregation in New York," p. 117.

43. In 1969 only 29 percent of Puerto Ricans indicated that English was the language usually spoken at home, compared to 94 percent of the total U.S. population; 60 percent of Puerto Ricans twenty five years and over reported that they were able to read and write in English, compared to 94 percent for the total U.S. population (Kal Waghenheim, *A Survey of Puerto Ricans on the U.S. Mainland in the 1970's* [New York: Praeger, 1975], p. 87). A study by the National Commission for Employment Policy, *Hispanics and Jobs: Barriers to Progress* (Washington, D.C.: National Commission for Employment Policy, 1982), pp. 46–47, documented the occupational crowding of Hispanics.

44. Fitzpatrick, *Puerto Rican Americans,* p. 57.

45. Adalberto López, "The Puerto Rican Diaspora," in *The Puerto Ricans*, ed. Adalberto López (Cambridge, Mass.: Schenkman, 1980), p. 326; Handlin, *The Newcomers*, p. 118.

46. Fitzpatrick, *Puerto Rican Americans*, p. 58; Jennings and Rivera, *Puerto Rican Politics in Urban America*, pp. 3–4.

47. Steven Cohen and Robert E. Kapsis, "Participation Rates of Blacks, Puerto Ricans, and Whites in Voluntary Associations: A Test of Current Theories," *Social Forces* 56 (June 1978): 1051–71; Dale Nelson, "The Political Behavior of New York Puerto Ricans: Assimilation or Survival," in Rodríguez, Sánchez-Korrol, and Alers, *The Puerto Rican Struggle*.

48. P. K. Eisenger, "Black Employment in Municipal Jobs: The Impact of Black Political Power," *American Political Science Review*, June 1982.

49. Thomas R. Dye and James Renick, "Political Power and City Jobs: Determinants of Minority Employment," *Social Science Quarterly* 62 (September 1981): 484.

50. Block, *The Circle of Discrimination*, chap. 10, recounts various campaigns carried out during 1950–65.

51. Charles Abrams, "Recommendations and Report Summary," in *Discrimination and Low Incomes*, ed. Aaron Antonovsky and Lewis Lorwin (New York: New School for Social Research, 1959), p. 30.

52. New York City Commission on Human Rights, *The Ethnic Survey* (New York: Commission on Human Rights, 1964), p. 3.

53. Julian Ellison, "The New York Fiscal Crisis and Its Economic Impact on Minority Communities," *Review of Black Political Economy* 4 (Spring 1976): 339, Table 5.

54. Public unions had traditionally opposed reforms in personnel procedures that would have increased jobs for minorities. These reforms were pushed through finally in the late 1960s, by Mayor John Lindsay, who modified many regulations and opened the positions to greater numbers of African Americans and Puerto Ricans. (Martin Shefter, *Political Crisis, Fiscal Crisis* [New York: Basic Books, 1987], pp. 75, 90). Michael Oreskes points out the growing influence of minority leadership in the postal, health, and garment unions as well as the municipal labor sector ("Is It Still a Union Town?" *Dissent* 34, no. 4 [1987]: 490).

55. One such project, initiated by Lillian Roberts of District Council 37, created educational and training programs to improve career opportunities for union women; see Jewell Bellush, "Room at the Top: Black Women and District Council 37," *Dissent* 34, no. 4 (1987): 488–89.

56. A. Ortíz, "Puerto Rican Workers in the Garment Industry," p. 119.

57. "The holistic world view of black nationalism produced demands that in two respects were radically different from the usual articulation of urban issues. First, it did not respect traditional boundaries between issues. School, welfare, police and housing issues were treated together, as aspects of a total

condition. . . . Second, these policy areas were the objects of demands for a radical redistribution of resources and opportunities. . . . These demands could not be resolved at the urban level within the assumptions of the prevailing political economy" (Ira Katznelson, *City Trenches* [Chicago: University of Chicago Press, 1981], pp. 120–21).

58. The educational struggles are recounted in Diane Ravitch, *The Great School Wars: New York City, 1805–1973* (New York: Basic Books, 1974); and Marilyn Gittell, "Education: the Decentralization-Community Control Controversy," in *Race and Politics in New York City* ed. Jewell Bellush and Stephen M. David (New York: Praeger, 1971). The welfare movements are analyzed in Frances Fox Piven and Richard A. Cloward, *Poor People's Movements* (New York: Vintage, 1977). For a review of the community action programs, see Stephen M. David, "Welfare: The Community-Action Program Controversy," in Bellush and David, *Race and Politics in New York City*; Charles Morris, *The Cost of Good Intentions: New York City and the Liberal Experiment, 1960–1975* (New York: Norton, 1980); and Daniel P. Moynihan, *Maximum Feasible Misunderstanding* (New York: Free Press, 1969).

59. New York City Board of Education, *The Puerto Rican Study:* 1953–1957 (New York: Board of Education, 1958.

60. Isaura Santiago, *A Community's Struggle for Equal Opportunity: ASPIRA vs. Board of Education* (Princeton, N.J.: Educational Testing Service, 1978), p. 23.

61. Ibid., pp. 17, 19, 105.

62. Gittell, "Education," p. 160.

63. David, "Welfare," p. 29.

64. "Probably the most important contribution [of the antipoverty program] was simply the provision of jobs—middle class, civil service, white-collar jobs—for large numbers of blacks and Puerto Ricans, a service not unlike that performed for the Irish by an even crasser system of patronage a couple of generations earlier" (Morris, *The Cost of Good Intentions*, p. 66).

65. This term is from a clause in the legislation creating the Equal Opportunity Act, providing for direct involvement of community representatives at all levels of planning and administration of antipoverty programs. Each local jurisdiction was to determine the actual mechanisms by which such participation would be implemented (David, "Welfare," p. 30). See Moynihan, *Maximum Feasible Misunderstanding*, for a skeptical assessment of this program.

66. Morris, *The Cost of Good Intentions*, p. 65; David, "Welfare," p. 48.

67. David, "Welfare," pp. 52–53, citing several journalistic reports.

68. Luis Fuentes, "The Struggle for Local Political Control," in Rodríguez Sánchez-Korrol, and Alers, *The Puerto Rican Struggle for Survival*.

69. Green and Wilson, *The Struggle for Black Empowerment*, pp. 26–27. Jewell Bellush describes the interplay of class and racial rationales in the community's opposition to the plan; while acknowledging the undertone of racial prejudice, she points out that "arguments [against the plan] were generally phrased in

economic and class terms; that is, that public housing threatened property values and the community's economic and social stability" ("Housing: The Scattered-Site Controversy," in Bellush and David, *Race and Politics in New York City,* p. 124.)

70. Martin Kilson believes that unless ethnic political incorporation is strong (not weak) and stable (not cyclical), and maximizes intra-ethnic (black) and systemic (white) sources of political clout, it remains vulnerable and ineffective. He contends that as late as the mid-1980s black political incorporation had not attained these characteristics ("The Weakness of Black Politics," *Dissent* 34, no. 4 [1987]: 527).

71. Ibid., p. 524; Green and Wilson, *The Struggle for Black Empowerment,* p. 108.

72. Kilson, "The Weakness of Black Politics," pp. 527–28.

73. Angelo Falcón, *Black and Latino Politics in New York City* (New York: Institute for Puerto Rican Policy, 1985), pp. 8–9; Katznelson, *City Trenches,* pp. 171–72. Congressman Robert García noted that immigration issues were a major stumbling block to black acceptance of a Latino political agenda ("Hispanics Have to Work Closely with Blacks," *New York Times,* May 30, 1980).

74. Falcón, *Black and Latino Politics,* pp. 11–12; Institute for Puerto Rican Policy, Inc., *The Dinkins Administration and the Puerto Rican Community* (New York: Institute for Puerto Rican Policy, 1990).

75. Institute for Puerto Rican Policy, *Proceedings of a Conference on Black/Hispanic Dialogue* (New York: Institute for Puerto Rican Policy, 1990), p. 3.

76. Moynihan (*Maximum Feasible Misunderstanding,* p. 138) and David ("Welfare," p. 44) comment on interethnic conflict in the antipoverty programs; Katznelson (*City Trenches,* p. 171) describes the school board election process in Washington Heights; and the observation on the IS 201 case is made by Ravitch (*The Great School Wars,* p. 393).

77. Green and Wilson, *The Struggle for Black Empowerment,* pp. 105–6; Shefter, *Political Crisis, Fiscal Crisis,* pp. xv–xvi; Kilson, "The Weakness of Black Politics," pp. 528–29; *New York Times,* November 11, 1985.

78. Herbert Bienstock, "New York City's Labor Market: Past Trends, Current Traditions, Future Prospects," *City Almanac* 12, no. 4 (1977): 5.

79. Abraham Beame, *Economic Recovery: New York City's Program for 1977–1981* (New York: Department of City Planning, 1976), pp. 9–10.

80. U.S. Department of Labor, Bureau of Labor Statistics, *The Labor Force Experience of the Puerto Rican Worker* (Washington, D.C.: Government Printing Office, 1968), p. 14.

81. Lois Gray, "The Jobs Puerto Ricans Hold in New York City," *Monthly Labor Review* 98 (October 1975): Table 1.

82. Rosemary Santana-Cooney contends that Puerto Rican females have been especially vulnerable to structural change in New York, pointing to the fact that in other cities they have consistently shown much higher participation

rates ("Intercity Variations in Puerto Rican Female Participation," *Journal of Human Resources* 14 [Spring 1979]: 222–35. Other explanations for the low participation rates of Puerto Rican women have relied on cultural issues. According to one version, Hispanic culture and male chauvinist traditions ("machismo") encourage a purely household role for females. In another vein, some informal studies and anecdotal reports suggest that Latinas are particularly reluctant to transfer child-care duties to nonfamily members and thus resist the use of day-care facilities, especially where staff are not Hispanic. Presumably, a different set of customs and practices are operative in African American culture, but I am not aware of any study that analyzes comparative participation rates for African American and Puerto Rican women from this perspective.

83. Center for Puerto Rican Studies, *Characteristics of Persons, Families, and Households Living in New York City,* 1980 (New York: Center for Puerto Rican Studies, Hunter College, 1986), Table 16.

84. Bienstock, "New York City's Labor Market." A study by Raymond Horton disclosed that "Police Officers, a representative group because of the numerous horizontal and vertical pay relationships throughout the civil service, achieved real wage gains of 21.3 percent in the 1965–1976 period, an increase far in excess of any that were realized among private sector workers" ("People, Jobs, and Public Finance in New York City," *City Almanac* 12, no. 2 [1977]: 7).

85. Walter Stafford, *Racial, Ethnic, and Sexual Stratification and Affirmative Action Planning in New York City's Public and Private Sectors.* (Washington, D.C.: U.S. Commission on Civil Rights, 1983), p. 59.

Chapter Four

1. This chapter is a revised and expanded version of Andrés Torres, "Labor Market Segmentation: African American and Puerto Rican Labor in New York City, 1960–1980," *Review of Black Political Economy* 20 (Summer 1991): 59–77.

2. All references to sample data are taken from Andrés Torres, "Human Capital, Labor Market Segmentation and Inter-Minority Status" (Ph.D. diss., New School for Social Research, 1988).

3. Community Service Society, *Worlds Apart: Housing, Race/Ethnicity, and Income in New York City, 1978–87* (New York: Community Service Society, 1989); Community Service Society, *Poverty in New York City: 1980–1985* (New York: Community Service Society, 1987).

4. See Torres, "Labor Market Segmentation," pp. 67–68 and n. 20.

5. This not to deny that African Americans have benefited from rising returns to human capital, as the data show. Rather it is to say that, in comparative terms, their mobility was influenced positively by segmentation (i.e., there was an effective movement into primary jobs), while Puerto Rican mobility was

slowed down by segmentation; *at the same time,* both groups saw increasing returns to human capital.

6. It is fair to say, however, that the human capital tradition has accorded only slight importance to the political dimension in determining racial wage differentials. The primary concern was to examine the decision-making process that led to differences in marketable skills, paying only negligible attention to collective group behavior and agency in the political realm. (For a representative statement of this human capital approach, see James P. Smith and Finis R. Welch, "Racial Discrimination: A Human Capital Perspective," in *Labor Economics: Modern Views,* ed. William A. Darity [Boston: Kluwer-Nijhoff, 1984].) Furthermore, this interpretation of the results would not be consistent with the argument, made earlier, that the political factor was not so prominent within the Puerto Rican experience during the period examined.

Another explanation for the rising returns to human capital for Puerto Ricans would stress their rising English-language proficiency. Other results (reported in Torres, "Labor Market Segmentation") show that this variable attained significance for Puerto Rican males in 1970 and for Puerto Rican females in 1980. Also, the variables measuring language interaction with education and with labor force experience were both significant for Puerto Rican females in 1980. Greater English-language proficiency may have increased the quality of both education and experience for this group, thus helping to raise returns to human capital.

7. Barry Bluestone, "The Impact of Schooling and Industrial Restructuring on Recent Trends in Wage Inequality in the United States," *American Economic Review* 80, no. 2 (1990):304.

8. This issue was addressed by analyzing the explained variance in regression results. The approach used is to compare the percentage of explained variance accounted for by each vector of variables in each of the equations over time (see Torres, "Human Capital," chap. 6 and Table 54). These values are calculated from the results of the human capital earnings function taken on the six race/gender classifications (including white male and white female) of each decennial sample. The aggregate value for a given vector is calculated as the sum of changes in explanatory power (R^2) accounted for by all of the variables in that vector. The amount of each vector's contribution to the total R^2 is then expressed as the "percentage of explained variance" attributable to each vector.

9. Ibid., chap. 5 and Table 48, for complete reporting of results.

10. See ibid., pp. 207–17, for methodology and results.

11. William J. Wilson, *The Declining Significance of Race* (Chicago: University of Chicago Press, 1978).

12. The unexplained residual is that portion of the variation in the dependent variable (wages) that remains unaccounted for by the estimated regression equation. Other studies of wage differences have shown a similar decline in this

component for the period; see Leonard A. Carlson and Caroline Swartz, "The Earnings of Women and Ethnic Minorities, 1959–1979," *Industrial and Labor Relations Review* 41, no.4 (1988): 530–52.

13. David M. Gordon, Richard C. Edwards, and Michael Reich, *Segmented Work, Divided Workers* (Cambridge: Cambridge University Press, 1982); Sam Rosenberg, "From Segmentation to Flexibility: A Selective Survey," *Review of Radical Political Economics* 23, nos. 1–2 (1991).

14. Michael Wachter, "Primary and Secondary Labor Markets: A Critique of the Dual Approach," *Brookings Papers on Economic Activity* 3 (1974): 637–80. Glen Cain, "The Challenge of Segmented Labor Market Theories to Orthodox Theories: A Survey," *Journal of Economic Literature* 14 (December 1976): 1215–57; William T. Dickens and Kevin Lang, *Neoclassical and Sociological Perspectives on Segmented Labor Markets*, Working Paper no. 2127 (Cambridge, Mass.: National Bureau of Economic Research, 1987).

15. Paul Ryan, "Segmentation and the Internal Labor Market," in *The Dynamics of Labour Market Segmentation*, ed. Frank Williamson (London: Academic Press, 1981), p. 5.

16. Ryan, "Segmentation and the Internal Labor Market," p. 6.

17. Ryan (ibid., p. 11) describes a taxonomy of scenarios in which in-market segmentation is at least implied. Unfortunately, because of the interactions between in-market and pre-market segmentation, rigorous tests are not easily established; we would need to work with sample data in which comparable qualities of labor are distributed across segments. Under certain conditions, however, in-market segmentation is compatible with a finding of significant dispersion of pay for similar labor quality, when labor quality is measured by job requirements.

18. This inference is dependent on the extent to which these two groups of workers are generally equivalent in skill levels.

Chapter Five

1. Institute for Puerto Rican Policy, Inc., *The Puerto Rican and Latino Vote in the* 1984 New York State Democratic Presidential Primary (New York: Institute for Puerto Rican Policy, 1984).

2. A failed effort at black-Latino unity occurred during the New York City mayoralty race of 1985. The Coalition for a Just New York (CJNY), initiated primarily by black elected officials, tried to build an electoral slate that would depose Koch. When Basil Patterson, the generally preferred candidate, declined to run, Herman Badillo emerged as the most promising opponent to the incumbent mayor. But most African Americans in the coalition opposed turning leadership over to the Puerto Rican (some of them remembered that in 1977 Badillo had spoiled Percy Sutton's chances for election by declaring himself a candidate), and their decision now to nominate Herman D. Farrell, a state

assemblyman with little chance of defeating Koch, wrecked the coalition. Koch won the election in a landslide. See Martin Shefter, *Political Crisis, Fiscal Crisis* (New York: Basic Books, 1987), p. 186; and Charles Green and Basil Wilson, *The Struggle for Black Empowerment in New York City* (New York: Praeger, 1989), pp. 105–6.

3. In New York City, the campaign gained the endorsement from disparate quarters: Democratic Party figures such as John Conyers, David Dinkins, Enoch Williams, and Archie Spigner; dissidents within the regular Democratic machinery such as Al Vann and Roger Green; and nationalists and activists not usually associated with electoral politics, such as Alton C. Maddox, Herbert Daughtry, and Al Sharpton (Green and Wilson, *The Struggle for Black Empowerment*, p. 111).

4. The "Latinos for Jackson" coalition became a center of political insurgency within the Hispanic community and was revived in 1988. A key figure in this regard was then State Assemblyman José Serrano, who broke with Koch in 1985 when the mayor refused to endorse him for the borough presidency of the Bronx. Serrano joined City Councilman José Rivera, who had been an early supporter of Jackson. Michael Dukakis however, retained the support of Puerto Rican establishment figures, including Herman Badillo, Olga Mendez, and Ramon Velez.

5. In the 1988 primary, 93 percent of black voters supported Jackson (compared with 80 percent in 1984), along with 17 percent of whites (compared with 9 percent in 1984); see *New York Times*, April 21, 1988, p. D25.

6. Jack Newfield and Wayne Barrett, in *City for Sale* (New York: Harper & Row, 1988), detail the key episodes of these events, involving such well-known figures as Stanley Friedman, Meade Esposito, Donald Mannes, and Bess Myerson. For broader, analytical treatments of Koch's fall from power, see Asher Arian et al. *Changing New York City Politics* (New York: Routledge, 1991); and John H. Mollenkopf, *A Phoenix in the Ashes* (Princeton, N.J.: Princeton University Press, 1993).

7. As his close adviser Percy E. Sutton said of him, "David learned a long time ago, that as a black person you couldn't afford to get angry if you're going to exercise power" (quoted in Sam Roberts, "Mayor Dinkins: Every Day a Test," *New York Times Magazine*, April 7, 1991, p. 44).

8. Two other candidates shared the remaining 8 percent: Harrison Goldin and Richard Ravitch. Dinkins's primary victory was based on a 94 percent level of support from blacks and 56 percent from Latinos, according to estimates based on a CBS–*New York Times* exit poll taken on primary day, September 12, 1989 (cited in Arian et al., *Changing New York City Politics*, p. 230 n. 12). Note that Latinos actually gave less support to Dinkins than they gave Jackson (63 percent) in 1988.

9. Arian et al., *Changing New York City Politics*, pp. 109–12.

10. Ibid., p. 134.

11. Quoted in "Dinkins Ushers in History," *New York Newsday* p. 3.

12. "Mapping Out the New Mayor's Course," *New York Newsday,* December 22, 1989; "Dinkins Wanted an Unusual Group to Run His City, and Here It Is," *New York Times,* April 1, 1990.

13. As chairman of the Municipal Assistance Corporation (MAC), the financial watchdog agency established in the aftermath of the city's 1975 brush with bankruptcy, Rohatyn was the city's principal liaison with the financial markets that lend money to the municipal government.

14. This dichotomy was reproduced even within the inner circle. As his two chief deputy mayors, Dinkins named Norman Steisel and William Lynch. Steisel had been a commissioner during the Koch years and later an investment banker with ties to Rohatyn. Lynch had headed Dinkins's borough president staff and had been a key organizer for various Rainbow Coalition campaigns during the 1980s. The mayor made sure there would be little confusion over the chain of command: he named Steisel, representative par excellence of the status quo, first deputy mayor.

15. Richard Levine, "A New Mayor, Just in Time for the Hard Time after the Boom," *New York Times,* October 29, 1989, p. E5.

16. "Between 1986 and 1989 . . . four of the city's biggest sources of revenue were cut. First to fall was the personal income tax. To help out top rate payers, it was lowered from 4.3 to 3.4 per cent—it's 7 per cent in New Jersey—and the number of brackets was 'simplified.' The general corporation tax and utility sales taxes got shaved, too. And finally the city 'de-coupled' from federal tax law, allowing financial corporations to save an estimated $130 million since 1987" (Robert Fitch, "Mayor, the Sequel," *Village Voice,* July 31, 1990, p. 35).

17. Ibid., pp. 34–35. Specific proposals were contained in Arthur Cheliotes, *A Program for New York City Tax Reform* (New York: Communication Workers of America, Local 1180, 1991); City Project, *The AlterBudget Deficit Reduction and Investment Plan for New York City, Fiscal Year* 1992 (New York: City Project, 1990).

18. Quoted in Richard Levine, "Dinkins Faces the Painful: More Taxes," *New York Times,* November 2, 1990, p. B4.

19. Felix Rohatyn, "New York Can Be Made to Work," *New York Times,* November 2, 1990, p. B4.

20. Maggie Mahar, "Mr. Dinkins's Dilemma," *Barron's,* March 12, 1990, pp. 25–26; Levine, "Dinkins Faces the Painful," p. B1.

21. Quoted in Roberts, "Mayor Dinkins," p. 50.

22. Interview with Kenneth Clark in *Boston Globe,* May 31, 1993, p. 74.

23. This discussion is drawn from Andrés Torres and Frank Bonilla, "Decline within Decline," in *Latinos in a Changing U.S. Economy,* ed. Rebecca Morales and Frank Bonilla (Newbury Park, Calif.: Sage, 1993).

24. According to census statistics, there were 332,713 Dominicans living in New York City in 1990 (New York City Department of City Planning, "Total Population by Selected Hispanic Origin or Descent," July 1992).

25. Torres and Bonilla, "Decline Within Decline" pp. 94–98.

26. Roger Waldinger, *Through the Eye of the Needle: Immigrants and Enterprise in New York's Garment Trade* (New York: New York University Press, 1986); Sherri Grasmuck, "Immigration, Ethnic Stratification, and Native Working Class Discipline: Comparisons of Documented and Undocumented Dominicans," *International Migration Review* 18, no. 3 (1984).

27. Eugenia Georges, *New Immigrants and the Political Process: Dominicans in New York* (New York: Center for Latin American and Caribbean Studies, New York University, 1988); Manuel Gutierrez, "Desaliento y esperanza: La comunidad Dominicana en Manhattan," *Arieto* 1, no. 4 (1988); Guillermo Linares, "Dominicans in New York, " *Centro* 2, no. 5 (1989).

28. Silvio Torres-Saillant, "Dominicans as a New York Community: A Social Reappraisal," *Punto 7* 2, no. 1 (1989).

29. Gutierrez, "Desaliento y esperanza," p. 28.

30. Gutierrez (ibid.) echoes earlier studies of the Puerto Rican and other migrations in his comment that Dominicans exhibit a "transient mentality" regarding their position within U.S. society. With thoughts of returning to the Dominican Republic still very strong among community residents, commitment to U.S. political and social involvement remains tentative.

31. For my purposes, "West Indians" is defined as those persons who hail from the English-speaking Caribbean, although technically the West Indies encompasses all Caribbean islands, including Cuba, Puerto Rico, the Dominican Republic, Haiti, and several other former French and Dutch colonies. For further discussion of West Indian identity in the New York context, see Green and Wilson, *The Struggle for Black Empowerment;* and Philip Kasinitz, *Caribbean New York: Black Immigrants and the Politics of Race* (Ithaca, N.Y.: Cornell University Press, 1992).

32. This figure is calculated from an unpublished report issued by the New York City Planning Commission and cited in Betty Liu Ebron, "Trying to Make Sense of Census," *New York Daily News*, June 24, 1993, p. 8. The estimate is based on the number of non-Hispanic Caribbean blacks (389,000) as a proportion of African Americans (1,050,000) in New York City (1990 census). The total number of persons identified as black—of all national origins—was 2,088,000. Of these a large number, 345,000, did not respond to the question on national origin, making it impossible to know the true size of each ethnic group among black New Yorkers.

33. Nancy Foner, "The Jamaicans: Race and Ethnicity among Migrants in New York City," in *New Immigrants in New York*, ed. Nancy Foner (New York: Columbia University Press, 1987), p. 200; Kasinitz, *Caribbean New York*, chap. 3.

34. Thomas Morgan, "Caribbean Verve Brightens New York," *New York Times*, June 3, 1988, p. B1.

35. Commentary in defense of this view can be sampled in Thomas Sowell, *Ethnic America* (New York: Basic Books, 1981), pp. 219–20. See Green and

Wilson, *The Struggle for Black Empowerment*, pp. 123–24; Foner, "The Jamaicans," p. 215 n. 7; and Kasinitz, *Caribbean New York*, p. 93, for coverage of this controversy.

36. The historical record suggests that the experience of slavery was less pernicious for West Indians than for African Americans. Sowell, *Ethnic America*, summarizing comparative research on slave systems, points out that West Indian slaves were allocated *land* and *time* to farm for themselves. They were even permitted to sell surplus products. Meanwhile, U.S. slaves were issued food rations and divorced from any notion of property. Also, the British abolition of slavery (twenty-five years before the U.S. Emancipation Proclamation) followed a transitional period in which slaves were prepared for freedom.

37. "In general, the exploitative colonies of the West Indies and West Africa had substantial native black majorities and rather small white, European administration-entrepreneurial upper classes, so that whatever the form of white racism expressed by the latter, the former had their native communities and culture to draw upon and further were convinced that they could someday dominate the society" (Roy Bryce-LaPorte, "Black Immigrants: The Experience of Invisibility and Inequality," *Journal of Black Studies* 3, no.1 [1972]: 41.

38. The most important of several works is Calvin Holder, "The Rise of the West Indian Politicians in New York City," *Afro-Americans in New York Life and History* 4 (1980): 45–59.

39. For the early history of Chinese-Americans, see Benjamin Ringer, *"We, the People" and Others: Duality and America's Treatment of Its Racial Minorities* (New York: Tavistock, 1983); Rose Hum Lee, *The Chinese in the United States of America* (Hong Kong: Hong Kong University Press, 1960); Stanford Lyman, *Chinese Americans* (New York: Random House, 1974); Chinese Historical Society, *Chinese America: History and Perspectives* (San Francisco: Chinese Historical Society of America, 1987).

40. U.S. employers were permitted to recruit other Asians, and new immigration was stimulated from Japan, Korea, and the Philippines. Once here, those Asians too were subject to the discriminatory laws that had been designed for Chinese-Americans.

41. New York City Department of City Planning, 1990 Census, Summary Tape File *1A* (New York: Department of City Planning, 1993).

42. On Chinatown's economic transformation of the 1970s, see Peter Kwong, *The New Chinatown* (New York: Hill & Wang, 1987); Abeles, Schwartz, Haeckel and Silverblatt, Inc., *The Chinatown Garment Center Study* (New York, 1983); John Wang, "Behind the Boom: Power and Economics in Chinatown," *New York Affairs* 5, no. 3 (1979): 77–81.

43. Abeles, Schwartz, Haeckel and Silverblatt, *The Chinatown Garment Center Study*, p. 192.

44. Waldinger, *Through the Eye of the Needle*, p. 116.

45. Wang, "Behind the Boom," p. 81.

46. Sowell, *Ethnnic America*, chaps. 6–7; Robert Oxnam, "Why Asians Succeed Here," *New York Times Magazine*, September 30, 1986.

47. Setsuko Matsunaga Nishi, "The New Wave of Asian Americans," *New York Affairs* 5, no. 3 (1979): 83.

48. The U.S. gets the cream of the crop from the highly competitive Taiwanese educational system, where the ultimate sign of achievement is qualifying for study abroad. "Students in Taiwan are taught English beginning in junior high school and the system encourages them to specialize in fields needed in the American job market. The best students are pushed by teachers and parents into math, physics, or engineering, even if they are more talented and interested in literature or the social sciences. Taiwan tailors its curriculum to the American system, so that its graduates can easily adjust to American graduate schools. It trains its best students for 'export' " (Kwong, *The New Chinatown*, p. 61).

Chapter Six

1. Emmanuel Tobier, of New York University, quoted in Richard Levine, "Young Immigrant Wave Lifts New York Economy," *New York Times*, July 30, 1990, p. B4.

2. William Serrin, "After Years of Decline, Sweatshops Are Back," *New York Times*, October 12, 1983, p. A1.

3. Americo Badillo-Veiga, Josh DeWind, and Julia Preston, "Undocumented Immigrant Workers in New York City," *NACLA* 12, no. 6 (1979): 18.

4. Another troubling result is that "recent immigrant cohorts are much more likely to enter the welfare system than earlier cohorts . . . [and] the longer an immigrant household has resided in the United States, the more likely it is to receive welfare" (George J. Borjas and Stephen J. Trejo, "Immigrant Participation in the Welfare System," *Industrial and Labor Relations Review* 44, no. 2 [1991] 209–10.

5. Deborah Sontag, "Immigrants Forgoing Citizenship while Pursuing American Dream," *New York Times*, July 25, 1993.

6. Alejandro Portes and Min Zhou, "The New Second Generation: Segmented Assimilation and Its Variants among Post-1965 Immigrant Youth," *Annals of the American Academy of Political and Social Sciences* 122 (November 1993).

7. Eric Schmitt, "As the Suburbs Speak More Spanish, English Becomes a Cause," *New York Times*, February 26, 1989, p. 6.

8. Sarah Henry, "English Only: The Language of Discrimination," *Hispanic*, March 1990; James Crawford, *Bilingualism and the Politics of "English Only"* (New York: Addison-Wesley, 1992).

9. Special codes and vocabulary are used on job application forms to screen out less-preferred individuals. See Miguel Perez, "So, Job Barriers Were

Man-Made," *Daily News*, October 14, 1989; D. D. Guttenplan, "City, State Allege Bias at Jobs Firm," *Daily News*, February 21, 1990, p. 18.

10. New York City Commission on Human Rights, *Tarnishing the Golden Door* (New York: Commission on Human Rights, 1989).

11. Diane Ravitch, *The Great School Wars: New York City, 1805–1973* (New York: Basic Books, 1974).

12. Ira Katznelson, *City Trenches* (Chicago: University of Chicago Press, 1981), pp. 114–15.

13. N. R. Kleinfield, "Leader Presses Changes at CUNY, but Some See Threat to Its Mission," *New York Times*, July 7, 1992, p. A1.

14. A leaflet issued by students in the fall of 1990 displays the comprehensive scope of their analysis: "The United CUNY Federation (UCF) was organized this past Spring. However the struggle for open access and educational reform is much older and related to those struggles since the 1960s that have resulted in gains for CUNY. We believe that it is essential to keep the student struggle alive and ongoing against the city, the state and the financial interests that continue to attack our right to an education, and in the process are trying to descroy our future. . . . For 129 years CUNY was tuition free; only with the enrollment of those groups historically excluded from public education was tuition introduced, thus taking the teeth out of open access. . . . The UCF stands for and defends the rights of all students to a quality education that includes access for the multiplicity of cultures and ethnic groups that compose CUNY. The UCF upholds democratic process in decision making at all levels and is open to all CUNY students" (United CUNY Federation [UCF], "Statement of Purpose," Fall 1990).

15. Interview with a second-generation Puerto Rican woman in New York, quoted in David Vidal, "Study Shows Hispanic Residents in Favor of Bilingual Way of Life," *New York Times*, May 13, 1980.

16. New York City Department of City Planning, *Socioecoomic Profiles: A Portrait of New York City's Community Districts from the 1980 and 1990 Censuses of Population and Housing* (New York: Department of City Planning, 1993), p. 8. These data include immigrants of European origin as well.

17. The city's total population in 1990 stood at 7,322,564, of whom 1,217,515 were unnaturalized (but legal) residents (New York City Department of City Planning, *Socioeconomic Profiles*, p. 8). Adding 500,000 undocumented persons brings the proportion of noncitizens to 22 percent.

18. Felicity Barringer, "Ethnic Pride Confounds the Census," *New York Times*, May 9, 1993, p. E3.

19. The tendency of many Puerto Ricans—officials and lay public—to condone this downplaying of multiracial origins has induced critical commentary from scholars. See Samuel Betances, "The Prejudice of Having No Prejudice in Puerto Rico," *The Rican* (Winter 1972): 41–54; Frank Bonilla, "Beyond Survival: Porqué seguiremos siendo Puertorriqueños," in *The Intellectual Roots of Indepen-*

dence: An Anthology of Puerto Rican Political Essays, ed. Iris M. Zavala and Rafael Rodríguez (New York: Monthly Review Press, 1980); Palmira Ríos, "Black Latinos' Double Jeopardy," *New York Newsday*, October 25, 1991, p. 54.

20. Clara E. Rodríguez, *Puerto Ricans: Born in the U.S.A.* (Boston: Unwin Hyman, 1989), pp. 63–65.

21. Anemona Hartocollis, "Latinos Caught in a Color Bind," *New York Newsday*, November 18, 1991, p. 8.

22. Papo Colo, Puerto Rican art exhibitor, quoted in Hartocollis, "Latinos Caught in a Color Bind," p. 18.

23. A growing sense of a common Caribbean ancestry has also been noted. Although separated by geography and distinct histories, people from the various island nations are more likely to intermingle in the new environment. Nancy Foner reports that Jamaicans refer to themselves simultaneously as "Jamaican" and "West Indian" ("The Jamaicans: Race and Ethnicity among Migrants in New York City," in *New Immigrants in New York*, ed. Nancy Foner (New York: Columbia University Press, 1987), p. 211. Dr. Lemuel Stanislaus, a native of Grenada and a U.S. citizen for decades, agreed that a Pan-Caribbean solidarity was arising among New York immigrant groups. In an interview, the one-time Grenadan representative to the United Nations stated, "There never was much intercommunication among the island nations. . . . But here in New York City, we've been able to develop a strong Caribbean community" (quoted in Thomas Morgan, "Caribbean Verve Brightens New York," *New York Times*, June 3, 1988, p. B5).

24. Foner, "The Jamaicans," p. 205.

25. This was a 1982 election in the twenty-first senatorial district (Brooklyn). Marty Markowitz, a Jewish candidate, defeated Waldaba Stewart (West Indian) and Carl Andrews (African American). West Indian and African American operatives proved unable to agree on running a single candidate. According to Charles Green and Basil Wilson: "The inability of the incumbent African American politicians to share power with the Caribbean community was the critical factor in allowing Markowitz to win the seat" (*The Struggle for Black Empowerment in New York City* (New York: Praeger, 1989), p. 135.

26. Ibid., p. 132. This conclusion is based on two polls: one conducted by the Caribbean Research Center at Medgar Evers College of the City University of New York in 1987, and another by the Gallup organization in 1988.

27. Philip Kasinitz argues that the relation between race and ethnicity among black Caribbeans has passed through three phases: racial identity predominated through the 1970s, was subordinated through most of the next decade, and resumed prominence in the late 1980s (*Caribbean New York: Black Immigrants and the Politics of Race* [Ithaca, N.Y.: Cornell University Press, 1992], pp. 9–11; 251–55).

28. A sampling from the literature on Hispanics includes Douglas T. Gurak and Mary M. Kritz, "Hispanic Immigration to the Northeast in the 1970's,"

Migration Today 13, no. 2 (1985); Linda Chavez, *Out of the Barrio: Toward a New Politics of Hispanic Assimilation.* (New York: Basic Books, 1991); Rodolfo O. de la Garza et al., *Latino Voices: Mexican, Puerto Rican, and Cuban Perspectives* (Boulder, Colo.: Westview Press, 1992).

Chapter Seven

1. William J. Wilson, *The Truly Disadvantaged* (Chicago: University of Chicago Press, 1987), p. 12.

2. Oscar Lewis, *La Vida: A Puerto Rican Family in the Culture of Poverty* (New York: Random House, 1966); Oscar Lewis, "The Culture of Poverty," in *On Understanding Poverty,* ed. Daniel P. Moynihan (New York: Basic Books, 1968).

3. Ken Auletta, *The Underclass* (New York: Random House, 1982); Lawrence Mead, *Beyond Entitlement: The Social Obligations of Citizenship* (New York: Free Press, 1985); Charles Murray, *Losing Ground: American Social Policy, 1950–1980* (New York: Basic Books, 1984).

4. These activities and products are catalogued in William R. Prosser, "The Underclass: Assessing What We Have Learned," *Focus* 13, no. 2 (1991): 1–18; "Defining and Measuring the Underclass," *Focus* (Special Issue) 12, no. 1 (1989); and Isabel Sawhill, "Poverty in the U.S.: Why Is It So Persistent?" *Journal of Economic Literature* 26 (September 1988): 1073–1119.

5. Christopher Jencks, "What Is the Underclass and Is It Growing?" *Focus* 12, no. 1 (1989): 14.

6. Ibid., p. 25.

7. Michael Harrington, *The Other America: Poverty in the United States* (New York: Macmillan, 1962); Walter W. Stafford and Joyce Ladner, "Political Dimensions of the Underclass Concept," in *Sociology in America,* ed. Herbert J. Gans (Newbury Park, Calif.: Sage, 1990), p. 139.

8. Prosser, "The Underclass," p. 13.

9. Leslie Inniss and Joe R. Feagin, "The Black Underclass Ideology in Race Relations Analysis," *Social Justice* 16, no. 4 (1989); Mack Jones, "The Black Underclass as Systemic Phenomenon," in *Race, Politics, and Economic Development,* ed. James Jennings (New York: Verso, 1992); Stafford and Ladner, "Political Dimensions of the Underclass Concept"; Andrés Torres and Clara Rodríguez, "Latino Research and Policy: The Puerto Rican Case," in *Hispanics in the Labor Force: Issues and Policies* ed. Edwin Meléndez, Clara Rodríguez, and Janis Barry Figueroa (New York: Plenum Press, 1991).

10. Jason DeParle, "What to Call the Poorest Poor?" *New York Times,* August 26, 1990.

11. Wilson (*The Truly Disadvantaged,* chap. 1) cogently shows how ignoring the depth of inner-city poverty leads some to idealize ghetto life.

12. Robin Turner, "Los Angeles Riots Are a Warning, Americans Fear," *New York Times,* May 11, 1992, p. 1.

13. The case for letting market processes dictate allocation of resources is covered in any standard introduction to economic theory, usually with cautionary reminders about common instances of market failure and imperfections. Popular renditions of the conservative variant that precludes any but a minor role for government are George Gilder, *Wealth and Poverty* (New York: Basic Books, 1981); Milton and Rose Friedman, *Free to Choose* (New York: Harcourt Brace Jovanovich, 1990).

14. David Osbourne and Ted Gaebler, *Reinventing Government* (New York: Plume, 1993); E. S. Savas, "Considering Privatization," in *New York Unbound*, ed. Peter D. Salins (New York: Basil Blackwell, 1988).

15. Mark A. Willis, "New York's Renaissance," in Salins, *New York Unbound*.

16. John Chubb and Terry Moe, *Politics, Markets, and America's Schools* (Washington, D.C.: Brookings Institution, 1990).

17. Elizabeth Neuffer, "Cash-Hungry States Revamp Welfare," *Boston Globe*, July 2, 1992.

18. Phoebe H. Cottingham and David T. Ellwood, eds., *Welfare Policy for the 1990s* (Cambridge, Mass.: Harvard University Press, 1989); Theresa M. Hanafin, "Stubborn Welfare Rolls Spur Aid Alternatives," *Boston Globe*, June 21, 1992; "The Carrots and Stick of Welfare Reform," *The Economist*, March 13, 1993.

19. Gertrude Himmelfarb, *The Idea of Poverty* (New York: Random House, 1983); Michael B. Katz, *In the Shadow of the Poor House* (New York: Basic Books, 1986.

20. Christopher Jencks, *Rethinking Social Policy* (New York: Harper Collins, 1992), p. 204.

21. Such proposals are not to be confused with the version of communitarianism promulgated by Amitai Etzioni (and others), who feels that our society has shifted too far away from a concern with "responsibilities" by having privileged the principle of "rights." On one level, he appeals to a sense of unity: our society must instill a vision of sharing among all its participants, as if we were members of a common family. But for the poor and powerless, participation in this "social contract" is nonexistent, and calls for exercising greater responsibility ring hollow. As long as poverty limits the enjoyment of rights, the urging to assume greater duties will remain ineffective (*The Spirit of Community* [New York: Crown, 1993]).

22. Jacqueline Novogratz, *Hopeful Change: The Potential of Micro-Enterprise Programs as a Community Revitalization Intervention* (New York: Rockefeller Foundation, 1992).

23. A case study of Indiana's program found that only 15 percent of jobs went to inner-city residents; see Leslie Papke, *Tax Policy and Urban Development: Evidence from an Enterprise Zone Program* Working Paper no. 3945, (Cambridge, Mass.: National Bureau of Economic Research, 1992). Critics also claim that EZs essentially redistribute existing businesses among distressed areas without

creating a net addition to economic activity and jobs; see Mitchell Zuckoff, "Enterprise Areas Questioned as Agents of Change," *Boston Globe,* July 6, 1992.

24. In its original form, the idea of linkage was designed to offer local neighborhoods some of the benefits generated by development of the central business district (CBD) of a major city. Real estate developers and employers involved in office expansion were required to contribute to publicly monitored trust funds created for affordable housing, job training, and other "community benefits." The proposal here would extend the idea to enterprises receiving public subsidies for community enterprises.

25. Proprietary schools are private establishments providing specialized occupational training that is unaccredited by institutions of higher education. Commercial schools offering courses in clerical, secretarial, and computer skills or programs in electronic and other technical instruction are examples.

26. Recent studies have outlined the basic elements of a holistic plan for economic revival, one that presupposes a supportive role for inner cities. See Michael Albert and Robin Hahnel, *Looking Forward: Participatory Economics for the Twenty First Century* (Boston: South End Press, 1991); Samuel Bowles, David M. Gordon, and Thomas E. Weisskopf, *After the Wasteland: A Democratic Economics for the Year* 2000 (Armonk, N.Y.: M. E. Sharpe, 1990); Bennett Harrison and Barry Bluestone, *The Great U-Turn* (New York: Basic Books, 1988); Juliet B. Schor, *The Overworked American* (New York: Basic Books, 1992).

27. In formulating these ideas, I have benefited from participation in discussions sponsored by the Poverty and Race Research Action Council, a national network of researchers and advocates with headquarters in Washington, D.C.

28. One of the most fertile sources for the study of personal information, the Public Use Microdata Sample (PUMS) for 1990, was still unavailable to the public at the time of this writing.

Conclusion

1. Quoted in David Vidal, "Hispanic Newcomers in city Cling to Values of Homeland." *New York Times,* May 11, 1989, p. 42.

2. A sampling of recent works includes Derrick Bell, *Faces at the Bottom of the Well: The Permanence of Racism* (New York: Basic Books, 1992); Thomas Byrne Edsall and Mary D. Edsall, *Chain Reaction* (New York: Norton, 1992); Michael B. Katz, *The Undeserving Poor* (New York: Pantheon Books, 1989).

Appendix B

1. Jacob Mincer, *Schooling, Experience, and Earnings* (New York: National Bureau of Economic Research, 1974).

2. Ibid.; James D. Gwartney and James Long, "The Relative Earnings of Blacks and Other Minorities," *Industrial and Labor Relations Review* 31 (April):

336–46. Separate analyses (not reported here) were conducted using other dependent variables: hours worked per week (LNHOURS), weeks worked (LNWKSW), and annual income (LNINCOME1). Since the census does not report hourly wage directly, this variable is calculated from the hours, weeks, and income variables: wage rate = annual earnings/(hours worked × weeks worked). Thus regressions of the wage rate do not include the LNHOURS and LNWKSW expressions among the independent variables, as these latter terms are already factored into the LNWAGERT dependent variable. See Andrés Torres, "Human Capital, Labor Segmentation, and Inter-Minority Relative Status," (Ph.D. diss., New School for Social Research, 1988).

3. Geoffrey Carliner, "Returns to Education for Blacks, Anglos, and Five Spanish Groups," *Journal of Human Resources* 11 (Spring 1976): 172–84; Barry Chiswick, "An Analysis of the Earnings and Employment of Asian-American Men," *Journal of Labor Economics*, April 1983), 197–214.

4. Walter McManus, William Gould, and Finis Welch, "Earnings of Hispanic Men: The Role of English Language Proficiency," *Journal of Labor Economics* 1 (April 1983): 101–30.

5. Chiswick, "Analysis"; McManus, Gould, and Welch, "Earnings of Hispanic Men."

6. Barry Chiswick, "Sons of Immigrants: Are They at an Earnings Disadvantage?" *American Economic Review* 67 (February 1977): 376–80; George Borjas, "The Earnings of Male Hispanic Immigrants in the U.S.," *Industrial Labor Relations Review* 35 (April 1982): 343–53.

7. As U.S. citizens, Puerto Ricans are not counted among the foreign-born in census surveys.

8. McManus, Gould, and Welch, "Earnings of Hispanic Men."

9. Geoffrey Carliner, "Wages, Earnings, and Hours of First, Second, and Third Generation American Males," *Economic Inquiry* 18 (January 1980): 87–102.

10. David M. Gordon, "Procedures for Allocating Jobs into Labor Segments" (unpublished paper, New School for Social Research, 1986).

Appendix D

1. The approach used here is akin to that in Ronald L. Oaxaca, "Male-Female Wage Differentials in Urban Labor Markets," *International Economic Review* 14 (1973): 693–709, in which intergroup differences in earnings for a given year are decomposed and an analysis of the residual conducted. More precisely, the method used here decomposes the *intertemporal change in wage for each group separately*. It is drawn from David M. Gordon, "A Guide to Onerous Calculations" (unpublished paper, New School For Social Research, 1987). The calculations are based on the results of regressions taken on the wage equations of each decennial sample. The total value for a given vector is calculated as the sum of the change in explanatory power (R^2) accounted for by all the variables

in that vector. The amount of each vector's contribution to total R^2 is then expressed as the percentage of explained variance accounted for by each vector.

For example, in the case of Puerto Rican females during the 1960–70 period, changes in the level of human capital variables accounted for 15 percent of the increase ($0.4573) in the mean wage. Changes in the levels of *all* variables contributed 54 percent (15 + 23 + 16 percent) of the total increase in LN-WAGERT. These effects ere accompanied by the changes in regression coefficients which exerted both positive (human capital, segmentation) and negative (constant, demographic) effects, summing to 46 percent. Comparing the sum of percentage change by the two components, one can say that changing levels of independent variables had the dominant effect (54 percent) on the increase in LNWAGERT for Puerto Rican females during 1960–70.

The discussion in the text focuses on comparisons of human capital and segmentation variables, abstracting from the demographic variables.

2. Since this model is unable to test for the importance of changes in the *demand* for labor, the significance of the entered variables may be overestimated. For example, the rise in subordinate primary jobs for black women during 1960–70 may be due partially to shifts in labor demand from personal service to clerical and secretarial workers—traditionally female jobs that expanded significantly during this period. This would counter the notion that the political factor was the driving force behind changes in segment distribution.

3. Randall K. Filer, "Male-Female Wage Differences: The Importance of Compensating Differentials," *Industrial and Labor Relations Review* 38, no. 3 (1985): 426–37. The Public Use Microdata Sample (PUMS) used in this study (1980, 1970, 1960) does not provide information on working conditions or union status, measures that have been used in other attempts to estimate compensating payments. In a related effort, Janis Barry finds that women fail to receive compensating payments regardless of segment location; she attributes this pattern to gender inequality in bargaining power ("Women Production Workers: Low Pay and Hazardous Work," *American Economic Review, Papers and Proceedings* 75, no. 2 [1985]: 262–65).

4. Solomon W. Polacheck, "Occupational Self-Selection: A Human Capital Approach to Sex Differences in Occupational Structure," *Review of Economics and Statistics* 63, no. 1 (1981): 60–69.

5. To the best of my knowledge, there are no scholarly studies offering a comparative evaluation of union membership patterns among the two groups in the New York metropolitan area. There is a greater representation of African Americans than of Puerto Ricans within the unionized public sector (Walter Stafford, *Employment Segmentation in New York City Municipal Agencies* [New York: Community Service Society, 1990]). At the same time, Puerto Ricans are highly represented within manufacturing, hotel, restaurant, and building service industries in which unionization has been extensive. Surveys in the early

postwar period estimated that more than half of Puerto Rican workers belonged to unions (Edward González and Lois Gray, "Puerto Ricans, Politics, and Labor Activism," in *Puerto Rican Politics in Urban America,* ed. James Jennings and Monte Rivera [Westport, Conn.: Greenwood Press, 1984], pp. 117–27).

6. For detailed reporting of results, see Andrés Torres, "Labor Segmentation: African American and Puerto Rican Labor in New York City, 1960–1980," *Review of Black Political Economy* 20, no. 1 (1991): Table 4.

7. These interpretations abstract from the effects of demographic variables as well as the constant term.

BIBLIOGRAPHY

Abeles, Schwartz, Haekel and Silverblatt, Inc. *The Chinatown Garment Center Study*. New York, 1983.

Abrams, Charles. "Recommendations and Report Summary." In *Discrimination and Low Incomes*, ed. Aaron Antonovsky and Lewis Lorwin. New York: New School for Social Research, 1959.

Alba, Richard. *Ethnic Identity: The Transformation of White America*. New Haven, Conn.: Yale University Press, 1990.

———. *The Impact of Migration on New York State*. Albany: Center for Social and Demographic Analysis, State University of New York, 1984.

Albelda, Randy. "Nice Work If You Can Get It: Segmentation of White and Black Women Workers in the Post-War Period." *Review of Black Political Economy* 17 (Fall 1985): 72–86.

Albert, Michael, and Robin Hahnel. *Looking Forward: Participatory Economics for the Twenty-First Century*. Boston: South End Press, 1991.

Alcaly, Roger E., and David Mermelstein, eds. *The Fiscal Crisis of American Cities* New York: Vintage Books, 1977.

Anderson, Jervis. *This Was Harlem: 1900–1950*. New York: Farrar, Straus & Giroux, 1981.

Antonovsky, Aaron, and Lorwin, Lewis. *Discrimination and Low Incomes*. New York: New School For Social Research, 1959.

Arian, Asher, Arthur S. Goldberg, John H. Mollenkopf, and Edward T. Rogowsky. *Changing New York City Politics*. New York: Routledge, 1991.

Auletta, Ken. *The Underclass*. New York: Random House, 1982.

Badillo-Veiga, Americo, Josh DeWind, and Julie Preston. "Undocumented Immigrant Workers in New York City," *NACLA* 12, no. 6 (1979): 18.

Bailey, Robert W. *The Crisis Regime*. Albany: State University of New York Press, 1984.

Bailey, Thomas. "Black Employment Opportunities." in *Setting Municipal Priorities 1990*, ed. Charles Brecher and Raymond Horton. New York: New York University Press, 1989.

Bailey, Thomas, and Roger Waldinger. "The Changing Ethnic/Racial Division of Labor." In *Dual City: Restructuring New York,* ed. John H. Mollenkopf and Manuel Castells. New York: Russell Sage Foundation, 1991.

Bane, Mary Jo, and Paul A. Jargowsky. "Urban Poverty Areas: Basic Questions concerning Growth, Prevalence, and Dynamics." In *Urban Change and Poverty,* ed. Michael G. McGeary and Laurence E. Lynn, Jr. Washington, D.C.: Urban Institute Press, 1988.

Baron, Harold M. "Racial Domination in Advanced Capitalism: A Theory of Nationalism and Divisions in the Labor Market." In *Labor Market Segmentation,* ed. Richard C. Edwards, Michael Reich, and David M. Gordon. Lexington, Mass.: Heath, 1975.

———. "Racism Transformed: The Implications of the 1960's." *Review of Radical Political Economics* 17, no. 3 (1985): 10–33.

Barrera, Mario. *Race and Class in the Southwest.* Notre Dame, Ind.: Notre Dame University Press, 1979.

Barringer, Felicity. "Ethnic Pride Confounds the Census." *New York Times,* May 9, 1993, p. E3.

Barry, Janice. "Women Production Workers: Low Pay and Hazardous Work." *American Economic Review, Papers and Proceedings* 75, no. 2 (1985): 262–65.

Baver, Sherrie. "Puerto Rican Politics in New York City: Postwar II Period." In *Puerto Rican Politics in Urban America,* ed. James Jennings and Monte Rivera. Westport, Conn.: Greenwood Press, 1984.

Beame, Abraham. *Economic Recovery: New York City's Program for 1977–1981.* New York: Department of City Planning, 1976.

Beauregard, Robert A. *Economic Restructuring and Political Response.* New York: Sage, 1989.

Becker, Gary S. *Human Capital.* Chicago: University of Chicago Press, 1975.

Beechey, Veronica. "Women and Production: A Critical Analysis." In *Feminism and Materialism,* ed. Annette Kuhn and Ann Marie Wolpe. London: Routledge and Kegan Paul, 1978.

Bell, Derrick. *Faces at the Bottom of the Well: The Permanence of Racism.* New York: Basic Books, 1992.

Bellush, Jewell. "Housing: The Scattered Site Controversy." In *Race and Politics in New York City,* ed. Jewell Bellush and Stephen M. David. New York: Praeger, 1971.

———. "Room at the Top: Black Women and District Council 37." *Dissent* 34, no. 4 (1987): 488–89.

Bellush, Jewell, and Stephen M. David, eds. *Race and Politics in New York City.* New York: Praeger, 1971.

Betances, Samuel. "The Prejudice of Having No Prejudice in Puerto Rico". In *The Rican* 1 (Winter 1972): 41–54.

Bienstock, Herbert. "New York City's Labor Market: Past Trends, Current Conditions, Future Prospects." *City Almanac* 12, no. 4 (1977): 1–18.

Blaug, Mark. "The Empirical Status of Human Capital Theory: A Slightly

Jaundiced Survey." *Journal of Economic Literature* 14 (September 1976): 827–55.

Blauner, Robert. *Racial Oppression in America.* New York: Harper & Row, 1972.

Block, Herman. *The Circle of Discrimination: An Economic and Social Study of the Black Man in New York.* New York: New York University Press, 1969.

Bluestone, Barry. "The Impact of Schooling and Industrial Restructuring on Recent Trends in Wage Inequality in the United States." *American Economic Review* 80, no. 2 (1990): 304.

Bonacich, Edna. "Class Approaches to Ethnicity and Race." *Insurgent Sociologist* 10, no. 2 (1980): 9–23.

Bonilla, Frank. "Beyond Survival: Porqué seguiremos siendo Puertorriqueños." In *The Intellectual Roots of Independence: An Anthology of Puerto Rican Political Essays,* ed. Iris M. Zavala and Rafael Rodriquez. New York: Monthly Review Press, 1980.

Bonilla, Frank, and Ricardo Campos. "Ethnic Orbits: The Circulation of Capitals and Peoples." In *Industry and Idleness,* by Frank Bonilla and Ricardo Campos. New York: Center for Puerto Rican Studies, 1986.

———. "Evolving Patterns of Puerto Rican Migration." In *The Americas in the International Division of Labor,* ed. Steve Sanderson. Chicago: Holmes & Meier, 1985.

———. "Exclusion from Work: Race, Ethnicity, and Sex in the Formation of U.S. Labor Reserves." In *Industry and Idleness,* by Frank Bonilla and Ricardo Campos. New York: Center for Puerto Rican Studies, 1986.

———. "A Wealth of Poor: Puerto Ricans in the New Economic Order." *Daedulus* 110 (Spring 1981): 133–76.

Borjas, George. "The Earnings of Male Hispanic Immigrants in the U.S." *Industrial Labor Relations Review* 35 (April 1982): 343–53.

———. *Friends or Strangers? The Impact of Immigrants on the U.S. Economy.* New York: Basic Books, 1990.

Borjas, George, and Marta Tienda. *Hispanics in the U.S. Economy.* Orlando: Academic Press, 1985.

Borjas, George J., and Stephen J. Trejo. "Immigrant Participation in the Welfare System." *Industrial and Labor Relations Review* 44, no. 2 (1991): 195–211.

Boston, Thomas D. *Race, Class, and Conservatism.* Boston: Unwin Hyman, 1988.

Bowles, Samuel, and Herbert Gintis. "The Problem with Human Capital Theory: A Marxian Interpretation." *American Economic Review* 65 (May 1975): 74–82.

Bowles, Samuel, David M. Gordon, and Thomas E. Weisskopf. *After the Wasteland: A Democratic Economics for the Year 2000.* Armonk, N.Y.: M. E. Sharpe, 1990.

Brecher, Charles, and Raymond D. Horton, eds. *Setting Municipal Priorities 1990.* New York: New York University Press, 1989.

Brecher, Charles, and Emmanuel Tobier. *Economic and Demographic Trends in*

New York City: The Outlook for the Future. New York: Temporary Commission on City Finances, 1977.

Briggs, Vernon. *Chicanos and Rural Poverty*. Baltimore, Md.: Johns Hopkins University Press, 1973.

Bryce-LaPorte, Roy. "Black Immigrants: The Experience of Invisibility and Inequality." *Journal of Black Studies* 3, no. 1 (1972): 41.

Buchele, Robert. "Sex Discrimination and Labor Market Segmentation." In *The Dynamics of Labor Market Segmentation*, ed. Frank Williamson. Cambridge: Cambridge University Press, 1981.

Cabranes, José A. *Citizenship and the American Empire*. New Haven, Conn.: Yale University Press, 1979.

Cain, Glen. "The Challenge of Segmented Labor Market Theories to Orthodox Theory: A Survey." *Journal of Economic Literature* 14 (December 1976): 1215–57.

Calitri, Ronald, and Angelo Falcón. *Latino Voter Registration in New York City*. New York: Institute for Puerto Rican Policy, 1982.

Carliner, Geoffrey. "Returns to Education for Blacks, Anglos, and Five Spanish Groups." *Journal of Human Resources* 11 (Spring 1976): 172–84.

———. "Wages, Earnings, and Hours of First, Second, and Third Generation American Males." *Economic Inquiry* 18 (January 1980): 87–102.

Carlson, Leonard A., and Caroline Swartz. "The Earnings of Women and Ethnic Minorities, 1959–1979." *Industrial and Labor Relations Review* 41, no. 4 (1988): 530–52.

Carnavale, Anthony P. *America and the New Economy*. Washington, D.C.: American Society for Training and Development, 1991.

Carnoy, Martin, Hugh Daley, and Raul Hinojosa. "The Changing Economic Position of Hispanic and Black Americans in the U.S. Labor Market since 1959." Unpublished paper. Stanford University, Inter-University Program in Latino Research, 1989.

Carr, Raymond. *Puerto Rico: A Colonial Experiment*. New York: Vintage Books, 1984.

"The Carrots and Stick of Welfare Reform." *The Economist* 330 (March 13, 1993): 31–32.

Center for Puerto Rican Studies. *Characteristics of Persons, Families, and Households Living in New York City, 1980*. New York: Center for Puerto Rican Studies, Hunter College, 1986.

Chall, Daniel. "New York City's 'Skills Mismatch.'" *Federal Reserve Board of New York Quarterly*, Spring 1985, pp. 20–26.

Chavez, Linda. *Out of the Barrio: Toward a New Politics of Hispanic Assimilation*. New York: Basic Books, 1991.

Cheliotes, Arthur. *A Program for New York City Tax Reform*. New York: Communication Workers of America, Local 1180, 1991.

Chen, Hsiang-Shui. *Chinatown No More.* Ithaca, N.Y.: Cornell University Press, 1992.

Chenault, Lawrence. *Puerto Rican Migrant in New York City.* New York: Columbia University Press, 1938.

Chinese Historical Society. *Chinese America: History and Perspectives.* San Francisco: Chinese Historical Society of America, 1987.

Chiswick, Barry. "An Analysis of the Earnings and Employment of Asian-American Men." *Journal of Labor Economics* 1, no. 2 (1983): 197–214.

———. "The Effect of Americanization on the Earnings of Foreign-born Men." *Journal of Political Economy* 86, no. 5 (1978) 897–921.

———. *Income Inequality: Regional Analysis within a Human Capital Framework.* New York: National Bureau of Economic Research, 1974.

———. "Sons of Immigrants: Are They at an Earnings Disadvantage?" *American Economic Review* 67 (February 1977): 376–80.

Chubb, John, and Terry Moe. *Politics, Markets, and America's Schools.* Washington, D.C.: Brookings Institution, 1990.

City Project. *The AlterBudget Deficit Reduction and Investment Plan for New York City, Fiscal Year 1992.* New York: City Project, 1990.

Clark, Kenneth. *Dark Ghetto.* New York: Harper & Row, 1965.

Cohen, Robert B. "The New International Division of Labor, Multinational Corporations, and the Urban Hierarchy." In *Urbanization and Urban Planning in Capitalist Society,* ed. Michael Dear and Allen J. Scott, New York: Methuen, 1981.

Cohen, Steven, and Robert E. Kapsis. "Participation Rates of Blacks, Puerto Ricans, and Whites in Voluntary Associations: A Test of Current Theories." *Social Forces* 56 (June 1978): 1051–71.

Community Service Society. *Poverty in New York City: 1980–1985.* New York: Community Service Society, 1987.

———. *Worlds Apart: Housing, Race/Ethnicity, and Income in New York City, 1978–1987.* New York: Community Service Society, 1989.

Cordasco, Francesco, and Eugene Buchionne. *The Puerto Rican Experience.* Totawa, N.J.: Littlefield, Adams, 1975.

Cottingham, Phoebe H., and David T. Ellwood, eds. *Welfare Policy for the 1990's.* Cambridge, Mass.: Harvard University Press, 1989.

Cotton, Jeremiah. "A Comparative Analysis of Black-White and Mexican-American-White Male Wage differentials." *Review of Black Political Economy* 15 (Spring 1985): 51–69.

Crawford, James. *Bilingualism and the Politics of "English Only."* New York: Addison-Wesley, 1992.

Darity, William A. "The Human Capital Approach to Black-White Earnings Inequality: Some Unsettled Questions." *Journal of Human Resources* 17, no. 1 (1982): 72–93.

———. *Labor Economics: Modern Views.* Boston: Kluwer-Nijhoff, 1984.

Darity, William A., and Rhonda M. Williams. "Peddlers Forever? Culture, Competition, and Discrimination." *American Economic Review* 75 (May 1985): 256–61.

David, Stephen M., "Welfare: The Community-Action Program Controversy." In *Race and Politics in New York City*, ed. Jewell Bellush and Stephen M. David. New York: Praeger, 1971.

Dear, Michael, and Allen J. Scott. *Urbanization and Urban Planning in Capitalist Society.* New York: Methuen, 1981. "Defining and Measuring the Underclass." *Focus* (special issue) 12, no. 1 (1989).

de la Garza, Rodolfo O., F. Chris García, John A. García, and Angelo Falcón. *Latino Voices: Mexican, Puerto Rican, and Cuban Perspectives.* Boulder, Colo.: Westview Press, 1992.

DeParle, Jason. "What to Call the Poorest Poor?" *New York Times*, August 26, 1990.

Dickens, William T., and Kevin Lang. *Neoclassical and Sociological Perspectives on Segmented Labor Markets.* Working Paper no. 2127. Cambridge, Mass.: National Bureau of Economic Research, 1987.

———. "A Test of the Dual Labor Market." *American Economic Review* 75 (September 1985): 792–805.

Dietz, James. *Economic History of Puerto Rico: Institutional Change and Capitalist Development.* Princeton, N.J.: Princeton University Press, 1986.

Doeringer, Peter B., and Michael Piore. *Internal Labor Markets and Manpower Analysis.* Lexington, Mass.: Lexington Books, 1971.

Drennan, Matthew. "The Decline and Rise of New York's Economy." In *Dual City: Restructuring New York*, ed. John H. Mollenkopf and Manuel Castells. New York: Russell Sage Foundation, 1991.

Duncan, O., and B. Duncan. "A Methodological Analysis of Segregation Indices." *American Sociological Review* 20 (1955): 210–17.

Durbin, Elizabeth. "Public Assistance." In *Setting Municpal Priorities 1990*, ed. Charles Brecher and Raymond Horton. New York: New York University Press, 1989.

Dye, Thomas R., and James Resnick. "Political Power and City Jobs: Determinants of Minority Employment." *Social Science Quarterly*, September 1981.

Ebron, Betty Liu. "Trying to Make Sense of Census." *New York Daily News*, June 24, 1993, p. 8.

Edel, Matthew. "The New York Crisis as Economic History." In *The Fiscal Crisis of American Cities*, ed. Roger E. Alcaly and David Mermelstein. New York: Vintage Books, 1977.

Edsall, Thomas Byrne, and Mary D. Edsall. *Chain Reaction* New York: Norton, 1992.

Edwards, Richard C. *Contested Terrain* New York: Basic Books, 1979.

Edwards, Richard C., Michael Reich, and David M. Gordon. *Labor Market Segmentation*. Lexington, Mass.: Heath, 1975.

Ehrenhalt, Samuel M. "Changing Configurations in the Regional Labor Market." In *Proceedings of the 17th Annual Institute of the New York City Council on Economic Education*. New York: Council on Economic Education, 1984.

———. "Insight and Outlook: The New York City Economy as a Service Economy." Paper presented to the New York City Council on Economic Education, May 14, 1986.

———. *Looking to the 1990's: Continuity and Change*. New York: Bureau of Labor Statistics, Middle Atlantic Region, 1987.

———. "New York City's Changing Role in the Regional Economy." In *Proceedings of the 18th Annual Institute of the New York City Council on Economic Education*. New York: Council on Economic Education, 1985.

Eisenger, P. K. "Black Employment in Municipal Jobs: The Impact of Black Political Power." *American Political Science Review*, June 1982.

Ellison, Julian. "The New York City Fiscal Crisis and Its Economic Impact on Minority Communities." *Review of Black Political Economy* 4 (Spring 1976): 331–41.

Etzioni, Amitai. *The Spirit of Community*. New York: Crown, 1993.

Fabricant Lowell, Ruth. "Testing a Dual Labor Market Classification of Jobs." *Journal of Regional Science* 18, no. 1 (1978): 95–103.

Falcón, Angelo. *Black and Latino Politics in New York City*. New York: Institute for Puerto Rican Policy, 1985.

———. "A History of Puerto Rican Politics in New York City." In *Puerto Rican Politics in Urban America*, ed. James Jennings and Monte Rivera. Westport, Conn.: Greenwood Press, 1984.

Figueroa, Loida. *History of Puerto Rico*. New York: Anaya, 1974.

Filer, Randall. "Male-Female Wage Differentials: The Importance of Compensating Differentials." *Industrial and Labor Relations Review* 38, no. 3 (1985): 426–37.

Fitch, Robert. "Mayor, the Sequel." *Village Voice*, July 31, 1990, pp. 34–35.

Fitzpatrick, Joseph. *Puerto Rican Americans*. Englewood Cliffs, N.J.: Prentice-Hall, 1971.

Foner, Nancy. "The Jamaicans: Race and Ethnicity among Migrants in New York City." In *New Immigrants in New York*, ed. Nancy Foner. New York: Columbia University Press, 1987.

Franklin, Raymond S., and Solomon Resnick. *The Political Economy of Racism*. New York: Holt, Rinehart & Winston, 1973.

Frederickson, George. *White Supremacy*. New York: Oxford University Press, 1982.

Freedman, Marcia. "The Labor Market for Immigrants in New York City." *New York Affairs* 4 (1983): 94–111.

———. "Urban Labor Markets and Ethnicity: Segments and Shelters Reexamined." In *Urban Ethnicity in the U.S.,* ed. Lionel Maldonado and Joan Moore. Beverly Hills, Calif.: Sage, 1985.

Friedman, Milton, and Rose Friedman. *Free to Choose.* New York: Harcourt Brace Jovanovich, 1990.

Friedman, Samuel. "Structure, Process and the Labor Market." In *Labor Economics: Modern Views,* ed. William Darity. Boston: Kluwer-Nifkoff, 1984.

Frobel, Folker, Jurgen Heinrichs, and Otto Kreye. *The New International Division of Labor.* New York: Cambridge University Press, 1980.

Fuentes, Luis. "The Struggle for Local Political Control." In *The Puerto Rican Struggle for Survival,* ed. Clara E. Rodríguez, Virginia Sánchez-Korrol, and José Oscar Alers. Maplewood, N.J.: Waterfront Press, 1980.

Garcia, Mario. "Racial Dualism in the El Paso Labor Market: 1880–1920." *Aztlan,* Summer 1975, pp. 197–218.

García, Robert. "Hispanics Have to Work Closely with Blacks." *New York Times,* May 30, 1980.

Georges, Eugenia. *New Immigrants and the Political Process: Dominicans in New York.* Occasional Paper 45. New York: Center for Latin American and Caribbean Studies, New York University, 1984.

Gilbert, Neil. *Capitalism and the Welfare State.* New Haven, Conn.: Yale University Press, 1983.

Gilder, George. *Wealth and Poverty.* New York: Basic Books, 1981.

Gittell, Marilyn. "Education: The Decentralization–Community Control Controversy." In *Race and Politics in New York City,* ed. Jewell Bellush and Stephen M. David. New York: Praeger, 1971.

Glazer, Nathan. "The New New Yorkers." In *New York Unbound,* ed. Peter D. Salins. New York: Basil Blackwell, 1989.

Glazer, Nathan, and Daniel P. Moynihan. *Beyond the Melting Pot.* Cambridge, Mass.: MIT Press, 1963.

González, Edward, and Lois Gray. "Puerto Ricans, Politics, and Labor Activism," in *Puerto Rican Politics in Urban America,* ed. James Jennings and Monte Rivera, 117–27. Westport, Conn.: Greenwood Press, 1984.

Gordon, David M. "Procedures for Allocating Jobs into Labor Segments." Unpublished paper, New School for Social Research, 1986.

———. *The Working Poor: Towards a State Agenda.* Washington D.C.: Council of State Planning Agencies, 1979.

Gordon, David M., Richard C. Edwards, and Michael Reich. *Segmented Work, Divided Workers.* Cambridge: Cambridge University Press, 1982.

Gordon, Milton. *Assimilation in American Life.* New York: Oxford University Press, 1961.

Grasmuck, Sherri. "Immigration, Ethnic Stratification, and Native Working Class Discipline: Comparisons of Documented and Undocumented Dominicans." *International Migration Review* 18, no. 3 (1984): 692–713.

Gray, Lois. "The Jobs Puerto Ricans Hold in New York City." *Monthly Labor Review* 98 (October 1975): 12–16.

Green, Charles, and Basil Wilson. *The Struggle for Black Empowerment in New York City.* New York: Praeger, 1989.

Gurak, Douglas T., and Mary M. Kritz. "Hispanic Immigration to the Northeast in the 1970's." *Migration Today* 13, no. 2 (1985): 6–12.

Gutierrez, Manuel. "Desaliento y esperanza: La comunidad Dominicana en Manhattan." *Areito* 1, no. 4 (1988).

Guttenplan, D. D. "City, State Allege Bias at Jobs Firm." *New York Daily News,* February 21, 1990, p. 18.

Gwartney, James D., and James Long. "The Relative Earnings of Blacks and Other Minorities." *Industrial and Labor Relations Review* 31 (April 1978): 336–46.

Hanafin, Theresa M. "Stubborn Welfare Rolls Spur Aid Alternatives." *Boston Globe,* June 21, 1992, pp. 1, 18.

Handlin, Oscar. *The Newcomers: Negroes and Puerto Ricans in a Changing Metropolis.* New York: Anchor Press, 1959.

Harrington, Michael. *The Other America: Poverty in the United States.* New York: Macmillan, 1962.

Harrison, Bennett, and Barry Bluestone. *The Great U-Turn.* New York: Basic Books, 1988.

Harrison, Bennett, and A. Sum. "The Theory of Dual or Segmented Labor Markets." *Journal of Economic Issues* 13 (1979): 687–706.

Hartocollis, Anemona. "Latinos Caught in a Color Bind." Interview with Papo Colo. *New York Newsday,* November 18, 1991, pp. 8, 25.

Heilbrun, James. *Urban Economics and Public Policy.* New York: St. Martin's Press, 1974.

Henry, Sarah. "English Only: The Language of Discrimination." *Hispanic,* March 1990, pp. 28–32.

Henry, William A., III. "Beyond the Melting Pot," *Time* 135 no. 15 (1990): 28–31.

Hiestand, Dale L., and Dean W. Morse. *Comparative Metropolitan Employment Complexes.* Montclair, N.J.: Allanheld Osmun, 1979.

Hill, Richard C. "State Capitalism and the Urban Fiscal Crisis in the U.S." *International Journal of Urban and Regional Research* 1 (1977): 37–43.

Himmelfarb, Gertrude. *The Idea of Poverty.* New York: Random House, 1983.

History and Migration Task Force, Centro de Estudios Puertorriqueños, ed. *Labor Migration under Capitalism.* New York: Monthly Review Press, 1979.

Holder, Calvin. "The Rise of the West Indian Politicians in New York City." *Afro-Americans in New York Life and History* 4 (1980): 45–59.

Horton, Raymond. "People, Jobs, and Public Finance in New York City." *City Almanac* 12, no. 2 (1977): 1–12.

Inniss, Leslie, and Joe R. Feagin. "The Black Underclass Ideology in Race Relations Analysis." *Social Justice* 16, no. 4 (1989): 13–34.

Institute for Puerto Rican Policy, Inc. *The Dinkins Administration and the Puerto Rican Community*. New York: Institute for Puerto Rican Policy, 1990.

———. *Proceedings of a Conference on Black/Hispanic Dialogue*. New York: Institute for Puerto Rican Policy, 1990.

———. *The Puerto Rican and Latino Vote in the 1984 New York State Democratic Presidential Primary*. New York: Institute for Puerto Rican Policy, 1984.

Jackson, Philip. "Paradoxes of Puerto Rican Segregation in New York." In *Ethnic Segregation in Cities*, ed. C. Peach, V. Robinson, and S. Smith. London: Croom Helm, 1981.

Jencks, Christopher. *Rethinking Social Policy*. New York: Harper Collins, 1992.

———. "What Is the Underclass and Is It Growing?" *Focus* 12, no. 1 (1989): 14–25.

Jennings, James. *Puerto Rican Politics in New York City*. Washington, D.C.: University Press of America, 1977.

Jennings, James, and Monte Rivera, eds. *Puerto Rican Politics in Urban America*. Westport, Conn.: Greenwood Press, 1984.

Jones, Mack. "The Black Underclass as Systemic Phenomenon." In *Race, Politics, and Economic Development*, ed. James Jennings. New York: Verso, 1992.

Jordan, Winthrop D. *White over Black: American Attitudes toward the Negro, 1550–1812*. 1968; New York: Norton, 1977.

Kantrowitz, Nathan, and Donnell M. Pappenfort. *Social Statistics for Metropolitan New York: 1960 Factbook for the New York-Northeastern New Jersey Standard Consolidated Area*. New York: New York University Graduate School of Social Work, 1966.

Kasinitz, Philip. *Caribbean New York: Black Immigrants and the Politics of Race*. Ithaca, N.Y.: Cornell University Press, 1992.

Katz, Michael. *In the Shadow of the Poor House*. New York: Basic Books, 1986.

———. *The Undeserving Poor*. New York: Pantheon Press, 1988.

Katznelson, Ira. *Black Men, White Cities*. London: Oxford University Press, 1973.

———. *City Trenches*. Chicago: University of Chicago Press, 1981.

Kilson, Martin. "The Weakness of Black Politics." *Dissent* 34, no. 4 (1987): 523–29.

Kleinfield, N. R. "Leader Presses Changes at CUNY, but Some See Threat to Its Mission." *New York Times*, July 7, 1992, p. A1.

Kotz, David M. *Bank Control of Large Corporations in the United States*. Berkeley: University of California Press, 1978.

Kwong, Peter. *The New Chinatown*. New York: Hill & Wang, 1987.

Lee, Rose Hum. *The Chinese in the United States of America*. Hong Kong: Hong Kong University Press, 1960.

Lever-Tracy, Constance. "The Paradigm Crisis of Dualism: Decay or Regeneration." *Politics and Society* 13, no. 1 (1984): 59–89.

Levine, Richard. "Dinkins Faces the Painful: More Taxes." *New York Times*, November 2, 1990, pp. B1, B4.

———. "A New Mayor, Just in Time for the Hard Time after the Boom." *New York Times*, October 29, 1989, p. E5.

———. "Young Immigrant Wave Lifts New York Economy." *New York Times*, July 30, 1990, p. B4.

Lewis, Oscar. "The Culture of Poverty." In *On Understanding Poverty*, ed. Daniel P. Moynihan. New York: Basic Books, 1968.

———. *La Vida: A Puerto Rican Family in the Culture of Poverty*. New York: Random House, 1966.

Linares, Guillermo. "Dominicans in New York." *Centro* 2, no. 5 (1989): 77–84.

Linkh, Richard M. *American Catholicism and European Immigrants, 1900–1924*. Staten Island, N.Y.: Center for Migration Studies, 1975.

López, Adalberto. "The Puerto Rican Diaspora." In *The Puerto Ricans*, ed. Adalberto López. Cambridge, Mass.: Schenkman, 1980.

Lyman, Stanford. *Chinese Americans*. New York: Random House, 1974.

McGowan, Brenda, and Elaine Walsh. "Services to Chıldren." In *Setting Municipal Prioritites 1990*, ed. Charles Brecher and Raymond D. Horton. New York: New York University Press, 1989.

McManus, Walter, William Gould, and Finis Welch. "Earnings of Hispanic Men: The Role of English Language Proficiency." *Journal of Labor Economics* 1 (April 1983): 101–30.

McWilliams, Carey. *North from Mexico*. New York: Greenwood Press, 1968.

Mahar, Maggie. "Mr. Dinkins's Dilemma." *Barron's*, March 12, 1990, pp. 6–28.

Maldonado, Rita. "Why Puerto Ricans Migrated to the United States in 1947–1973." *Monthly Labor Review* 99 (September 1976): 7–18.

Mann, Evelyn S., and Joseph J. Salvo. "Characteristics of New Hispanic Immigrants to New York City: A Comparison of Puerto Rican and Non-Puerto Rican Hispanics." Unpublished paper, New York City Department of City Planning, 1984.

Mann, Seymour Z., and Handman, Edward. "The Role of Municipal Unions." *City Almanac* 12, no. 1 (1977).

Masters, Stanley. *Black-White Income Differentials*. New York: Academic Press, 1975.

Mead, Lawrence. *Beyond Entitlement: The Social Obligations of Citizenship*. New York: Free Press, 1985.

Meléndez, Edgardo. *Puerto Rico's Statehood Movement*. Westport, Conn.: Greenwood Press, 1988.

Meléndez, Edwin. *Labor Market Structure and Wage Inequality in New York City: A Comparative Analysis of Hispanics, Non-Hispanic Blacks, and Whites*. Cambridge, Mass.: MIT Department of Urban Studies and Planning, 1988.

Mincer, Jacob. "The Distribution of Labor Incomes: A Survey." *Journal of Economic Literature* 8 (March 1970): 1–26.

———. *Schooling, Experience, and Earnings*. New York: National Bureau of Economic Research, 1974.

Mollenkopf, John H. *The Contested City.* Princeton, N.J.: Princeton University Press, 1983.

———. *A Phoenix in the Ashes.* Princeton, N.J.: Princeton University Press, 1993.

———. *The Wagner Atlas: New York City Politics 1989.* New York: Robert F. Wagner, Sr., Institute of Urban Public Policy, City University of New York Graduate School and University Center, 1989.

Mollenkopf, John H., and Manuel Castells, eds. *Dual City: Restructuring New York.* New York: Russell Sage Foundation, 1991.

Morales, Rebecca, and Frank Bonilla, eds. *Latinos in a Changing U.S. Economy.* Newbury Park, Calif.: Sage, 1993.

Morales Carrión, Arturo. *Puerto Rico: A Political and Cultural History.* New York: Norton, 1983.

Morgan, Thomas. "Caribbean Verve Brightens New York." *New York Times,* June 3, 1988, pp. B1, B5.

Morris, Charles. *The Cost of Good Intentions: New York City and the Liberal Experiment, 1960–1975.* New York: Norton, 1980.

Moynihan, Daniel P. *Maximum Feasible Misunderstanding.* New York: Free Press, 1969.

———. "Patterns of Ethnic Succession: Blacks and Hispanics in New York City." *Political Science Quarterly* 94 (Spring 1979): 1–14.

Murray, Charles. *Losing Ground: American Social Policy, 1950–1980.* New York: Basic Books, 1984.

Naison, Mark. *Communists in Harlem during the Depression.* Urbana: University of Illinois Press, 1983.

Nakano-Glenn, Evelyn. "Racial Ethnic Women's Labor: The Intersection of Race, Gender, and Class Oppression." *Review of Radical Political Economy* 17 (Fall 1985): 86–108.

National Commission for Employment Policy. *Hispanics and Jobs: Barriers to Progress.* Washington D.C.: National Commission for Employment Policy, 1982.

Nelson, Dale. "The Political Behavior of New York Puerto Ricans: Assimilation or Survival." In *The Puerto Rican Struggle,* ed. Clara Rodríguez, Virginia Sánchez-Korrol, and José Oscar Alers. Maplewood, N.J.: Waterfront Press, 1984.

Netzer, Dick. "The Cloudy Prospects for the City's Economy." *New York Affairs* 1, no. 4 (1974): 22–35.

———. "New York's Mixed Economy: Ten Years Later." *Public Interest* 16 (Summer 1969): 188–202.

Neuffer, Elizabeth. "Cash-Hungry States Revamp Welfare." *Boston Globe,* July 2, 1992, pp. 1, 17.

Newfield, Jack, and Wayne Barrett. *City for Sale.* New York: Harper & Row, 1988.

New York City Board of Education. *The Puerto Rican Study: 1953–1957*. New York: Board of Education, 1958.

New York City Bureau of Labor Statistics. *Perspectives on Minorities in the N.Y.C. Resident Labor Force*. New York: Bureau of Labor Statistics, 1987.

New York City Commission on Human Rights. *The Ethnic Survey*. New York: Commission on Human Rights, 1964.

———. *Tarnishing the Golden Door*. New York: Commission on Human Rights, 1989.

New York City Department of City Planning. "Components of Population Change by Race and Hispanic Origin or Descent, 1980–1990." Population Division, unpublished report, May 1991.

———. *1990 Census, Summary Tape File 1A*. New York: Department of City Planning, 1993.

———. *The Puerto Rican New Yorkers*. New York: Department of City Planning, 1985.

———. *Socioeconomic Profiles: A Portrait of New York City's Community Districts from the 1980 and 1990 Censuses of Population and Housing*. New York: Department of City Planning, 1993.

———. "Total Population by Selected Hispanic Orgin or Descent." Unpublished report, July 1992.

New York City Human Resources Agency. *Dependency: Economic and Social Data for New York City*. New York: Human Resources Administration, 1988.

New York City Temporary Commission on City Finances. *The City in Transition: Prospects and Policies for New York*. New York: Temporary Commission on City Finances, 1977.

Niemi, Albert M., Jr. "Wage Discrimination against Negroes and Puerto Ricans in the New York SMSA: An Assessment of Educational and Occupational Differences." *Social Science Quarterly* 55 (June 1974): 112–20.

Nishi, Setsuko Matsunaga. "The New Wave of Asian Americans." *New York Affairs* 5, no. 3 (1979): 82–97.

Novogratz, Jacqueline. *Hopeful Change: The Potential of Micro-Enterprise Programs as a Community Revitalization Intervention*. New York: Rockefeller Foundation, 1992.

Noyelle, Thierry. "New York's Competitiveness." In *New York's Financial Markets*, ed. Thierry Noyelle. Boulder, Colo.: Westview Press, 1989.

Oaxaca, Ronald L. "Male-Female Wage Differentials in Urban Labor Markets." *International Economic Review* 14 (October 1973): 693–709.

Omi, Michael, and Howard Winant, eds. *Racial Formation in the United States*. New York: Routledge, 1986.

O'Neill, Hugh, and Mitchell L. Moss. *Reinventing New York*. New York: Urban Research Center, New York University, 1991.

Oreskes, Michael. "Is It Still a Union Town?" *Dissent* 34, no. 4 (1987): 486–91.

Ortíz, Altagracia. "Puerto Rican Workers in the Garment Industry of New York City, 1920–1960." In *Labor Divided: Race and Ethnicity in U.S. Labor Struggles, 1835–1960,* ed. Robert Asher and Charles Stephenson. Albany: State University of New York Press, 1990.

Ortiz, Vilma. "Changes in the Characteristics of Puerto Rican Migrants, from 1955–1980." *International Migration Review* 20 (Fall 1986): 612–28.

Osbourne, David, and Ted Gaebler. *Reinventing Government.* New York: Plume, 1993.

Osofsky, Gilbert. *Harlem: The Making of a Ghetto.* New York: Harper & Row, 1971.

Osterman, Paul. "An Empirical Study of Labor Market Segmentation." *Industrial and Labor Relations Review* 28 (July 1975): 508–22.

Ottley, Roi, and Weatherby, William J. *The Negro in New York.* Dobbs Ferry, N.Y.: Oceania, 1967.

Oxnam, Robert. "Why Asians Succeed Here." *New York Times Magazine,* September 30, 1986.

Papke, Leslie. *Tax Policy and Urban Development: Evidence from an Enterpise Zone Program.* Working Paper no. 3945. Cambridge, Mass.: National Bureau of Economic Research.

Pérez-Stable, Marifel, and Miren Uriarte. "Cubans and the Changing of Miami." In *Latinos in a Changing U.S. Economy,* ed. Rebecca Morales and Frank Bonilla. Newbury Park, Calif.: Sage, 1993.

Peterson, Paul E. *City Limits.* Chicago: University of Chicago Press, 1981.

Piore, Michael J. "Notes for a Theory of Labor Market Stratification." In *Labor Market Segmentation,* ed. Richard C. Edwards, Michael Reich, and David M. Gordon. Lexington, Mass.: Heath, 1975.

———. "The Technological Foundations of Dualism." In *Dualism and Discontinuity in Industrial Societies,* ed. Suzanne Berger and Michael J. Piore, New York: Cambridge University Press, 1980.

Piore, Michael J., and Charles F. Sabel. *The Second Industrial Divide: Possibilities for Prosperity.* New York: Basic Books, 1984.

Piven, Frances Fox. "The Fiscal Crisis: Who Got What and Why." In *The Fiscal Crisis of American Cities,* ed. Roger Alcaly and David Mermelstein. New York: Vintage Books, 1977.

Piven, Frances Fox, and Richard A. Cloward. *Poor People's Movements.* New York: Vintage, 1977.

———. *Regulating the Poor.* New York: Vintage, 1971.

Polocheck, Solomon W. "Occupational Self-Selection: A Human Capital Approach to Sex Differences in Occupational Structure." *Review of Economics and Statistics* 63, no. 1 (1981): 60–69.

Port Authority of New York and New Jersey. *Comprehensive Annual Financial Report.* New York: Port Authority of New York and New Jersey, 1987.

———. *Demographic Trends—Income Distribution and Poverty.* New York: Port Authority of New York and New Jersey, 1994.

———. *Report.* New York: Port Authority of New York and New Jersey, 1980, 1984, 1992.

Portes, Alejandro. "Modes of Structural Incorporation and Present Theories of Labor Immigration." In *Global Trends in Migration,* ed. Mary Kritz, Charles B. Keeley, and Silvano M. Tomasi. New York: Center for Migration Studies, 1981.

Portes, Alejandro, and Min Zhou. "The New Second Generation: Segmented Assimilation and Its Variants among Post-1965 Immigrant Youth." *Annals of the American Academy of Political and Social Sciences* 98 (November 1993).

Poston, Dudley. "The Economic Attainment Patterns of Foreign-Born Cubans, Mexicans, and Puerto Ricans, and Other Foreign-born Workers in the U.S." Unpublished paper, Department of Rural Sociology, Cornell University, 1989.

Prosser, William R. "The Underclass: Assessing What We Have Learned." *Focus* 13, no. 2 (1991): 1–18.

Ravitch, Diane. *The Great School Wars: New York City, 1805–1973,* New York: Basic Books, 1974.

Rebitzer, James B. "Radical Political Economy and the Economics of Labor Markets." *Journal of Economic Literature* 31 (September 1993): 1394–1434.

Reed, Adolph. *The Jesse Jackson Phenomenon: The Crisis of Purpose in Afro-American Politics.* New Haven, Conn.: Yale University Press, 1986.

Regional Plan Association. *The Growing Latino Presence in the Tri-State Region.* New York: Regional Plan Association, 1988.

———. *Metropolis in the Making.* New York: Regional Plan Association, 1955.

———. *Outlook for the Tri-State Region through 2000.* New York: Regional Plan Association, 1986.

Reich, Michael. *Racial Inequality.* Princeton, N.J.: Princeton University Press, 1981.

———. "Segmented Labour: Time Series Hypotheses and Evidence." *Cambridge Journal of Economics* 8 (1984): 63–81.

Reich, Michael, David M. Gordon, and Richard C. Edwards. "A Theory of Labor Market Segmentation." In *Problems in Political Economy,* ed. David M. Gordon. Lexington, Mass.: Heath, 1977.

Reimers, Cordelia. "Cultural Differences in Labor Force Participation among Married Women." *American Economic Review* 75 (May 1985): 251–55.

———. "Labor Market Discrimination against Hispanics and Black Men." *Review of Economics and Statistics* 65 (November 1983): 570–79.

Ringer, Benjamin. *"We, the People" and Others: Duality and America's Treatment of Its Racial Minorities.* New York: Tavistock, 1983.

Ríos, Palmira. "Black Latinos' Double Jeopardy." *New York Newsday,* October 25, 1991, p. 54.

Rodríguez, Clara E. "Economic Factors Affecting Puerto Ricans in New York." In *Labor Migration under Capitalism*, ed. History and Migration Task Force, Centro de Estudios Puertorriqueños. New York: Monthly Review Press, 1979.

———. *Puerto Ricans: Born in the U.S.A.* Boston: Unwin Hyman, 1989.

Rodríguez, Clara E., Virginia Sánchez-Korrol, and José Oscar Alers. *The Puerto Rican Struggle: Essays on Survival*. Maplewood, N.J.: Waterfront Press, 1984.

Rohatyn, Felix. "New York Can Be Made to Work." *New York Times*, November 2, 1990, p. B4.

Rosen, Sherwin. "Human Capital: A Survey of Empirical Research." In *Research in Labor Economics*, ed. R. G. Ehrenberg. Greenwich, Conn.: JAI Press, 1977.

Rosenberg, Sam. "From Segmentation to Flexibility: A Selective Survey." *Review of Radical Political Economics* 23, nos. 1–2 (1991).

Rosenberg, Terry J., and R. W. Lake. "Toward a Racial Model of Residential Segregation and Succession: Puerto Ricans in N.Y.C., 1960–1970." *American Journal of Sociology* 81 (1976): 1142–50.

Ross, Robert, and Trachte, Kent. "Global Cities and Global Classes: The Peripheralization of Labor in New York." *Review* 6, no. 3 (1983): 393–431.

Rubery, Jill. "Structured Labor Markets, Worker Organization, and Low Pay." *Cambridge Journal of Economics* 2 (1978): 17–36.

Rubinstein, Richard E., and Robert M. Fogelson. *The Harlem Riot of 1935*. New York: Arno Press, 1969.

Rumberger, Russell, and Martin Carnoy. "Segmentation in the U.S. Labor Market: Its Effects on the Mobility and Earnings of Whites and Blacks." *Cambridge Journal of Economics* 4 (1980): 117–32.

Ryan, Paul. "Segmentation and the Internal Labor Market." In *The Dynamics of Labour Market Segmentation*, ed. Frank Wilkinson. London: Academic Press, 1981.

Salins, Peter D., ed. *New York Unbound*. New York: Basil Blackwell, 1988.

Salle, Omer R., et al. "Racial Mix and Industrial Productivity." *American Sociological Review* 50, no. 1 (1985).

Sanabria, Carlos. "Patriotism and Class Conflict." *Latino Studies Journal* 2, no. 2 (1991): 1–14.

Sánchez, José Ramón. "Residual Work and Residual Shelter." In *Critical perspectives on Housing*, ed. Rachel G. Bratt, Chester Hartmann, and Ann Meyerson. Philadelphia: Temple University Press, 1986.

Sánchez-Korrol, Virginia. *From Colonia to Community: The History of Puerto Ricans in New York City, 1917–1948*. Westport, Conn.: Greenwood Press, 1983.

———. "The Survival of Puerto Rican Women in New York before World War II." In *The Puerto Rican Struggle: Essays on Survival*, ed. Clara Rodríguez,

Virginia Sánchez-Korrol, and José Oscar Alers. Maplewood, N.J.: Waterfront Press, 1984.

Sanders, Ronald. *Lost Tribes and Promised Lands: The Origins of American Racism.* New York: HarperCollins, 1978.

Santana-Cooney, Rosemary. "Intercity Variations in Puerto Rican Female Participation." *Journal of Human Resources* 14 (Spring 1979): 222–35.

Santiago, Isaura. *A Community's Struggle for Equal Opportunity: ASPIRA vs. Board of Education.* Princeton, N.J.: Educational Testing Service, 1978.

Sassen-Koob, Saskia. "Changing Composition and Labor Market Location of Hispanic Immigrants in New York City: 1960–1980." In *Hispanics in the U.S. Economy,* ed. George Borjas and Marta Tienda. Orlando: Academic Press, 1982.

———. *The Mobility of Labor and Capital.* New York: Cambridge University Press, 1988.

———. "The New Labor Demand in Global Cities." In *Urban Affairs Annual Reviews,* ed. M. P. Smith. Beverly Hills, Calif.: Sage, 1984.

Savas, E. S. "Considering Privatization." In *New York Unbound,* ed. Peter D. Salins. New York: Basil Blackwell, 1988.

Sawhill, Isabel. "Poverty in the U.S.: Why Is It So Persistent?" *Journal of Economic Literature* 26 (September 1988): 1073–1119.

Schaller, Bruce. "The Employment Outlook for Minorities in a Changing Economy: Evidence from New York City's Financial Services Sector." Unpublished paper. New York City Office for Economic Development, 1983.

Scheiner, Seth M. *Negro Mecca: A History of the Negro in New York City, 1865–1920.* New York: New York University Press, 1965.

Schor, Juliet B. *The Overworked American.* New York: Basic Books, 1992.

Serrin, William. "After Years of Decline, Sweatshops Are Back." *New York Times,* October 12, 1983, p. A1.

Shefter, Martin. *Political Crisis, Fiscal Crisis.* New York: Basic Books, 1987.

Shuman, Steven. "Race, Class, and Occupational Stratification: A Critique of W. J. Wilson's *The Declining Significance of Race.*" *Review of Radical Political Economics* 13, no. 3 (1981): 21–31.

Simon, Julian. *The Economic Consequences of Immigration.* Cambridge, Mass.: Basil Blackwell, 1989.

Smith, James P. "Race and Human Capital." *American Economic Review* 74 (September 1984): 685–98.

Smith, James P., and Finis R. Welch. "Racial Discrimination: A Human Capital Perspective." In *Labor Economics: Modern Views,* ed. William A. Darity. Boston: Kluwer-Nijhoff, 1984.

Sontag, Deborah. "Immigrants Forgoing Citizenship while Pursuing American Dream." *New York Times,* July 25, 1993.

Sowell, Thomas. *Ethnic America*. New York: Basic Books, 1981.

———. *Markets and Minorities*. New York: Basic Books, 1981.

Spero, Sterling D., and Abram L. Harris. *The Black Worker*. New York: Atheneum, 1974.

Stafford, Walter. *Closed Labor Markets: The Underrepresentation of Blacks, Hispanics, and Women in New York City's Core Industries*. New York: Community Service Society, 1985.

———. *Employment Segmentation in New York City Municipal Agencies*. New York: Community Service Society, 1990.

———. *Racial, Ethnic, and Sexual Stratification and Affirmative Action Planning in New York City's Public and Private Sectors*. Washington, D.C.: U.S. Commission on Civil Rights, 1983.

Stafford, Walter, and Joyce Ladner. "Political Dimensions of the Underclass Concept." In *Sociology in America*, ed. Herbert J. Gans. Newbury Park, Calif.: Sage, 1990.

Steinberg, Stephen. "Human Capital: A Critique." *Review of Black Political Economy* 14 (Summer 1985): 67–74.

Sternlieb, George, and James W. Hughes. "Metropolitan Decline and Inter-Regional Job Shifts." In *The Fiscal Crisis of American Cities*, ed. Roger E. Alcaly and David Mermelstein. New York: Vintage Books, 1977.

Stevens-Arroyo, Antonio. "Puerto Rican Struggles in the Catholic Church." In *The Puerto Rican Struggle: Essays on Survival*, ed. Clara Rodríguez, Virginia Sánchez-Korrol, and José Oscar Alers. Maplewood, N.J.: Waterfront Press, 1984.

Swinton, David H. "Economic Theory and Working Class Poverty: Toward a Reformulation." *American Economic Review* 77, no. 2 (1987): 223–28.

Syzmanski, Al. "Trends in Economic Discrimination against Blacks in the U.S. Working Class." *Review of Radical Political Economics* 7 (Fall 1975): 1–22.

Tabb, William K. *The Long Default*. New York: Monthly Review Press, 1982.

Tabb, William K., and Larry Sawyers, eds. *Marxism and the Metropolis*. New York: Oxford University Press, 1984.

Teaford, Jon C. *The Twentieth Century American City: Problem, Promise, and Reality*. Baltimore, Md.: Johns Hopkins University Press, 1986.

Thompson, Wilbur R. *A Preface to Urban Economics*. Baltimore, Md.: Johns Hopkins University Press, 1965.

Thurow, Lester. *Dangerous Currents*. New York: Random House, 1983.

———. *Generating Inequality*. New York: Basic Book, 1975.

———. *Investment in Human Capital*. Belmont, Calif.: Wadsworth, 1970.

Tienda, Marta. "Puerto Ricans and the Underclass Debate." *Annals of the American Academy of Political and Social Science* 501 (January 1989): 105–19.

Tienda, Marta, and Lisa J. Niedart. "Language, Education, and the Socio-

Economic Achievement of Hispanic Origin Men." *Social Science Quarterly* 65 (June 1984): 519–36.

Tobier, Emmanuel. *The Changing Face of Poverty.* New York: Community Service Society, 1984.

———. "Foreign Immigration," In *Setting Municipal Priorities 1983*, ed. Charles Brecher and Raymond D. Horton. New York: Russell Sage Foundation, 1983.

———. "The Homeless." In *Setting Municipal Priorities 1990*, ed. Charles Brecher and Raymond D. Horton. New York: New York University Press, 1989.

Tomasi, Silvano. *Piety and Power: The Role of Italian Parishes in the New York Metropolitan Area (1889–1930).* Staten Island, N.Y.: Center for Migration Studies, 1975.

Torres, Andrés. "Human Capital, Labor Segmentation, and Inter-Minority Relative Status." Ph.D. diss., New School for Social Research, 1988.

———. "Labor Market Segmentation: African American and Puerto Rican Labor in New York City, 1960–1980." *Review of Black Political Economy* 20 (Summer 1991): 59–77.

Torres, Andrés, and Frank Bonilla. "Decline within Decline." In *Latinos in a Changing U.S. Economy*, ed. Rebecca Morales and Frank Bonilla. Newbury Park, Calif.: Sage, 1993.

Torres, Andrés, and Clara Rodríguez. "Latino Research and Policy: The Puerto Rican Case." In *Hispanics in the Labor Force: Issues and Policies*, ed. Edwin Meléndez, Clara Rodríguez, and Janis Barry Figueroa. New York: Plenum Press, 1991.

Torres-Saillant, Silvio. "Dominicans as a New York Community: A Social Reappraisal." *Punto 7* 2, no. 1 (1989): 7–25.

U.S. Bureau of the Census. *Census of Population and Housing 1960: NYSMSA No. 1, Parts 1 and 2, Series PHC-1.* Washington, D.C.: Government Printing Office, 1968.

———. *1970–1980 Census Comparability, Detailed Occupation and Industry Sorted by 1980 Codes.* Washington, D.C.: Government Printing Office, 1983.

———. *1980 Census of Population: Detailed Population Characteristics.* Washington, D.C.: Government Printing Office, 1980.

———. *1980 Census of Population: General Population Characteristics, New York.* Washington, D.C.: Government Printing Office, 1980.

———. *1980 Census of Population: General Social and Economic Characteristics, New York.* Washington, D.C.: Government Printing Office, 1980.

———. *Occupational and Industry Classification Systems in Terms of Their 1960 Occupation and Industry Elements.* Technical Paper 26, Washington, D.C.: Government Printing Office, 1970.

———. *Public Use Microdata Samples from the 1980 Census: Technical Documentation..* Washington, D.C.: Government Printing Office, 1983.

———. *A Public Use Sample of Basic Records from the 1960 Census: Description and Technical Documentation.* Washington, D.C.: Government Printing Office, 1975.

———. *Public Use Samples of Basic Records from the 1970 Census: Description and Technical Documentation.* Washington, D.C.: Government Printing Office, 1972.

———. *The Social and Economic Status of the Black Population in the United States: An Historical View 1770–1978.* Special Studies Series no. 80. Washington, D.C.: Government Printing Office, 1979.

U.S. Commission on Civil Rights. *Puerto Ricans in the Continental United States: An Uncertain Future.* Washington, D.C.: Government Printing Office, 1976.

U.S. Department of Labor, Bureau of Labor Statistics. *The Labor Force Experience of the Puerto Rican Worker.*. Washington, D.C.: Government Printing Office, 1968.

———. *New York in Transition: Population, Jobs, Prices and Pay in a Decade of Change.* Washington, D.C.: Government Printing Office, 1973.

———. *A Socio-Economic Profile of Puerto Rican New Yorkers.* Washington, D.C.: Government Printing Office, 1975.

Vernon, Raymond. *Metropolis 1985.* Cambridge, Mass.: Harvard University Press, 1960.

Vidal, David. "Hispanic Newcomers in City Cling to Values of Homeland." *New York Times,* May 11, 1980, pp. 1, 42.

Wachter, Michael. "Primary and Secondary Labor Markets: A Critique of the Dual Approach." *Brookings Papers on Economic Activity* 3 (1974): 637–80.

Waghenheim, Kal. *Puerto Rico: A Profile.* New York: Praeger, 1970.

———. *A Survey of Puerto Ricans on the U.S. Mainland in the 1970's.* New York: Praeger, 1975.

Waldinger, Roger. "Immigration and Urban Change." *American Review of Sociology* 15 (1989): 211–32.

———. *Through the Eye of the Needle: Immigrants and Enterprise in New York's Garment Trade.* New York: New York University Press, 1986.

Wang, John. "Behind the Boom: Power and Economics in Chinatown." *New York Affairs* 5, no. 3 (1979): 77–81.

Weisbrot, Robert. *Father Devine.* Boston: Beacon Press, 1983.

Weitzman, Philip. *Worlds Apart: Housing, Race/Ethnicity and Income in New York City, 1978–87.* New York: Community Service Society, 1989.

Wilkinson, Frank, ed. *The Dynamics of Labour Market Segmentation.* London: Academic Press, 1981.

Williams, Rhonda M. "Capital, Competition, and Discrimination: A Reconsideration of Racial Earnings Inequality." *Review of Radical Political Economics* 19, no. 2 (1987): 1–15.

Willis, Mark A. "New York's Renaissance." In *New York Unbound,* ed. Peter Salins. New York: Basil Blackwell, 1988.

Wilson, James Q. *Negro Politics: A Search for Leadership.* Glencoe, Ill.: Free Press, 1960.

Wilson, William J. *The Declining Significance of Race.* Chicago: University of Chicago Press, 1978.

———. "Race Specific Policies and the Truly Disadvantaged." *Yale Law Policy Review* 11 (1988): 272–90.

———. *The Truly Disadvantaged.* Chicago: University of Chicago Press, 1987.

Wright, Erik Olin. "Race, Class and Income Inequality." *American Journal of Sociology* 83, no. 6 (1978): 1368–97.

Zhou, Min. *Chinatown: The Socioeconomic Potential of an Urban Enclave.* Philadelphia: Temple University Press, 1992.

INDEX